KERBER ART

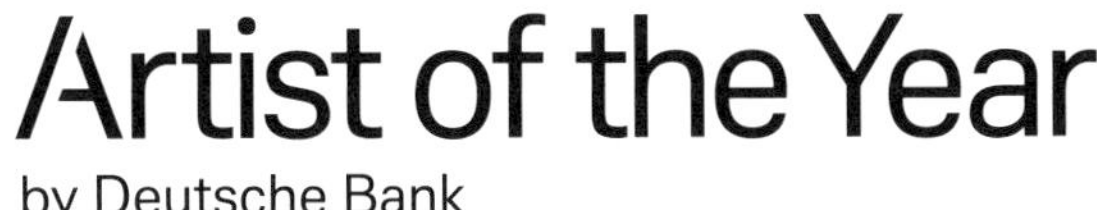

CALINE AOUN
SEEING IS BELIEVING

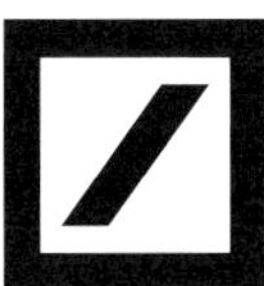

GREETING

Amidst the constant flood of images and information, Caline Aoun's exhibition *seeing is believing* is a place of contemplation, a counterpoint to "media noise." This does not mean it is a secluded retreat, however, but a free space in which art inspires us to think differently about reality— and not least to deal with it differently. The artist, who lives and works in Beirut, deals with the phenomenon of virtualization, with the difficulty of understanding and grasping the circulation of data in a new way. Aoun's reduced and poetic works lend the supposedly "invisible" process of data traffic physicality, feel, and sensuality.

The "Artist of the Year" award has been presented by Deutsche Bank for almost a decade now. And if we look at the positions of the award-winning artists, we see a mirror image of the social debates and themes that move the world. This includes a confrontation with racism, migration, and environmental destruction as well as technological and social visions of the future. As the current "Artist of the Year," Caline Aoun poses fundamental and philosophical questions about our altered concept of reality in the digitized world.

Looking back, it is apparent how much this award has contributed to firmly establishing our "Artists of the Year" and their ideas in the international art world. While artists such as Yto Barrada, Wangechi Mutu, and Kemang Wa Lehulere were previously known only to insiders, artists, and curators, today they are an indispensable part of biennials and major international museum exhibitions. They have a decisive influence on global art discourse.

Like her predecessors, Caline Aoun refers specifically to the situation in her home country. But she cannot be limited to her nationality and categorized as a "Lebanese" artist. Her work always communicates has universal, existential meaning and understood all over the world.

From the very beginning, the declared aim of our commitment to art, culture, and sports has been to unite different cultures, life stories, and social backgrounds, to overcome boundaries and entrenched ideas. These topics help us develop new perspectives, to think in a new and lateral way—something that is reflected in the PalaisPopulaire's interdisciplinary program.

Thorsten Strauß
Global Head of Art, Culture & Sports
Deutsche Bank

GRUSSWORT

Inmitten der ständigen Bilder- und Informationsflut ist Caline Aouns Ausstellung *seeing is believing* ein Ort der Kontemplation, ein Gegenpol zum „medialen Lärm". Damit ist kein abgeschotteter Rückzugsort gemeint, sondern ein Freiraum, in dem uns die Kunst dazu anregt, anders über die Wirklichkeit nachzudenken – und nicht zuletzt auch anders mit ihr umzugehen. Die bei Beirut lebende und arbeitende Künstlerin setzt sich auf neue Weise mit dem Phänomen der Virtualisierung auseinander, mit der Schwierigkeit, die Zirkulation von Daten zu begreifen und zu erfassen. Aouns reduzierte und poetische Arbeiten verleihen dem vermeintlich „unsichtbaren" Prozess des Datenverkehrs Körperlichkeit, Haptik und Sinnlichkeit.

Seit beinahe einem Jahrzehnt wird die Auszeichnung „Artist of the Year" von der Deutschen Bank verliehen. Und betrachtet man die Positionen der ausgezeichneten Künstlerinnen und Künstler, sieht man hier auch ein Spiegelbild der gesellschaftlichen Debatten und Themen, die die Welt bewegen. Dazu gehörte die Auseinandersetzung mit Rassismus, Migration und Umweltzerstörung ebenso wie technologische und soziale Zukunftsvisionen. Als aktuelle „Artist of the Year" gelingt es Caline Aoun in ihrem Werk, ganz grundsätzliche, auch philosophische Fragen zu unserem veränderten Begriff der Wirklichkeit in der digitalisierten Welt zu stellen.

Schaut man heute zurück, sieht man zugleich, wie sehr diese Auszeichnung auch dazu beigetragen hat, unsere „Artists of the Year" und ihre Ideen fest im internationalen Kunstbetrieb zu etablieren. Waren Künstlerinnen und Künstler wie Yto Barrada, Wangechi Mutu oder Kemang Wa Lehulere zuvor zwar Insidern, Künstlern und Kuratoren bekannt, sind sie heute nicht mehr aus Biennalen und großen internationalen Museumsausstellungen wegzudenken. Sie prägen den globalen Kunstdiskurs ganz entscheidend mit.

Wie auch ihre Vorgängerinnen und Vorgänger nimmt Caline Aoun ganz spezifisch auf die Situation in ihrem Heimatland Bezug. Doch sie lässt sich nicht auf ihre Nationalität begrenzen, als „libanesische" Künstlerin kategorisieren. Was ihre Arbeit mitteilt, hat auch immer allgemeingültige, existenzielle Bedeutung, wird auf der ganzen Welt verstanden.

Unterschiedliche Kulturen, Lebensgeschichten und soziale Hintergründe zu vereinen, Grenzen und festgefahrene Vorstellungen zu überwinden, war von Anfang an das erklärte Ziel unseres Engagements für Kunst, Kultur und Sport. Denn alle diese Themen helfen, neue Perspektiven zu entwickeln, neu und quer zu denken – so wie es das interdisziplinäre Programm des PalaisPopulaire widerspiegelt.

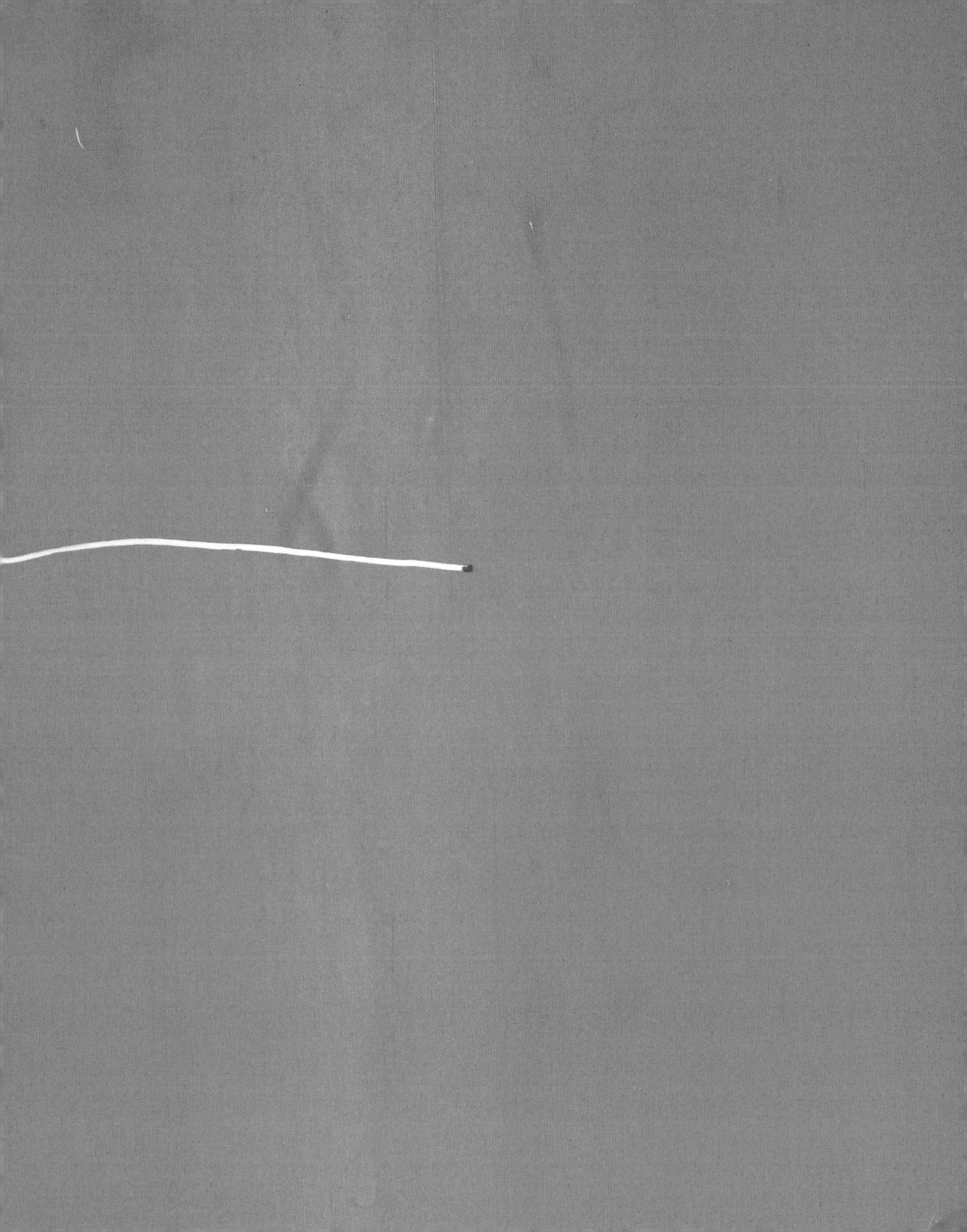

BRITTA FÄRBER

SEEING IS BELIEVING
ON THE ABSTRACT STATE OF EMERGENCY
IN CALINE AOUN'S WORK

"We don't see more, we see less. It's almost like there is a breakdown in the overall system of representation and this is when the abstraction comes in. This is why I go back to the material because I try to see a new potential," says Caline Aoun referring to her methodology.[1] Pure materiality and accelerated abstraction—these parameters also characterize her exhibition at the PalaisPopulaire: Her expansive, picturesque "wallpaper" made of assembled, color-printed DIN A3+ sheets, for instance, looks like a test print for a Constructivist-Minimalist stained glass window consisting of hundreds of brightly colored rectangles. But not everything is hunky-dory here. An almost tar black, velvety surface splinters into more and more color fields: inky grayish blue, rich cranberry red, violet. The feeling of opulence and warmth subsides; the ornament decomposes increasingly into narrowing beams of light blue, turquoise, and yellow. Finally, only white remains, covered with the streaks and traces of empty printer heads that have scraped over the paper.

The fading colors, the ever-deteriorating quality of the prints, and mechanical traces, all make it clear that Aoun is not primarily concerned with creating abstract, aesthetic forms or perfect symmetries and color effects. Rather, the Lebanese artist explains, a process becomes visible here, "the image struggling to appear through the process of its own making."[2] In fact, Aoun feeds her printers an overload of data, prints giga-bytes of images, even though the ink cartridges are almost empty. The exhausted device tries to produce another picture with all its might and uses all available ink remnants, but they gradually run dry.

The same applies to the four formally reduced fountains in the room, each of which bubbles with one color from the CMYK color model: cyan, magenta, yellow, and black—traditionally referred to as the "key." The fountains are connected by a system of tubes and exchange fluids with one another at a very slow, barely perceptible pace pp. 40–43. At first, pure colors still effervesce from the ink heads, but in the course of time they meld into a cloudy dark sludge that coagulates, clogs the ink heads, and finally dries up completely, thus interrupting the cycle. Asked whether the

1   Caline Aoun in conversation with Hou Hanru, *Deutsche Bank ArtMag* (2018), https://db-artmag.de/en/104/feature/we-dont-see-more-we-see-less-caline-aoun-in-conversation-with-ho/
2   Ibid.

SEEING IS BELIEVING

ÜBER DEN ABSTRAKTEN AUSNAHMEZUSTAND IN CALINE AOUNS WERK

„Wir sehen nicht mehr, sondern weniger. Es ist fast so, als würde ein alles umfassendes Repräsentationssystem abstürzen. Und an diesem Punkt kommt die Abstraktion ins Spiel. Hier greife ich auf alles Materielle zurück, denn ich versuche, darin ein neues Potenzial zu entdecken", so Caline Aoun zu ihrer Methodik.[1] Pure Materialität und beschleunigte Abstraktion – dies sind auch die Parameter, die ihre Ausstellung im PalaisPopulaire auszeichnen: So ist da eine raumfüllende, malerisch wirkende „Tapete" aus zusammenmontierten, farbig bedruckten DIN-A3+-Blättern. Diese Wandarbeit wirkt wie der Probedruck für ein konstruktivistisch-minimalistisches Glasfenster, das aus Hunderten von farbig leuchtenden Rechtecken besteht. Doch scheint hier nicht alles rundzulaufen. Eine fast teerschwarze, samten wirkende Fläche splittert sich in immer mehr Farbfelder auf, in tintiges Graublau, sattes Cranberry-Rot, Violett. Das Gefühl von Opulenz und Wärme weicht: Immer mehr zersetzt sich das Ornament in schmaler werdende Balken aus Hellblau, Türkis und Gelb. Schließlich bleibt nur noch Weiß, übersät mit Schlieren und Spuren der leeren Druckerköpfe, die über das Papier geschabt sind.

Schon anhand der auslaufenden und verblassenden Farben, der immer schlechter werdenden Qualität der Drucke und der Spuren der Maschine wird deutlich, dass es Aoun weniger darum geht, abstrakte, ästhetische Formen oder perfekte Symmetrien und Farbwirkungen zu schaffen. Vielmehr handelt es sich, wie die libanesische Künstlerin erklärt, um einen Prozess, der hier sichtbar wird – um den „Kampf eines Bildes, das mit allen Kräften zu erscheinen versucht".[2] Tatsächlich füttert Aoun ihre Drucker mit einem Overload aus Daten, druckt Gigabytes von Bildern aus, obwohl die Farbpatronen fast leer sind. Das erschöpfte Gerät versucht, mit aller Kraft noch ein weiteres Bild zu produzieren und bedient sich dabei aller verfügbaren Farbreste, die aber allmählich versiegen.

Ähnlich ergeht es den vier Brunnen im Raum. Aus jeder der formal reduzierten Fontänen sprudelt eine Farbe, die im CMYK-Farbmodell für den Vierfarbdruck eingesetzt wird: Cyan, Magenta, Yellow und Schwarz, das traditionell als „Key" bezeichnet wird. Die Brunnen sind durch ein Röhrensystem miteinander verbunden und tauschen sich in einem sehr langsamen, kaum wahrnehmbaren Tempo aus S. 40–43. Zunächst sprudeln noch reine Farben aus den Düsen, im Laufe der Zeit zerfließen sie aber zu einer trüben dunklen Brühe, die gerinnt, die Düsen verklebt, schließlich eintrocknet und so den Kreislauf zu unterbrechen droht. Auf die Frage, ob die Brunnen, ähnlich wie die Drucke, mit der Übertragung und Zirkulation von Daten zu tun haben, antwortet Aoun: „Was sind Daten? Sie sind pure Information. Doch anstatt mich lediglich um die Information zu kümmern, die Daten in sich tragen, interessiere ich mich mehr für die materielle Dimension der

1   Caline Aoun im Gespräch mit Hou Hanru, *Deutsche Bank ArtMag* 2018: https://db-artmag.de/de/104/feature/wir-sehen-nicht-mehr-sondern-weniger-caline-aoun-im-gespraech-mi/
2   Ebd.

fountains, like the prints, also have to do with the transfer and circulation of data, Aoun replies: "What is data? It is pure information. But instead of merely caring about the information that data carry, I am more interested in the material dimension of digitization—how this proton of information carries a vision, of faith, of the future, and what tangible, palpable consequences it has."[3] Aoun's works do not depict or symbolize. Rather, they are the material result of an invisible process made visible, and thus, perceptible. So the exhibition title *seeing is believing* is meant quite literally.

Traveling Data

In its dialectic, Aoun's work seems made for an era in which economic, political, and ecological contexts are becoming less and less tangible, while at the same time an infinite amount of data is circulating on the internet. Although more and more people have virtually unlimited access to more and more pictures, numbers, and facts, this data remains mostly abstract to us. It simply cannot be connected with our perception and our own reality.

A good example of this is climate change. It is not for nothing that activists stress that climate change is not a subjective perception or an individual interpretation, but based on scientific data and research. But why is it so difficult to accept climate change as a reality? Climate change "is not a concrete, singular event, but a concatenation of dynamic processes," wrote Tobias Haberkorn in a much discussed 2018 article in the German weekly newspaper *Die Zeit*. "It does not only mean fires, floods, poor harvests, climate flight; all the horror scenarios we read about in the media. It also means nice weather outside the window."[4] And then he quotes the artist Roni Horn: "The pleasant, the beautiful, shows itself immediately and individually; the wrong lies in the system." Horn argues that the climate is like a collective self-portrait, reflecting our global situation. However, we experience it as a singular phenomenon, or better said, its beautiful side, like the endless blue sky. The worst consequences of climate change therefore still sound like fiction to us, says Haberkorn. "If you want to get the creeps you can start with this forest fire video of the Hollywood area and then let YouTube's algorithm, with its characteristic overbidding logic, demonstrate how bad the climate might become or actually has been for a long time."

This decoupled, alienated perception and the transfer of problems into an ominous "system" also affects other pressing global issues related to climate change, including migration and the refugee crisis, growing nationalism, digital surveillance, and the resulting handling of big data. It is becoming increasingly clear that these problems cannot be negotiated, let alone solved, separately. They are the phenomena of disjointed global geopolitical systems. Here, as with Aoun's fountain, everything is interconnected. And as in her works, this system is characterized by contradictory states that occur simultaneously and often suddenly: extreme lack and excessive abundance, circulation and congestion. Her abstract works engage with these dynamics, which always occur when systems are unstable and threatening to change into a completely different, unforeseen state.

A central motif for Aoun is the image conveyed and reproduced by the media of a material visualization of reality. Yet, like many other artists

3   In conversation with the author, February 2, 2019.
4   Tobias Haberkorn, "Die Sintflut kommt," in *Die Zeit*, November 4, 2018, https://www.zeit.de/kultur/2018-10/klimawandel-schuld-anerkennung-klimakrieg-weltklimakonferenz/komplettansicht

Digitalisierung – wie dieses Proton von Information eine Vision in sich trägt, von Glauben, Zukunft und welche ganz handfesten, greifbaren Konsequenzen es in sich birgt."[3] Aouns Arbeiten bilden nicht ab, sie symbolisieren nicht, sondern sind selbst das materielle Ergebnis eines eigentlich unsichtbaren Prozesses, der sichtbar und damit wahrnehmbar wird. Der Ausstellungstitel *seeing is believing* ist also ganz wörtlich gemeint.

Traveling Data

Aouns Werk erscheint in seiner Dialektik wie gemacht für eine Ära, in der die ökonomischen, politischen und ökologischen Zusammenhänge immer weniger begreifbar sind, während gleichzeitig unendlich viele Daten im Netz zirkulieren. Obwohl immer mehr Menschen einen scheinbar unbegrenzten Zugriff auf immer mehr Bilder, Zahlen und Fakten haben, bleiben diese Daten für uns meist abstrakt, nicht verknüpfbar mit unserer Wahrnehmung und unserer eigenen Lebenswirklichkeit.

Ein gutes Beispiel dafür ist der Klimawandel. Nicht umsonst betonen Aktivisten, dass die Tatsache des Klimawandels keine subjektive Wahrnehmung oder individuelle Deutung ist, sondern auf wissenschaftlichen Daten und Forschungsergebnissen beruht. Warum ist es dann so schwierig, den Klimawandel als Realität zu akzeptieren? Der Klimawandel „ist kein konkretes, singuläres Ereignis, sondern eine Verkettung dynamischer Prozesse", schreibt Tobias Haberkorn 2018 in einem viel diskutierten Beitrag in der *Zeit*: „Er bedeutet nicht nur Feuersbrünste, Überflutungen, Missernten, Klimaflucht; all die Horrorszenarien, über die wir in den Medien lesen. Er bedeutet auch das schöne Wetter vor dem Fenster."[4] Dann zitiert er die Künstlerin Roni Horn: „Das Angenehme, Schöne zeigt sich unmittelbar und individuell, das Falsche liegt im System." Das Klima, so Horn, sei wie ein kollektives Selbstporträt, es spiegelt unsere globale Lage wider. Wir erleben es jedoch als singuläres Phänomen oder besser, seine schönen Seiten, wie den endlos blauen Himmel. Die schlimmsten Folgen des Klimawandels klingen deshalb für uns noch immer wie Fiktionen sagt Haberkorn: „Wer sich ein bisschen gruseln will, kann mit diesem Waldbrandvideo aus der Gegend um Hollywood beginnen und sich dann vom YouTube-Algorithmus in seiner charakteristischen Überbietungslogik vorführen lassen, wie schlimm das mit dem Klima einmal werden könnte oder eigentlich längst ist."

Diese entkoppelte, entfremdete Wahrnehmung und die Verlegung der Probleme in ein ominöses „System" betrifft auch andere drängende globale Fragen, die ihrerseits mit dem Klimawandel zusammenhängen – Migration und Flüchtlingskrise, der zunehmende Nationalismus, digitale Überwachung und der darauf basierende Umgang mit Big Data. Es wird zunehmend deutlicher, dass man diese Probleme nicht getrennt voneinander verhandeln oder gar lösen kann. Sie sind Phänomene von geopolitischen, aus den Fugen geratenen, globalen Systemen. Hier ist, ähnlich wie bei Aouns Brunnen, alles mit allem verbunden. Und wie in Aouns Werken ist dieses System gekennzeichnet durch widersprüchliche Zustände, die gleichzeitig und häufig auch plötzlich auftreten: extremer Mangel und exzessiver Überfluss, Zirkulation und Anstauung. Aouns abstrakte Werke beschäftigen sich mit diesen Dynamiken, die immer dann auftreten, wenn Systeme zu kippen und in einen anderen, unvorhergesehenen Zustand überzugehen drohen.

3   Im Gespräch mit der Autorin, 20. Februar 2019.
4   Tobias Haberkorn, „Die Sintflut kommt", in: *Die Zeit*, 4. November 2018. https://www.zeit.de/kultur/2018-10/klimawandel-schuld-anerkennung-klimakrieg-weltklimakonferenz/komplettansicht

of her generation, Aoun radically questions this notion of the supposedly objective recording and reproduction of reality through the image. She focuses on the technology and the economic and social conditions of the people who are a physical part of the process of image formation. In a lecture titled "Is the Internet Dead?" Hito Steyerl gives a historical example of this: the uprising in Romania in 1989, when demonstrators invaded state television studios to write history. "At that moment, images changed their function. Broadcasts from occupied TV studios became active catalysts of events—not records or documents. Since then it has become clear that images are not objective or subjective renditions of a preexisting condition, or merely treacherous appearances. They are rather nodes of energy and matter that migrate across different supports, shaping and affecting people, landscapes, politics, and social systems."[5]

Aoun's works are situated precisely where the illusion of digital perfection implodes. In a world in which data is leaked, in which masses of goods and people are moved via digital processes, she treats data "as matter, as pure material."[6] In this sense, the pigment particles of the printing ink are just as much data carriers as the digitally stored information that the printer transfers onto the paper as an image. When Aoun casts pine needles she finds on the street outside her front door in copper and exhibits them, this is also a data transfer. Just as when she transmits live footage from the sea in Beirut to her Berlin exhibition via webcam p. 39. "The livestream forms something like the background for the installation of the fountains," says Aoun. "It embodies exactly the opposite, because the data cannot really be recorded in the stream. They only appear as 'traveling data' for a very short moment before disappearing again. The 'traveling data' or information that comes metaphorically from the printer behaves differently. It is like the ink that flows through the tubes and then lands on the paper. This journey has a very different physicality and carries a very different vision."[7]

Rooted in Beirut

Born in Beirut in 1983, Deutsche Bank's "Artist of the Year" belongs to a generation of young Lebanese artists who grew up abroad after the outbreak of civil war in 1975 and completed training outside of Lebanon. Caline Aoun studied in London at the Central Saint Martin's School of Art and Design and the Royal Academy Schools, before graduating from the University of East London in 2012 with a Professional Doctorate in Fine Arts. Originally, she used painting as a conceptual strategy to add a level of mediation to the omnipresence of media images. Shortly after graduating, however, she decided to give up painting and began experimenting with photography and digital printing techniques. She soon focused on urban space. "In my work I deal with urbanism, advertising space, and image making, but also what these things produce in terms of environmental noise," explains Aoun. "I am interested in the feeling we get out of the saturation they produce, or the exhaustion they create."[8] She always takes a look at the data that is closest to her physically:[9] "It could just as well be an Apple Watch as an urban environment." She began collecting freight data from the port of Beirut for her work *Datascape 2003–2014* (2016)—her

5   Hito Steyerl, "Is the Internet Dead?," in *Duty Free Art: Kunst in Zeiten des Globalen Bürgerkriegs* (Zurich, 2018), p. 151, (translated as *Duty Free Art: Art in the Age of Planetary Civil War,* London, 2017).
6   In conversation with the author, February 20, 2019.
7   Ibid.
8   Aoun in conversation with Hanru, cf. 1.
9   In conversation with the author, February 20, 2019.

Ein zentrales Motiv ist für Aoun das medial vermittelte und reproduzierte Bild als materielle Sichtbarmachung der Realität. Doch genau diese Vorstellung von der vermeintlich objektiven Aufzeichnung und Wiedergabe der Wirklichkeit durch das Bild zieht Aoun, wie viele andere Künstlerinnen und Künstler ihrer Generation, radikal in Zweifel. Dabei lenkt sie den Fokus auf die Technologie und die ökonomischen und sozialen Konditionen der Menschen, die physischer Teil des Prozesses der Bildwerdung sind. Hito Steyerl gibt dafür in ihrem Vortrag „Ist das Internet tot?" ein historisches Beispiel: den Aufstand in Rumänien 1989. Damals seien Demonstranten in die staatlichen Fernsehstudios eingedrungen, um Geschichte zu schreiben: „In diesem Augenblick änderten die Bilder ihre Funktion. Sendungen aus den besetzten Fernsehstudios wurden zu aktiven Katalysatoren von Ereignissen – statt Aufzeichnung oder Dokumente zu sein. Seither ist deutlich geworden, dass Bilder keine objektiven oder subjektiven Wiedergaben eines vorbestehenden Zustands sind und auch kein bloßer trügerischer Schein. Vielmehr sind sie Verknotungen von Energie und Materie, die über verschiedene Träger wandern und Menschen, Landschaften, politische Maßnahmen und Gesellschaftssysteme formen und beeinflussen."[5]

Aouns Werke entstehen genau dort, wo die Illusion der digitalen Perfektion in sich zusammenfällt. In einer Welt, in der Daten geleakt werden, also durchsickern und auslaufen, in der Massen von Waren und auch Menschen über digitale Prozesse bewegt werden, behandelt sie Daten „als Materie, als pures Material".[6] In diesem Sinne sind die Pigmentpartikel der Druckertinte genauso Datenträger wie die digital gespeicherten Informationen, die der Drucker als Bild auf das Papier bringt. Wenn Aoun die Piniennadeln auf der Straße vor ihrer Haustür in Kupfer nachgießt und ausstellt, ist das auch ein Datentransfer. Und zwar genauso, wie wenn sie mit einer Webcam Aufnahmen vom Meer in Beirut live in ihre Berliner Ausstellung überträgt S.39. „Der Livestream bildet so etwas wie den Hintergrund für die Installation der Brunnen", sagt Aoun. „Er verkörpert genau das Gegenteil, weil die Daten im Stream nicht wirklich festgehalten werden können. Sie erscheinen nur für einen ganz kurzen Moment als ‚Traveling Data' und verschwinden dann wieder. Die ‚Traveling Data' oder Informationen, die metaphorisch aus dem Drucker kommen, verhalten sich anders. Sie sind wie die Tinte, die durch die Leitungen strömt und dann auf dem Papier landet. Diese Reise hat eine ganz andere Körperlichkeit und trägt eine ganz andere Vision in sich."[7]

Verortung in Beirut

1983 in Beirut geboren, zählt die „Künstlerin des Jahres" der Deutschen Bank zu einer Generation junger libanesischen Künstlerinnen und Künstler, die nach dem Ausbruch des Bürgerkrieges 1975 im Ausland aufwuchsen und dort auch ihre Ausbildung absolvierten. Caline Aoun studierte in London an der Central Saint Martins School of Art and Design und den Royal Academy Schools, um 2012 an der University of East London ihren Meisterschülerabschluss in Bildender Kunst zu machen. Ursprünglich nutzte sie die Malerei als konzeptuelle Strategie, um den omnipräsenten Medienbildern eine andere Ebene medialer Vermittlung hinzuzufügen. Kurz nach ihrem Abschluss entschloss sie sich jedoch, die Malerei aufzugeben, um

5   Hito Steyerl, „Ist das Internet tot?", in: *Duty Free Art: Kunst in Zeiten des globalen Bürgerkriegs*, Zürich 2018, S. 151.
6   Im Gespräch mit der Autorin.
7   Ebd.

gallery was located directly at the port: "I had to respond to the information around me."[10] The port of Beirut plays a major role in the Lebanese economy and the city's infrastructure. In an interview with Hou Hanru, the artistic director of MAXXI in Rome and a member of Deutsche Bank's Global Art Advisory Council, Aoun explains: "I've collected data on 55 different types of goods that are handled in the port—the tonnage, the weight of goods, from natural produce to animals, from cars to construction materials. I was keeping track of the tonnage of every product per month and per year from 2003 to 2014. The graphs transformed into these muted landscapes. I transformed the data into a very sensual and physical mass on the surface of the paper. But at the same time these graphs would tell a story about Beirut."[11] This story appears in the hills and plains of Aoun's data landscape, but not only in an abstract poetic way. While the data for most years—the movements of ships, containers, and goods—result in an almost harmonious rhythm of ups and downs, the data pertaining to the beginning of the war in the summer of 2006 is radically interrupted: While the total declared freight drops to zero, the curve of the weight of the undeclared goods, i.e., the goods whose actual contents do not become transparent, rises from zero to a true mountain range. One can only speculate about the contents of these containers.

Disruptions

Such radical interruptions and disturbances appear in Aoun's works time and time again: Fountains spray ink; ink heads clog; paper gets stuck in the printer; and ink runs or fades. At first glance, Aoun's creations seem to stand aesthetically in a Minimalist abstract tradition. Many of her works are reminiscent of Concrete Art or seem to have been created in the spirit of German Minimalism of the 1960s and 1970s. The simple, industrial, and standardized materials that Aoun uses—the folds and geometries—are reminiscent of works by Blinky Palermo or Charlotte Posenenske, in which the fragmentary is confronted with classical Minimalist aesthetics. In addition, the work has a critical dimension, which is particularly pronounced in Posenenske's paintings: "When Ch. P. reaches for the spray can and sprays over an industrially produced relief, when she follows lines drawn with the ruler with colored Scotch tape and squashes the adhesive tape at the angles, etc., the barbs are suddenly there, and you suddenly see them shining through in the perfect industrial sculptures," Jochem Hendricks wrote in 2000 on the occasion of a Posenenske exhibition. "What I realized was that consistency alone does not make good art; the impurities are also important."[12]

The impurities in Aoun's fragile, Minimalist paper works—cracks, creases, perforations—are sometimes quite brutal, almost destructive. For her *Paperplanes* (2018) from the Deutsche Bank Collection, she pushed folded paper through an industrial printer inevitably jamming it pp. 50 \ 51, 68 \ 69. It was an act of violence, also for the artist, who had to pull the snagged paper out of the printer. Instead of creating an image, the printer left ink residue on the folded edges and sprayed the paper in fine blue shades. Impressions of

10   Ibid.
11   *Lands of Matter 2003–2018* (2019) relies on an even larger database of commodities than *Datascape*. In her current work at the PalaisPopulaire, 99 different categories are presented, and in contrast to *Datascape*, with 55 categories, there are no longer unknown goods. The wares include processed stones for construction, coffee, iron parts, books, brochures and leaflets, carbon and copy paper, propane gas, cane sugar, corn, wheat and grain, potatoes, and automobiles.
12   Quoted from Verena Kuni, "Charlotte Posenenske," in *Kunstbulletin* 1–2/2000, https://www.artlog.net/de/kunstbulletin-1-2-2000/charlotte-posenenske

mit Fotografie und digitalen Drucktechniken zu experimentieren. Im Fokus
stand dabei für sie schon bald der städtische Raum. „In meiner Arbeit
beschäftige ich mich mit Urbanistik, aber auch mit Werbeflächen und der
Erzeugung von Bildern und wie diese Dinge unterschwellig die gesamte
städtische Umgebung prägen", sagt Aoun. „Mich interessiert, wie sich diese Übersättigung, diese Erschöpfung, die daraus resultiert, auf unsere
Gefühle auswirken."[8] Sie sehe sich dabei immer die Daten genau an, die ihr
persönlich am nächsten seien.[9] Das meint Aoun räumlich: Es kann ebenso
gut eine Apple Watch wie auch eine urbane Umgebung sein. So begann sie
für ihre Arbeit *Datascape 2003–2014* (2016) Frachtdaten aus dem Hafen
in Beirut zu sammeln – ihre Galerie lag direkt am Hafen. „Ich musste auf die
Informationen um mich herum reagieren."[10] Der Hafen in Beirut spielt eine
maßgebliche Rolle für die libanesische Wirtschaft und die Infrastruktur
der Stadt. So erzählt Aoun im Gespräch mit Hou Hanru, dem Künstlerischen
Direktor des MAXXI in Rom und Mitglied des Global Art Advisory Council
der Deutschen Bank: „Ich habe die Daten von 55 unterschiedlichen Waren
gesammelt, die im Hafen umgeschlagen werden und habe alles festgehalten: die Tonnage, das Gewicht der Güter, vom Naturprodukt bis hin zum
Tier, vom Auto bis zum Baumaterial. Von 2003 bis 2014 habe ich die Tonnage, also das Volumengewicht, das monatlich und jährlich von jedem
einzelnen Produkt verladen wird, genau notiert. Die Grafiken dazu haben
sich dann in diese stummen Landschaften verwandelt. Dafür habe ich die
Daten sozusagen als sehr sinnliche und physikalische Masse auf das Papier übertragen. Doch zugleich erzählen die Grafiken auch eine Geschichte
über Beirut."[11] Diese Geschichte erscheint in den Hügeln und Ebenen von
Aouns Datenlandschaft nicht nur abstrakt-poetisch. Während sich aus
den Daten der meisten Jahre, aus den Bewegungen der Schiffe, Container
und Waren ein fast harmonischer Rhythmus von Höhen und Tiefen ergibt,
werden die Daten zu Beginn des Krieges im Sommer 2006 radikal unterbrochen: Die deklarierte Gesamtfracht sinkt auf null herab, die Kurve des
Gewichts der nicht deklarierten Waren, der Waren also, deren tatsächliche
Inhalte nicht transparent werden, steigt von null zu einem wahren Gebirge
auf – über die Inhalte dieser Container lässt sich nur spekulieren.

Disruptionen

Immer wieder tauchen in Aouns Arbeiten solche radikalen Einbrüche und
Störungen auf: Der Brunnen verspritzt Farbe und seine Düsen verkleben.
Das Papier bleibt im Drucker stecken, die Farbe verläuft oder verblasst.
Auf den ersten Blick scheinen Aouns Werke ästhetisch in einer minimalis-
tisch-abstrakten Tradition zu stehen. Viele ihrer Arbeiten erinnern an Kon-
krete Kunst oder wirken, als wären sie im Geist deutscher Minimalkunst
der 1960er- und 1970er-Jahre entstanden. Die einfachen, industriellen
und genormten Materialien, mit denen Aoun arbeitet, die Faltungen und
Geometrien erinnern an Werke von Blinky Palermo oder auch Charlotte
Posenenske, in denen auch das Fragmentarische, mit der klassischen
minimalistischen Ästhetik konfrontiert wurden. Hinzu kommt eine kritische
Dimension der Arbeit, die bei Posenenske besonders ausgeprägt ist:

8   Aoun, wie Anm. 1.
9   Im Gespräch mit der Autorin.
10   Ebd.
11   *Lands of Matter 2003–2018* (2019) greift auf eine noch größere Datenbasis von Handelsgütern zurück als
     Datascape. In ihrer aktuellen Arbeit im PalaisPopulaire sind 99 unterschiedliche Kategorien dargestellt, und
     im Gegensatz zu *Datascape* mit 55 Kategorien gibt es keine unbekannten Waren mehr. Zu den Gütern gehören
     u.a. bearbeitete Steine für den Bau, Kaffee, Eisenteile, Bücher, Broschüren und Faltblätter, Kohle- und Kopier-
     papier, Propangas, Rohrzucker, Mais, Weizen und Getreide, Kartoffeln, Automobile.

the machine, traces of pressure and tearing can be seen: an abstract state of emergency, so to speak. But this is not the result of a pre-planned compositional idea. It is, as Aoun points out, the natural result of her experimental arrangements. It's not just about the outcome; it's about the process. "My works may be quite abstract," says Aoun, "but at the same time they resemble something very real."[13] Where the digital image is supposed to appear as if by magic, Aoun brings the hardware into play: the body, the machine, and the paper. The transfer of data that leads to the image, which is barely noticed by the user, becomes a very uncertain, physical matter.

This is reminiscent of the concept of disruption that has been introduced in the economic sphere in recent years, particularly in the context of startups. The basic idea is that business models or even entire markets are broken open by innovations: With more effective, simple, or practical innovation completely replacing the old system. Examples include the replacement of DVDs by streaming services or the threat online mail order companies pose to the brick and mortar retail trade. Although these disturbances can destroy companies, they are not evaluated negatively by the economy, but positively, as a kind of natural process that is inevitable and necessary for progress. Through disruption, evolution turns into revolution; thus, a given product is not redesigned or further developed, but immediately discarded. At the same time, the term has also taken a completely different turn and is used in relation to climate change and politics, albeit under different auspices.

Noise and Silence

According to Aoun, the live stream, which she transfers from the shore of Beirut to the exhibition, refers to the central theme of the exhibition: cycles and the idea that data circulates like water. "When we look at the sea, we usually forget how much it is polluted by plastic waste or the oil industry. We are not thinking about the migration crisis and many other things. This work was so important to me because it shows something inside that actually only happens outside. It also deals with the gentrification of the Lebanese coastline and with access to one of the most important natural resources available to us today."[14] But why does Aoun deliberately interrupt these cycles again and again?

"I deal with this question, which also concerns my work: What happens if one day the hunger for data is completely saturated or even oversaturated?" says Aoun.[15] She describes the overload of images and data as "noise," which more or less subliminally shapes our entire environment. For her, the Minimalist, abstract appearance of her art is akin to breaking down this noise. "This is a way for me to create new experiences, forms of silence, and voids." Instead of adding more volume to the media noise, she condenses it in her work and gives it a material form, a form that makes it possible to sensually grasp and rethink otherwise intangible connections. Aoun's works can be read as abstract symbols for digital processes. They do not merely represent something, but are physical events themselves. You can feel the mechanical force she applies to her printers to silence the noise.

The disruption in Aoun's work is so great that, in contrast to the current economic, ecological, and social upheavals, it no longer "goes on somehow."

13   In conversation with the author, February 20, 2019.
14   Ibid.
15   Ibid.

„Wenn Ch. P. zur Spraydose greift und ein industriell gefertigtes Relief
überspritzt, wenn sie mit dem Lineal gezogene Linien mit farbigem Tesa-
band nachgeht und das Klebeband dabei in den Winkeln zerquetscht
usw., sind die Widerhaken auf einmal da, und man sieht sie plötzlich auch
in den perfekten Industrieskulpturen durchscheinen“, schreibt Jochem
Hendricks im Jahr 2000 anlässlich einer Posenenske-Ausstellung.
„Was mir klar wurde, ist, dass Konsequenz alleine noch keine gute Kunst
ausmacht, die Unreinheiten sind auch wichtig.“[12]

Die Unreinheiten auf Aouns fragilen, minimalistisch anmutenden
Papierarbeiten sind zum Teil ziemlich brutal, fast zerstörerisch: Risse,
Knicke, Perforationen. Für ihre *Paperplanes* (2018) aus der Sammlung
Deutsche Bank schob sie gefaltetes Papier durch einen Industriedrucker,
der zwangsläufig blockierte S. 50\51, 68\69. Ein Akt der Gewalt, auch für die
Künstlerin, die das verhakte Papier aus dem Drucker zerren musste. Statt
ein Bild zu machen, hinterließ der Drucker Farbreste an den Faltkanten
und besprühte das Papier in feinen Blauabstufungen. Es sind die Abdrücke der Maschine, Druck- und Reißspuren zu sehen, sozusagen ein
abstrakter Ausnahmezustand. Doch dieser entspringt keiner vorgeplanten
Kompositionsidee – er ist, wie Aoun betont, das natürliche Ergebnis ihrer
Versuchsanordnungen. Es geht nicht nur um das Ergebnis, sondern
vielmehr um den Prozess. „Meine Werke mögen ziemlich abstrakt sein“,
sagt Aoun, „doch zugleich ähneln sie etwas sehr Realem.“[13] Da, wo das
digitale Bild wie von Zauberhand aufscheinen soll, bringt Aoun die Hardware ins Spiel: den Körper, die Maschine und das Papier. Der eigentlich
vom Nutzer kaum bemerkte Transfer von Daten, der zum Bild führt, wird
zu einer sehr unsicheren, physischen Angelegenheit.

Das lässt an den Begriff der Disruption denken, der im Bereich der
Wirtschaft in den letzten Jahren besonders im Kontext von Startups ein-
geführt wurde. Die Grundidee dabei ist, dass Geschäftsmodelle oder auch
ganze Märkte durch Innovationen aufgebrochen werden: Die effektivere,
einfachere oder praktischere Innovation ersetzt das alte System komplett.
Als Beispiele dienen etwa die Ablösung von DVDs durch Streaming-
Dienste oder die Gefährdung des Einzelhandels durch Online-Versand-
häuser. Diese Störungen können Firmen vernichten. Sie werden von der
Wirtschaft jedoch nicht negativ, sondern positiv bewertet, als eine Art
natürlicher Prozess, der unvermeidlich und notwendig für den Fortschritt
ist. Durch Disruption schlägt die Evolution um in Revolution, das Produkt
wird nicht umgestaltet oder weiterentwickelt, sondern gleich abgeschafft.
Zugleich hat der Begriff auch eine ganz andere Wendung genommen
und wird in Bezug auf den Klimawandel und die Politik genutzt, allerdings
unter anderen Vorzeichen.

Rauschen und Ruhe

Der Livestream, den sie von der Küste in Beirut in die Ausstellung überträgt, verweist laut Aoun auf das zentrale Thema der Ausstellung: auf
Kreisläufe und auf die Idee, dass Daten genauso wie Wasser zirkulieren:
„Wenn wir auf das Meer schauen, vergessen wir meistens, wie sehr es
durch Plastikmüll oder die Erdölindustrie verschmutzt wird. Wir denken
nicht an die Migrationskrise und viele andere Dinge. Für mich war diese
Arbeit so wichtig, weil sie im Innenraum etwas zeigt, das sich eigentlich

12   Verena Kuni, „Charlotte Posenenske“, in: *Kunstbulletin*, 1-2/2000, https://www.artlog.net/de/kunst-
bulletin-1-2-2000/charlotte-posenenske
13   Im Gespräch mit der Autorin.

The overload and collapse of an old system creates a reduced beauty. From a distance, Aoun's works evoke a meditative serenity. The fountains could suggest public squares, meeting places, a stylized form of the agora where community is formed and debated—germ cells of democracy. Politics is not made visible and comprehensible in back rooms, but in public. For Homer, the absence of an agora is a sign of corruption and lawlessness. But as you get closer to Aoun's works, the damage caused by simultaneous excess and lack becomes discernible. If the installation with the four fountains, *Infinite Energy, Finite Time* (2019), was viewed symbolically, the fountains could be a reminder of the disappearance of democratic processes and public spaces.

The silence that reigns in Aoun's work also forces us to think about its causes. The oversaturation of her fountain system, which gradually turns the ink black, mirrors the oversaturation of big data being collected through advertising, cookies, and the monitoring of systems in networks of companies on social media platforms. "The more you watch videos on YouTube, on Google, receive data; the more you give away data without noticing," declares Aoun. "And this is the reason why everything is free and so easily accessible, because they need the information from you."[16] Recent debates about the 2018 Facebook-Cambridge Analytica data scandal, manipulated elections, and apps that tap biometric data also bear witness to this. Data has now overtaken oil in value, claims Brittany Kaiser, a former director at the now defunct political consulting firm Cambridge Analytica, in *The Great Hack* (2019).[17] Although there is no objective yardstick for this increase in profits, this too, is of course reflected in the black printing ink circulating through Aoun's fountains. Data, including our personal data, does not simply disappear: It materializes, becomes a product, represents power, and can be monetized. Whoever possesses big data increasingly determines what we buy and how we see the world. The enormous amount of data generated and transmitted manifests itself in the ecosystem: In the installation of fiber-optic cables, the construction of data centers and server farms, ultimately resulting in significantly increased energy needs and the concomitant climate-damaging CO_2 emissions.

Aoun's exhibition *seeing is believing* does not merely illustrate this. Through abstraction, it creates sensitivity for the material dimension of data and information and for how it is hacked. Aoun demonstrates not only how political and economic powers shape, abuse, and deploy our matrix, but also how we can appropriate it in an act of self-empowerment. While Aoun acts as an investigator in *Datascape* and *Lands of Matter 2003–2018* (2019) pp. 38 \ 39, depicting data as a landscape, she sabotages the system in other works, allowing it to fail due to disturbances and involuntarily producing completely new, abstract images. Aoun's fountains, which spill and spray ink on the floor, also create abstract images.

On the wall above the fountains, the artist installs the contours of their round basins, made visible on the floor during previous exhibitions as ink spilled out beyond their confines pp. 41–43. The circular forms, running along the edges in a mist of splashes and ink, have the character of informal postwar modernism. They recall the fire and soot pictures of Otto Piene and the group ZERO, which he founded together with Günther Uecker and Heinz Mack. As a reaction to the horrors of World War II and the Third

16   Ibid.
17   Trailer for *The Great Hack,* YouTube video, 2:27 min, uploaded by "Netflix," July 11, 2019, https://www.youtube.com/watch?v=iX8GxLP1FHo
All online links accessed on September 2, 2019.

nur im Außenraum abspielt. Sie befasst sich auch mit der Gentrifizierung
der Küstenlinie des Libanons und mit dem Zugang zu einer der wichtigsten
natürlichen Ressourcen, die uns heute noch zur Verfügung stehen."[14]
Warum jedoch werden eben diese Kreisläufe bei Aoun immer wieder unterbrochen und zwar vorsätzlich?

„Ich beschäftige mich mit dieser Frage, die auch meine Arbeit betrifft:
Was passiert, wenn eines Tages der Hunger nach Daten völlig gesättigt
oder sogar übersättigt ist?",[15] sagt Aoun. Sie bezeichnet den Overload an
Bildern und Daten als „Lärm", der mehr oder weniger unterschwellig
unsere gesamte Umgebung prägt. Das minimalistische, abstrakte Erschei-
nungsbild ihrer Kunst ist für sie so etwas wie das Herunterbrechen dieses
Rauschens. „Das ist ein Weg für mich, neue Erfahrungen, Formen von
Stille und Leerstellen zu erzeugen." Anstatt dem medialen Lärm noch mehr
Lautstärke hinzuzufügen, kondensiert sie ihn in ihrer Arbeit und gibt ihm
eine materielle Form. Eine Form, die es ermöglicht, sonst kaum greifbare
Zusammenhänge sinnlich zu erfassen und so zu überdenken. Aouns Werke
können als abstrakte Sinnbilder für digitale Prozesse gelesen werden.
Dabei bilden sie nicht lediglich etwas ab, sondern sind selbst physische
Ereignisse. Man spürt die mechanische Gewalt, die sie ihren Druckern
antut, um das Rauschen zum Schweigen zu bringen.

Die Disruption in Aouns Arbeiten ist so groß, dass es im Gegensatz
zu den aktuellen ökonomischen, ökologischen und sozialen Umbrüchen
nicht mehr „irgendwie weitergeht". Die Überforderung und der Zusam-
menbruch eines alten Systems lässt eine reduzierte Schönheit entstehen.
Aus der Entfernung suggerieren Aouns Werke eine meditative Heiterkeit.
Die Brunnen könnten öffentliche Plätze, Treffpunkte suggerieren, eine
stilisierte Form der Agora, an denen sich Gemeinschaft bildet und debat-
tiert wird – Keimzellen der Demokratie. Politik wird nicht in Hinterzimmern,
sondern öffentlich sichtbar, begreifbar gemacht. Bei Homer gilt das Feh-
len einer Agora als Anzeichen für Korruption, Recht- und Gesetzlosigkeit.
Doch tritt man näher an Aouns Werke heran, wird der Schaden sichtbar,
den gleichzeitiger Exzess und Mangel angerichtet haben. Würde man
die Installation mit vier Brunnen – *Infinite Energy, Finite Time* – symbolisch
betrachten, könnten sie eine Mahnung über das Verschwinden von demo-
kratischen Prozessen und öffentlichen Räumen sein.

Die Stille, die in Aouns Werk herrscht, zwingt auch zum Nachdenken
über ihre Ursachen. Die Übersättigung des Brunnensystems, die die Tinte
allmählich schwarz färbt, ähnelt der Übersättigung an Big Data, die im
Netz von Firmen auf Social-Media-Plattformen, durch Werbung, Cookies
und dem Mithören von Systemen abgeschöpft wird. „Je mehr man Videos
auf YouTube ansieht, googelt, Daten empfängt, umso mehr gibt man
auch Daten her, ohne es zu merken", sagt Aoun. „Das ist auch der Grund,
weshalb alles umsonst und so leicht zugänglich ist, weil sie die Informationen von dir brauchen."[16] Davon zeugen auch die aktuellen Debatten über
die Datenskandale von Facebook und Cambridge Analytica, manipulierte
Wahlen, Apps, die biometrische Daten abzapfen. Daten hätten in ihrem
Wert mittlerweile Erdöl überholt, behauptet Brittany Kaiser, die ehemalige
Direktorin bei Cambridge Analytica, in der Dokumentation *The Great
Hack* (2019).[17] Auch wenn es tatsächlich keinen objektiven Maßstab für

14   Ebd.
15   Ebd.
16   Ebd.
17   Netflix-Trailer für *The Great Hack*. YouTube-Video, 2:27 Min., 11. Juli 2019, https://www.youtube.com/
watch?v=iX8GxLP1FHo
Online-Verweise abgerufen am 2. September 2019.

Reich, their performances, sculptures, and paintings in the 1950s exuded a utopian spirit of departure associated with technological progress, internationalism, and the spiritual-cosmic dimension of space travel. Many abstract ZERO works are reminiscent of starry skies and planets, of elements of the microcosm and the macrocosm. That poetic dream of boundless transcendence and social optimism also flickers in the bright colors of Aoun's wall work, in the network of fountains, in the almost cheerful undulations of the diagrams, and in her fragile cast copper pine needles. They convey the hope that humans will not destroy the earth, that everything will still come together after all: civilization and nature, virtuality and reality, networking and personal freedom. Aoun's disruptive hacks suggest that the old system could be replaced by a new, more humane one. The excessive demands and noise must stop, because we need a space for contemplation to find new systems and ourselves.

diesen Gewinnzuwachs gibt, lässt das natürlich an die schwarze Druckerfarbe denken, die durch Aouns Brunnen zirkuliert. Daten, und zwar auch unsere persönlichen Daten, verschwinden nicht einfach irgendwo. Sie materialisieren sich, sind Ware, Macht und damit Geld. Wer in den Besitz von Big Data kommt, bestimmt zunehmend darüber, was wir kaufen und wie wir die Welt sehen. Die ungeheuren Mengen von Daten, die erzeugt und übertragen werden, manifestieren sich im Ökosystem: in der Installation von Glasfaserkabeln, der Errichtung von Rechenzentren und Serverfarmen, die für erheblich steigenden Energiebedarf und damit verbundene klimaschädliche CO_2-Emissionen sorgen.

Aouns Ausstellung *seeing is believing* ist weit davon entfernt, dies lediglich illustrieren zu wollen. Sie schafft durch die Abstraktion Sensibilität für die materielle Dimension von Daten und Informationen und dafür, wie sie gehackt werden. Aoun führt nicht nur vor, wie politische und ökonomische Mächte unsere Matrix formen, missbrauchen und nutzen, sondern auch, wie wir sie uns in einem Akt der Selbstermächtigung aneignen können. Während Aoun in *Datascape* und *Lands of Matter 2003–2018* (2019) S. 30\39 als investigative Ermittlerin fungiert und Daten wie eine Landschaft abbildet, sabotiert sie in anderen Arbeiten das System, lässt es durch Störungen scheitern und unfreiwillig völlig neue, abstrakte Bilder hervorbringen. Auch Aouns Brunnen, die kleckern und Farbe auf den Boden spritzen, schaffen abstrakte Bilder.

An der Wand über den Brunnen installiert die Künstlerin die Umrisse der runden Becken, die sich beim Lackieren der Stahlkonstruktionen mit Sprühfarbe auf dem Boden abgezeichnet haben S. 41–43. Die kreisrunden, an den Rändern in einem Nebel aus Spritzern und Farbe verlaufenden Formen haben die Ausstrahlung informeller Kunst der Nachkriegsmoderne. Sie erinnern an die Feuer- und Rauchbilder von Otto Piene und der von ihm gemeinsam mit Günther Uecker und Heinz Mack gegründeten Gruppe ZERO. Als Reaktion auf die Gräuel des Zweiten Weltkrieges und des Dritten Reichs verströmten sie in den späten 1950er-Jahren in ihren Performances, Skulpturen und Bildern einen utopischen Aufbruchsgeist, der mit technologischem Fortschritt, Internationalität und der spirituellkosmischen Dimension der Raumfahrt verbunden war. Viele der abstrakten ZERO-Werke erinnern an Sternenhimmel und Planeten, an Elemente des Mikro- und des Makrokosmos. Auch in den leuchtenden Farben von Aouns Wandarbeit, im Netzwerk der Brunnen, den fast heiteren Wellenformen der Diagramme und den fragilen, aus Kupfer gegossenen Piniennadeln flackert dieser poetische Traum von grenzenloser Transzendenz und gesellschaftlichem Optimismus auf. Da ist die Hoffnung, dass der Mensch die Erde nicht zerstört, dass alles doch noch zusammenfindet: Zivilisation und Natur, Virtualität und Wirklichkeit, Vernetzung und persönliche Freiheit. Aouns disruptive Hacks deuten an, dass das alte System durch ein neues, humaneres ersetzt werden könnte. Die Überforderung und der Lärm müssen aufhören, denn wir brauchen einen Raum für Kontemplation, um neue Systeme und zu uns selbst zu finden.

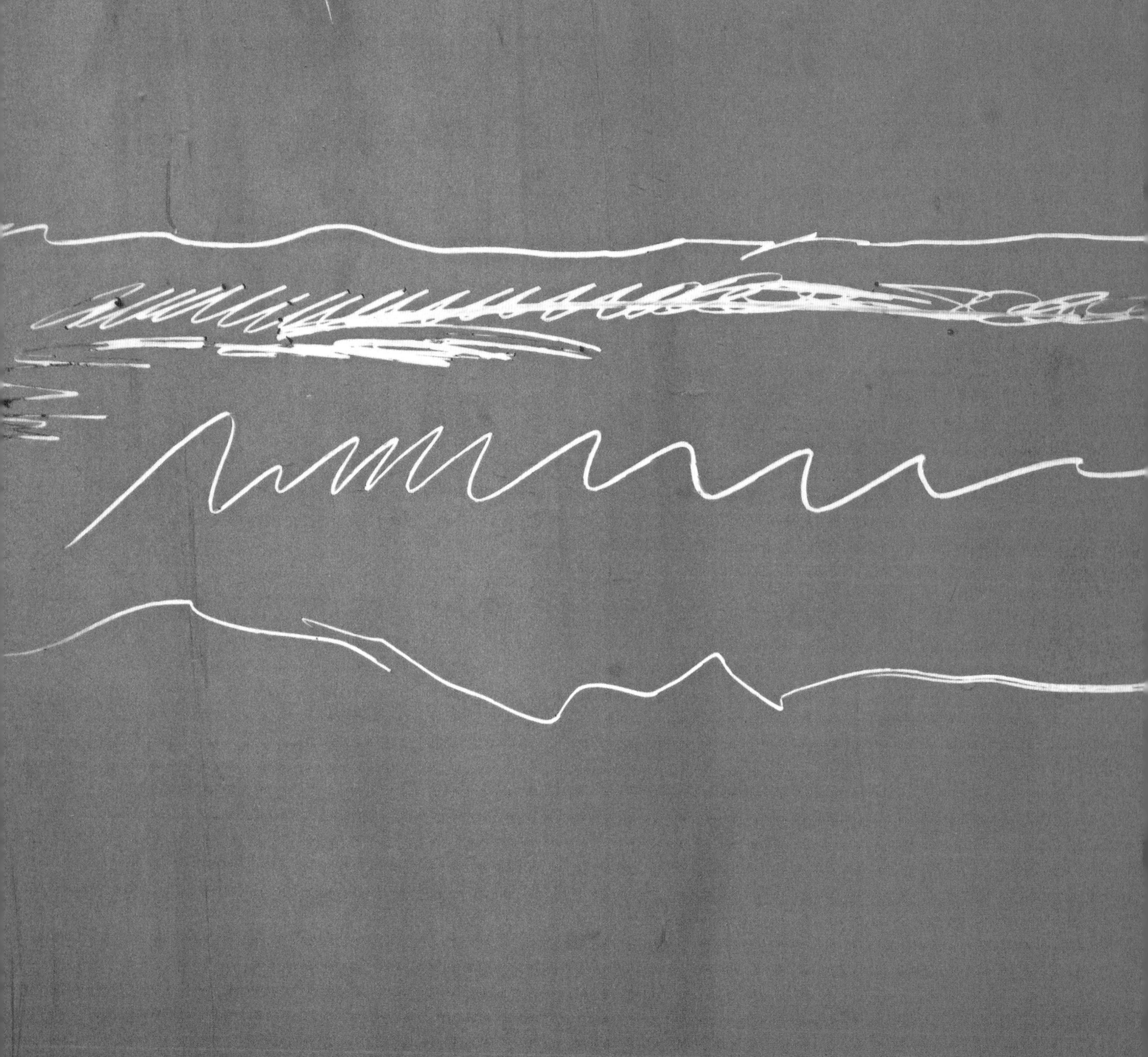

MURTAZA VALI

THE MATTER OF FACT

One of the central theses of pioneering media theorists like Marshall McLuhan and Friedrich Kittler is that technological progress, especially paradigmatic shifts in the medium and apparatus through which information is recorded, circulated and consumed, engenders profound changes in society and culture.[1] According to McLuhan, each new media technology "massages" us differently, producing a distinct set of effects on our sensorial and perceptual capacities and habits.[2] The global transition from analogue to digital media, and the attendant virtualization of data, information, images and even economic, political and social relations has acutely unsettled our conventional understandings of time and space, attention and memory, reality and artifice, self and community. It has recalibrated our ways of seeing and being, knowing and doing, looking and living, perceiving and remembering.

While Caline Aoun's art seeks to respond to the wide-ranging effects of this technological revolution her investigations rarely appear in the formats, platforms and interfaces one commonly associates with the digital and virtual: computers and smartphones, social media and websites, LCD screens, video projections and virtual reality headsets. Instead, she prefers inkjet prints on paper or vinyl, pulped paper, and, most recently, bubbling fountains of ink. Using these mediums, which are all resolutely physical and tactile, she attempts to rematerialize the invisible and intangible flow of digital data by revealing the very real, substantial and bodily substructure that enables it. Aoun is less interested in the aesthetics or politics of digital images per se—their "poorness," their vulnerability to manipulation and artifice, their democratic ubiquity—than the speed and ease with which digitized data and information disseminates and circulates, flitting effortlessly and endlessly between and across various formats, supports and interfaces.[3] She interrupts these never-ending loops by orchestrating

1   Marshall McLuhan, *Understanding Media: The Extensions of Man* (New York, 1964); Friedrich A. Kittler, *Gramophone, Film, Typewriter* (Stanford, 1999).
2   Marshall McLuhan and Quentin Fiore, *The Medium is the Massage: An Inventory of Effects* (New York, 1967).
3   Hito Steyerl, "In Defense of the Poor Image," *e-flux Journal*, no. 10 (November, 2009), accessed August 3, 2019, https://www.e-flux.com/journal/10/61362/in-defense-of-the-poor-image/.

TATSACHEN

Eine der zentralen Thesen wegweisender Medientheoretiker wie Marshall McLuhan und Friedrich Kittler lautet, dass technologischer Fortschritt tiefgreifende Veränderungen in Gesellschaft und Kultur zur Folge hat. Das gelte vor allem für paradigmatische Weiterentwicklungen von Medien und Geräten, über die sich Informationen aufzeichnen, in Umlauf bringen und konsumieren lassen.[1] Nach McLuhan beeinflusst uns jede neue Medientechnologie auf ihre eigene Art und Weise und übt eine Reihe von Wirkungen auf unsere Sinnes- und Wahrnehmungsfähigkeiten und -gewohnheiten aus.[2] Der weltweite Wechsel von analogen zu digitalen Medien und die damit einhergehende Virtualisierung von Daten, Informationen, Bildern und sogar ökonomischen, politischen und sozialen Beziehungen hat unsere hergebrachten Auffassungen von Zeit und Raum, Aufmerksamkeit und Erinnerung, Realität und Künstlichkeit, von Selbst und Gemeinschaft grundlegend ins Wanken gebracht. Es hat unsere Art und Weise, zu sehen und zu sein, zu wissen und zu handeln, zu schauen und zu leben, wahrzunehmen und uns zu erinnern, neu kalibriert.

Obwohl Caline Aoun versucht, mit ihren Werken auf die umfassenden Auswirkungen dieser technologischen Revolution zu reagieren, stehen ihre Arbeiten nicht im direkten Kontext der Formate, Plattformen und Schnittstellen, die zumeist mit dem Digitalen und Virtuellen assoziiert werden, wie etwa Computer und Smartphone, Soziale Medien und Websites, LCD-Bildschirme, Videoprojektionen oder Virtual-Reality-Headsets. Stattdessen arbeitet sie vorzugsweise mit Inkjetdrucken auf Papier oder Vinyl, mit Papierpulpe und jüngst auch mit Brunnen, aus denen Druckertinte sprudelt. Indem sie diese Werkstoffe verwendet, die ausgesprochen materiell und taktil zu erfahren sind, versucht sie den unsichtbaren und nichtgreifbaren Strom der digitalen Daten zu rematerialisieren. Dabei lenkt sie den Blick auf die sehr reale, substanzielle und körperliche Substruktur, die das „Nichtsichtbare" überhaupt erst ermöglicht. Aouns Interesse richtet sich weniger auf die Ästhetik oder die Bezüge von digitalen Bildern per se, auf ihre „Armseligkeit" und Anfälligkeit für Manipulation und Fälschung oder auf ihre demokratische Verfügbarkeit, vielmehr beobachtet sie die Geschwindigkeit und Leichtigkeit, in der sich digitalisierte Daten und Informationen verbreiten und zirkulieren, wie mühe- und endlos sie zwischen und über verschiedene Formate, Supports und Schnittstellen hin- und herhuschen.[3] Aoun unterbricht diese endlosen Loops, indem sie Momente der Störung inszeniert. So schafft sie Bilder und Objekte, die den Kreislauf so sehr verlangsamt haben, dass Daten – seien es Informationen oder Bilder – wieder tatsächlich gesehen und gefühlt werden können. Ihre Arbeit hebt die Lebendigkeit des Materials als Mittel gegen die Dematerialisierung des täglichen Lebens hervor.[4]

1   Marshall McLuhan, *Die magischen Kanäle, Understanding Media*, Dresden 1992, und Friedrich A. Kittler, *Grammophon / Film / Typewriter*, Berlin 1986.
2   Marshall McLuhan und Quentin Fiore, *Das Medium ist die Massage: Ein Inventar medialer Effekte*, Stuttgart 2011.
3   Hito Steyerl, „In Defense of the Poor Image", in: *e-flux Journal*, Nr. 10, November 2009, Zugriff 3. August 2019, https://www.e-flux.com/journal/10/61362/in-defense-of-the-poor-image/
4   Jane Bennett, *Vibrant Matter: A Political Ecology of Things*, Durham 2010.

moments of friction, creating images and objects that slow the cycle down enough for that data—be it information or image—to be seen and felt again. Her work foregrounds the vibrancy of matter as an antidote against the digital dematerialization of everyday life.[4]

Though not immediately evident in its final presentation, Aoun's art demands a substantial investment of time and manual labor to produce, from the mind-numbingly laborious task of repeatedly printing the same computer file to the meticulous care and sustained effort required to cast a surface twice, first in silicone, and then in pulped paper, diligently squeezing out all excess liquid to end up with a thin but solid form. Her minimal language—non-representational forms, simple geometries, and a preference for bold, flat colors—focuses the viewer's attention, drawing us in to the minute and easily overlooked details. The absence of recognizable content in the final work makes clear that what is at stake for Aoun is not *what* is being looked at but *how* we look. In contrast to the disinterested and fleeting glances we use when we scroll through our social media feeds, her works demand sustained acts of close looking. And, somewhat counterintuitively, this refined syntax is particularly apt for investigating the effects of an epistemological transformation that is itself an abstraction of sorts, a reduction of the complexities and contingencies of the real physical world into strings of binary code and algorithmic functions. Originally exhibited at Beirut's Marfa' Projects,—located close to the city's port—the work *Datascape* (2016) consists of a series of graphs that show the monthly tonnage in the port of Beirut of various goods imported between 2003–2014. While some track common foodstuffs like coffee, sugar, corn, potatoes, wheat and grain, or materials related to the artist's practice—such as carbon paper, books and other printed matter—others record industrial products and natural resources like motor vehicles and petroleum, or stone and iron, both commonly used in construction. For her exhibition in Berlin, Aoun continues this concept with *Lands of Matter 2003–2018* (2019) pp. 38 \ 39, a work that tracks all goods entering Beirut by sea and air between 2003 and 2018. In both works, Aoun succinctly translates quanta into qualia, visualizing numerical data as pared down graphs that have a heft to them that is undeniably haptic. Without identifying axes, the abstract measure of weight is made palpable. Displayed in rows, the graphs resemble the cross section of a landscape whose peaks and valleys track the shifting dynamics of international maritime trade. For Aoun, this largely out of sight material mercantile network is a suggestive analogue for the invisible and intangible circuits through which digital information travels. *Datascape* and *Lands of Matter 2003–2018* also present an abstract history of Lebanon through its specific patterns of trade and everyday consumption across years of peacetime prosperity, the disruptions of the 2006 invasion by Israel, and the ongoing conflict in neighboring Syria. Unsurprisingly, of all the imports, only wheat and grain spiked during wartime, quietly reminding us of how little is actually necessary for basic survival and how a reliance on foreign trade can leave a population particularly vulnerable to scarcity in times of crisis.

Like *Datascape* and *Lands of Matter 2003–2018*, much of Aoun's work to date has been created using an inkjet printer, a tool that is an integral part of our technological vernacular, albeit one whose utility is itself increasingly threatened by advances in digital technology. The printer functions as a threshold between the analogue and the digital, turning out

4   Jane Bennett, *Vibrant Matter: A Political Ecology of Things* (Durham, 2010).

Obwohl es in der finalen Installation nicht unmittelbar zu erkennen ist, erfordert Aouns Werk einen erheblichen Aufwand an Zeit und Handarbeit: von der unglaublich fordernden Tätigkeit, immer wieder die gleiche Datei auszudrucken, bis hin zur äußerst genauen und anhaltenden Aufmerksamkeit und Anstrengung, die sie von sich abverlangt, wenn sie eine Oberfläche zweifach sorgfältig abformt: erst in Silikon, dann mit Papierpulpe, aus der sie alle Flüssigkeit herauspresst, um einen dünnen, aber nach dem Trocknen festen Abdruck zu erhalten. Ihre minimalistische Formensprache – ungegenständliche Formen, reduzierte Geometrie und eine Präferenz von kräftigen matten Farben – zieht den Betrachter an, lässt ihn näher an die winzigen und leicht übersehenen Details rücken. Die Abwesenheit eines wiedererkennbaren Inhalts im finalen Werk macht deutlich, dass es Aoun nicht darum geht, „was" wahrgenommen wird, sondern „wie" wir es anschauen. Im Gegensatz zu den gelangweilten und flüchtigen Blicken, mit denen Social-Media-Feeds durchgescrollt werden, verlangen ihre Werke nach gründlicher Betrachtung aus der Nähe. Ein wenig gegen unsere Intuition – ist die verfeinerte Syntax ihres Werks besonders dazu geeignet, die Auswirkungen einer erkenntnistheoretischen Transformation zu untersuchen – der digitalen Umwälzung, die selbst quasi eine Abstraktion in ihrer Reduktion von Komplexitäten und Zufälligkeiten der realen physischen Welt auf Stränge binärer Codes und Algorithmusfunktionen verkörpert.

Zuerst in Beiruts Marfa' Projects in der Nähe des Hafens der Stadt ausgestellt, besteht *Datascape* (2016) aus einer Serie von Diagrammen, die die monatliche Tonnage verschiedener Importgüter in den Jahren 2003 bis 2014 darstellen. Während einige die Menge von Grundnahrungsmitteln wie Kaffee, Zucker, Mais, Kartoffeln, Weizen und Getreide aufzeichnen, oder von Materialien, die von der Künstlerin verwendet werden wie Kohlepapier, Bücher und andere Drucksachen, gehen weitere Diagramme auf Industriegüter und natürliche Ressourcen ein, darunter Kraftfahrzeuge, Erdgas, Steine und Eisen für die Bauindustrie. In ihrer Ausstellung in Berlin verfolgt Aoun dieses Konzept weiter in *Lands of Matter 2003–2018* (2019) S. 38 \ 39, nun mit noch umfassenderen Daten des Handels in Beirut. Aoun übersetzt in diesen Arbeiten prägnant abstrakte Mengen in Qualia – in subjektive Erlebnisinhalte. Sie visualisiert in Zahlen festgehaltene Daten in reduzierten Schaublättern, deren Ausdruckskraft unleugbar haptisch ist. Ohne die sonst üblichen erklärenden Achsen wird die abstrakte Maßeinheit des Gewichts regelrecht greifbar. In Reihen nebeneinander gehängt, ähneln die Diagramme dem Höhenprofil einer Landschaft, deren Gipfel und Täler die wechselnde Dynamik des internationalen Handels zur See nachzeichnen. Aoun sieht dieses merkantile Netzwerk, das unleugbar materiell ist, aber größtenteils außerhalb unserer alltäglichen Wahrnehmung liegt, als eine suggestive Analogie der unsichtbaren und ungreifbaren Kreisläufe, in denen sich digitale Informationen bewegen. Wegen der präzise ablesbaren Muster des Handels und täglichen Konsums in den Jahren des Friedens und wachsenden Wohlstands und den Brüchen durch die israelische Invasion im Jahr 2006 und den fortdauernden Konflikt im benachbarten Syrien sind *Datascape* und darauf aufbauend auch *Lands of Matter 2003–2018* auch eine abstrakte Geschichte des Libanons. Außer bei Weizen und Getreide sinken die Importe nicht überraschend zu Kriegszeiten, und erinnern uns so daran, wie wenig tatsächlich zum bloßen Überleben notwendig ist, und dass das Vertrauen der Bevölkerung in einen funktionierenden Außenhandel sie in Krisenzeiten besonders verwundbar macht.

tangible, hard copies of otherwise fugitive digital data. Aoun subverts the printer's primary function of reproducing textual and photographic information, instead using it to print abstractions that range from austere monochromes to gentle and not-so-gentle color gradations, some recalling the soft indeterminacies of Color Field Painting while others approximate the hazy sublimity of dawn and dusk, times of the day that Aoun returns to often in her work.[5] In early works like *Portals* (2009) and *Sliding Gazes* (2010) Aoun produced black voids by repeatedly printing differently colored rectangles on top of each other, their composite character only revealed at the edges due to slightly imprecise registrations between sequential layers, while in *Glow to Scatter* (2009), she used mostly empty printer cartridges, producing an evanescent field from the dregs of ink in them.

Similarly, to create *Contemplating Dispersions, 536 ml* (2018) pp. 52 \ 53, Aoun repeatedly printed the same all-black image on a CMYK inkjet printer until it ran out of ink, installing the product of each iteration of this process in a row, with multiple attempts brought together to form a mural-sized grid. Throughout history, technological innovation has been driven by the desire to overcome the limits of the human, ensuring greater efficiency and maximal profits. Aoun's process purposely and perversely imposes a particularly human quality back onto a mechanical tool: exhaustion. As the colored inks run out at varying rates or the printer heads clog, the velvety black monochrome, that zero degree of painting, disintegrates into striated fields of vivid color: deep and bright reds at first, then pinks, purples and occasional streaks of yellow and cyan and, finally, the pure white of the blank page. This chromatic disintegration reveals the composition of this printing process, the most commonly used today, foregrounding the material qualities of the different inks used.

Eschewing more conventional forms of facture, Aoun deploys the printer as a surrogate for her hand and body, reintroducing through its eventual failure—which is both intentional and incidental—the potential for a gesture of expressivity. Updating Andy Warhol's use of the silkscreen for the digital age, she uses repetition to produce difference not identity; the inevitable and irrepressible glitch is the very point of the work. This substitution of the human body for the mechanical tool is not an act of distancing, but is surprisingly intimate and tender. It collapses the historical dichotomy between human and machine by establishing an equivalence between them—through their shared capacity for exhaustion and failure—that the demands of capitalism and technological progress have disavowed.[6]

Aoun reverses the conceptual logic of *Contemplating Dispersions, 536 ml* in her elaborate new relay of fountains at the PalaisPopulaire, each filled with one of the four CMYK inks—cyan, magenta, yellow and black. Gradually, in tiny increments, each of the colored inks will be contaminated by the others, their hues changing and darkening over time into a muddy

5   Aoun's preoccupation with periods of transition between darkness and daylight, and how they affect our perception of a landscape, reappear across different media. A smooth, continuous shift in quality, be it light or color, can be particularly difficult to approximate in a digital format, in which information is broken down into discrete increments. This quality makes it an excellent abstraction through which to register the traces of process and test the limits of the apparatus, recording both manual manipulations and machine malfunctions, as is evident in *At a Glance* (2009), a monochrome print on the characteristic salmon pink newsprint of the *Financial Times*, and *Processing Days and Nights 1–4* (2015), a series of color prints on digital transfer film, which in their own ways approximate the soft pinkish hues of twilight. The waning light of the setting sun is also represented, through its reflection on a circular metallic disc, in the video *A Moment of Singularity in the Cyclical Rhythm of the Sun* (2013), while *Time Travel* (2019), Aoun's recent contribution to the 14th Sharjah Biennial, theatricalized the uncanny and disorienting effects of the space-time compression enabled by instantaneous digital communications, dissolving a live transmission of footage of the sunset in Beirut into a fragile and flickering panorama through the use of four fast spinning projectors.
6   Kerstin Stakemeier, "Crisis and Materiality in Art: On the Becoming of Form and Digitality," in *Power of Material / Politics of Materiality*, eds. Susanne Witzgall and Kerstin Stakemeier (Zurich-Berlin, 2014), 172–84.

Wie bei *Datascape* und *Lands of Matter 2003–2018* ist die Verwendung eines Inkjetdruckers bis heute häufig in Aouns Werk zu finden: Ein Werkzeug, das ein integraler Bestandteil unseres technologischen Alltags ist, allerdings eines, das selbst durch die Fortschritte in der digitalen Technologie in seinem Nutzwert zunehmend bedroht wird. Der Drucker funktioniert an der Grenze des Analogen und Digitalen, er produziert greifbare Papierkopien von ansonsten flüchtigen digitalen Daten. Aoun verwendet den Drucker entgegen seiner primären Funktion, textliche und fotografische Informationen zu reproduzieren. Stattdessen druckt sie Abstraktionen aus, die von streng monochromen bis hin zu zarten und nicht so zarten Farbabstufungen reichen. Einige erinnern an die weiche Unschärfe der Farbfeldmalerei, andere an die Morgen- und Abenddämmerung, Tageszeiten, zu denen Aoun in ihrem Werk Bezug nimmt.[5] In frühen Werken wie *Portals* (2009) und *Sliding Gazes* (2010) erzeugt Aoun schwarze Leerstellen, indem sie immer wieder verschiedenfarbige Rechtecke übereinander druckt, bis sie sich so miteinander verbinden, dass nur an den Rändern die fortlaufenden Farbschichten noch schwach zu erkennen sind. In *Glow to Scatter* (2009) verwendet sie dagegen fast leere Druckerpatronen, um ein immer schwächer werdendes Farbfeld aus den Tintenresten zu erzeugen.

Bei *Contemplating Dispersions, 536 ml* (2018) S. 52 \ 53 druckt Aoun in ähnlicher Weise wiederholt dasselbe Bild in Schwarz auf einem CMYK-Inkjetdrucker aus, bis dieser keine Tinte mehr hat. Die Druckergebnisse aller Schritte hängt sie in einer Reihe auf, so dass die vielfachen Versuche ein wandfüllendes Raster bilden. Im Lauf der Geschichte ist technologische Innovation immer vom Verlangen getrieben gewesen, die dem Menschen gesetzten Grenzen zu überwinden und so größere Effizienz und maximalen Profit zu ermöglichen. Aouns Werkprozess bürdet dagegen voller Absicht einem mechanischen Werkzeug einen menschlichen Zustand auf: den der Erschöpfung. So wie die Farbtinten in unterschiedlicher Geschwindigkeit zu Ende gehen oder den Drucker immer mehr verstopfen, löst sich das schwarz-samtige Monochrom, dieser Nullgrad der Malerei, in gestreifte Felder von lebendiger Farbigkeit auf: Zuerst erscheinen dunkle und helle Rottöne, dann Rosa, Violett und gelegentlich Schlieren in Gelb und Cyan, und zum Schluss das pure Weiß der leeren Blattseite. Diese chromatische Aufspaltung legt den Vorgang des Vierfarbdrucks offen, der heute am häufigsten verwendet wird, und stellt die Materialität der unterschiedlichen Tinten, die hier zum Einsatz kommen, in den Vordergrund.

Aoun setzt den Drucker anstelle ihrer Hände und ihres Körpers ein und vermeidet so die eher konventionelle Form einer persönlichen Handschrift. Durch sein gelegentliches Versagen, das sowohl absichtlich als auch durch den Zufall herbeigeführt wird, sind aber expressive Gesten möglich. Aoun überführt Andy Warhols Siebdruck in das digitale Zeitalter: Sie verwendet die Wiederholung, um eine Differenz zu erzeugen; es geht ihr nicht um die Wiedererkennbarkeit. In der unvermeidbaren und nicht zu

5   Das Phänomen der Dämmerung, den fließenden Übergängen von Licht zu Tagesbeginn und -ende, und wie es unsere Wahrnehmung einer Landschaft verändert, ist ein medienübergreifendes Thema im Werk von Aoun. Allerdings ist es schwierig, sich den sanften Veränderungen einer Eigenschaft – sei es Licht oder Farbe – in einem digitalen Format anzunähern. Aber mit dieser Technik können die Spuren eines Vorgangs erfasst oder die Grenzen von Geräten ausgelotet werden: durch manuelle Manipulation und durch das Auslösen von Fehlfunktionen der Apparate, wie es augenscheinlich in *At a Glance* (2009) geschehen ist, einem monochromen Druck auf das typische Lachsrosa der *Financial Times*, oder in *Processing Days and Nights 1–4* (2015), einer Serie von Farbdrucken auf Digitaltransferfilm, die sich auf ihre Weise an die zartrosafarbene Färbung der Dämmerung annähern. Auf das schwindende Licht der untergehenden Sonne verweist eine kreisförmige, reflektierende Metallscheibe im Video *A Moment of Singularity in the Cyclical Rhythm of the Sun* (2013). *Time Travel* (2019), Aouns Beitrag zur 14. Sharjah Biennial, hat die unheimlichen und in irreführenden Effekte der Verdichtung von Raum und Zeit zum Thema: Die Live-Übertragung des Sonnenuntergangs in Beirut wird durch vier, sich schnell drehende Projektoren in ein fragiles und flimmerndes Panorama aufgelöst.

black. The operative metaphor of this work is saturation, a process that eventually turns any signal into inchoate noise, compromising its legibility. By staging this process Aoun dramatizes and materializes the cognitive effects of the growing deluge of digital data we are subjected to on a daily basis, an oversaturation that weakens our capacity to retain information and construct meaning. While the installation of fountains might be temporary, the carpeting underneath it, which will soak up the unavoidable splatter of ink through the exhibition's run, ensures an enduring document of the work's unfolding. Floating on the gallery's far wall, the halo-like traces of the last iteration of this experiment are spectral reminders that if the speed and volume of circulation continues to grow unabated, such indifferent mottled stains might be all that is left for us to make sense of.

Aoun's other preferred medium is pulped paper, which she has used to hand cast replicas of sections of different architectural surfaces—a swimming pool, a road, the walls and floors of different spaces she has exhibited in, and the base of a shipping container. This technique is decidedly retro and low-tech, especially in light of the growing use by artists of scanning and modeling software and 3-D printers to investigate the impact of digital technologies on the ontological status of objects. Her super low-relief sculptures carefully transcribe the varying textures of these surfaces, from the incised grids of tilework and the knotty grain and interlocking planks of a hardwood floor to the very distinct feels of concrete, asphalt and metal. Embedded within these casts are the physical traces, albeit molecular and largely imperceptible to the human eye, of the histories, memories and experiences that have unfolded in these spaces and on these surfaces. Aoun carefully selects paper stock to achieve different colors for these casts. In an early iteration, *Beirut Art Center Square Meters* (2012) pp. 74–77, she cast sections of the floor of a former furniture factory using a variety of discarded paper found on site to create a series of differently colored monochromes: brown envelopes and pink invoice slips were combined to create two sandy brown parallelograms; phone books were transformed into pastel pink and yellow rectangles; a long horizontal grey band was made out of blue envelopes pulped together with other office paperwork, leaving fragments of letters and tables that appeared on them still visible in the final work; and the incorporation of CMYK ink waste to produce an almost black surface. In subsequent works, she has incorporated carbon paper to achieve a dark charcoal grey or deep blue. At the PalaisPopulaire, Aoun presents cast replicas of segments of the storied structure's walls before its recent renovation, resulting in works that are ontological contradictions: concrete flashbacks, physically present ghosts, material indexes of the building's forgotten and erased past.

As casts, though once removed, these works retain an indexical link to their subjects, much like analogue photography. The growing spread of digital technology has thrust this relationship to the real world into significant crisis. There is a subtle subversion to Aoun's sculptural transcriptions. While something weighty and permanent like a wall, floor or road is replicated in delicate papier-mâché, fragile pine needles collected outside her studio are reproduced in hardy copper (*Pine Needles* (2015) pp. 56 \ 57, 102 \ 103, 106 \ 107), or the fluidity of water is arrested as clear resin, tinted ever so slightly blue (*Still Water* (2015)). While her interest in replication as a process can also be traced back to the infinite reproducibility of digital information, these works intentionally introduce a material and physical discrepancy between the original and the copy. This difference, which is subtle but palpable, engenders a slightly distinct phenomenological

unterdrückenden Störung ihrer „Versuchsanordnung" kommt das Werk genau auf den Punkt. Die Substitution des menschlichen Körpers durch eine Maschine ist bei Aoun nicht ein Akt der Distanzierung, sondern überraschend intim und zärtlich. Die historische Dichotomie von Mensch und Maschine wird durch eine äquivalente Relation aufgelöst, denn Mensch und Maschine erfahren hier gemeinsam Erschöpfung und Scheitern; Funktionsstörungen, die der Kapitalismus und der technologische Fortschritt ihnen eigentlich nicht zugestehen.[6]

Aoun wendet die konzeptuelle Logik von *Contemplating Dispersions, 536 ml* auch in ihrer elaborierten neuen Anordnung der Brunnen im PalaisPopulaire an. Jeder der vier Brunnen ist mit einer Tinte des CMYK-Spektrums gefüllt – mit Cyan, Magenta, Gelb oder Schwarz. Nach und nach werden die farbigen Tinten in winzigen Schritten durch die jeweils anderen Farben kontaminiert. Ihre Farbtöne verändern sich und werden mit der Zeit immer dunkler bis hin zu einem trüben Schwarz. Diese Arbeit führt uns die Saturation vor Augen, den Prozess der Sättigung, der letzten Endes jedes Signal in undefinierbare Störgeräusche verwandelt und ihre Lesbarkeit unmöglich macht. Indem Aoun diesen Werkprozess inszeniert, dramatisiert und materialisiert sie die Effekte der steigenden Flut von digitalen Daten auf unsere Wahrnehmung. Eine Flut, der wir täglich ausgesetzt sind, eine Übersättigung, die unsere Fähigkeit, Informationen zu behalten und unsere Meinung von ihnen abzuleiten, beeinträchtigt. Die Installation der Brunnen mag temporär sein, aber der darunterliegende Teppich, der die unausweichlichen Tintenspritzer während der Ausstellungszeit aufsaugen soll, wird ein dauerhaftes Dokument der Werkentwicklung sein. Auf der hinteren Wand des Ausstellungsraums erinnern die heiligenscheinähnlichen geisterhaften Spuren der letztmaligen Wiederaufführung dieses Experiments daran, dass die Geschwindigkeit und das Volumen von zirkulierenden Daten unvermindert weiter anwachsen, während solche nichtigen und gesprenkelten Flecken alles sein mögen, was bleiben wird, um uns ein Bild zu davon machen.

Neben Drucker, Tinte und Papier ist Pappmaché der Werkstoff, den Aoun bevorzugt einsetzt. Hiermit formt sie von Hand unterschiedliche Architekturoberflächen ab – von einem Swimmingpool, einer Straße, von Wänden und Böden der Räume, in denen sie ausstellt, und vom Boden eines Schiffscontainers. Diese Technik ist ausgesprochen altmodisch und „low-tech", insbesondere vor dem Hintergrund, dass Künstler heute immer häufiger Software zum Scannen oder Modellieren verwenden und 3-D-Drucker nutzen, um zu untersuchen, wie die digitalen Technologien die Erscheinungsformen von Objekten beeinflussen. Aoun überträgt die unterschiedlichen Texturen der von ihr ausgewählten Oberflächen in superflache Reliefs: vom eingeschnittenen Raster von Fliesen und Einschlüssen von Holzfasern eines Parkettbodens bis hin zur ausgeprägten Haptik von Beton, Asphalt und Metall.

Wenn auch nur winzig und für das bloße Auge größtenteils nicht zu sehen, sind die Geschichten, Erinnerungen und Erfahrungen, die sich in diesen Räumen und auf diesen Oberflächen abgespielt haben, in den Abformungen eingeschrieben. Aoun sucht das Papiermaterial sorgfältig aus, um für die Abdrücke unterschiedliche Farbtöne zu generieren. In einer frühen Arbeit dieser Art, *Beirut Art Center Square Meters* (2012) S. 74–77, formt sie Teile des Bodens einer ehemaligen Möbelfabrik ab. Sie

---

6   Kerstin Stakemeier, „Krise und Materialität in der Kunst: über Formwerdung und Digitalität", in: Susanne Witzgall und Kerstin Stakemeier, *Macht des Materials / Politik der Materialität*, Zürich / Berlin 2014, S. 184–198.

response in the viewer, a shift that reminds us of the *jouissance* of sense and touch that is lost when we encounter yet another digital copy. Her quiet and contemplative works, which allow for a momentary respite from the incessant barrage of digital data, translate specific aspects of this condition—repetition, replication, oversaturation, transfer—into phenomenological, palpable, embodied experiences. They allow us to once again feel the gentle massaging touch of profound technological shifts whose effects are commonly understood and perceived as intangible and asomatous. In the face of the growing dominance of the virtual, her work softly reasserts the value of the real, returning again and again, to the matter of fact.

verwendet dazu unterschiedlichen Papierabfall, den sie vor Ort vorgefunden hat, und schafft so eine Serie verschiedenfarbiger Monochrome: Braune Umschläge und rosafarbene Rechnungsbelege werden zu zwei sandbraunen Parallelogrammen; Telefonbücher werden in Rechtecke in Pastellrosa und Gelb transformiert; ein langes, horizontal angebrachtes graues Band entsteht aus blauen Briefumschlägen, die mit anderem Büropapier so vermischt wurden, dass auch im fertiggestellten Werk noch Fragmente von Buchstaben und Tabellen zu erkennen sind. Und die Verwendung von CMYK-Tintenresten erzeugte eine fast schwarze Oberfläche. In weiteren Arbeiten nutzt Aoun Kohlepapier, um ein dunkles Kohlegrau oder ein tiefes Blau zu erzielen. Im PalaisPopulaire zeigt sie Abformungen von Wandsegmenten, die von der Zeit vor der kürzlich erfolgten Renovierung zeugen. Diese Abformungen verkörpern ontologische Gegensätze: Rückblenden aus Stein, Geister, die physisch vorhanden sind, Materialindexe der vergessenen und ausgelöschten Vergangenheit des Gebäudes.

Als Abformungen, auch wenn sie aus ihrem ursprünglichen Kontext herausgelöst sind, behalten diese Arbeiten eine indexikalische Verknüpfung an ihren ursprünglichen Gegenstand bei, ähnlich wie bei der analogen Fotografie. Die wachsende Verbreitung digitaler Technologien hat diesen Bezug zur realen Welt in eine beachtliche Krise gestürzt. In Aouns skulpturalen Übertragungen gibt es eine raffinierte Subversion: Während etwas Schweres und Dauerhaftes wie eine Wand, ein Boden oder eine Straße in fragilem Pappmaché reproduziert wird, lässt sie zarte Piniennadeln, die sie in der Nähe ihres Ateliers aufgelesen hat, in hartes Kupfer gießen (*Pine Needles*, 2015 S. 56 \ 57, 102 \ 103, 106 \ 107) oder fließendes Wasser in zartblau getöntem, klarem Kunstharz festhalten (*Still Water*, 2015). Ihr Interesse am Prozess der Nachbildung lässt sich auf die unendliche Reproduzierbarkeit digitaler Informationen zurückführen. Aber vor allem wird in diesen Werken die materielle und physische Diskrepanz von Original und Kopie offengelegt. Der Unterschied, der subtil, aber greifbar ist, bewirkt eine phänomenologische Reaktion des Betrachters, eine Verschiebung, die uns an die „Jouissance", den unmittelbaren sinnlichen und fühlbaren Genuss, erinnert, den wir vermissen, wenn wir heute auf eine weitere digitale Kopie treffen. Ihre ruhigen und kontemplativen Werke, die eine kurze Atempause im konstanten Datenrauschen erlauben, übertragen einige Aspekte dieses Befunds – Wiederholung, Kopie, Übersättigung, Transfer – in wahrnehm- und greifbare Erfahrungen. Sie erinnern uns an die sanft massierende Berührung grundlegender technologischer Veränderungen, deren Auswirkungen nicht greifbar und schwer zu fassen sind. Angesichts der wachsenden Übermacht des Digitalen verschafft ihr Werk der Realität neue Geltung, indem es sich wieder und wieder den Tatsachen zuwendet.

look at the moon

Hello

Lands of Matter 2003–2018, 2019
Seascape, 2016 / 2019
PalaisPopulaire, Berlin 2019

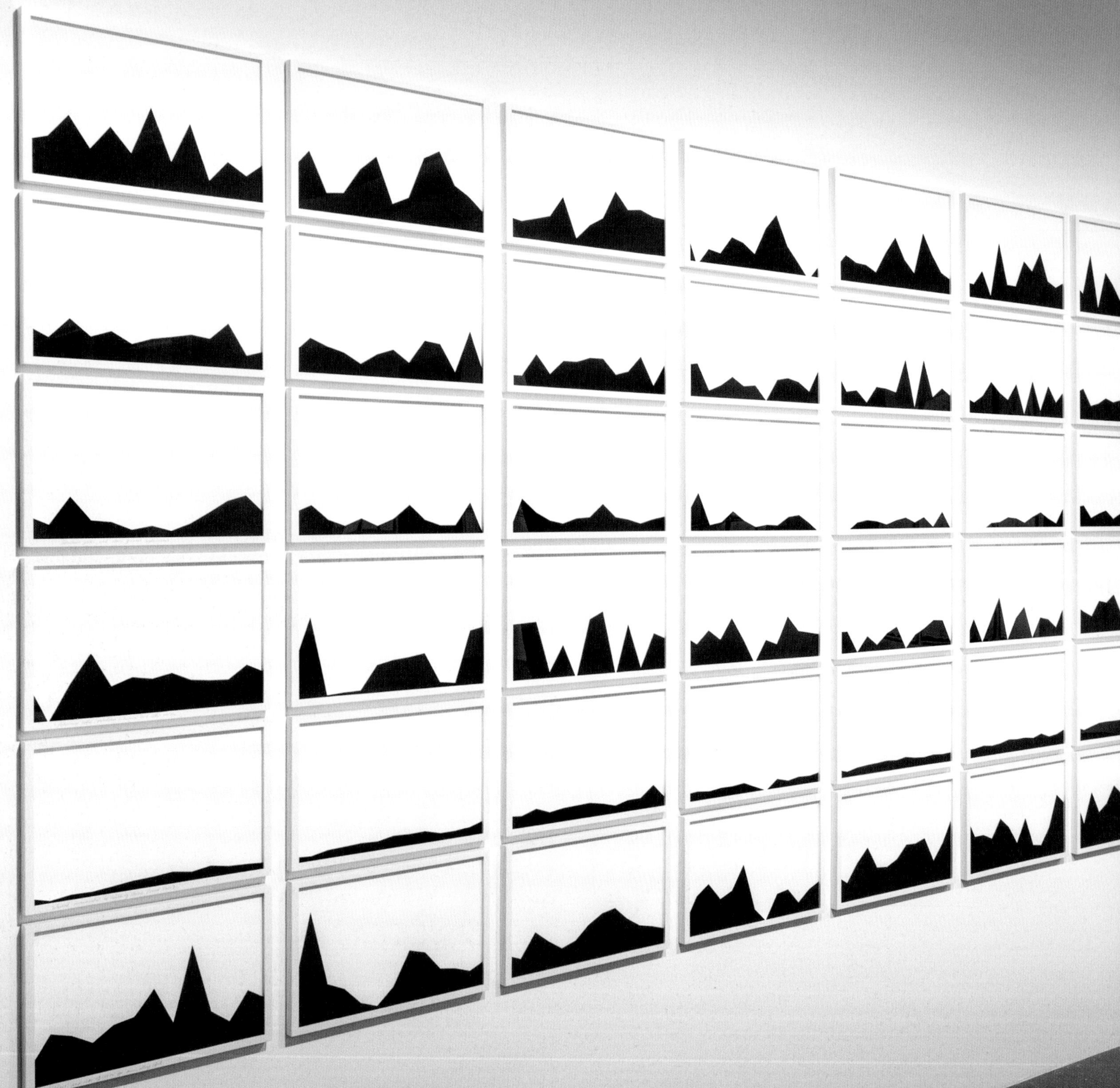

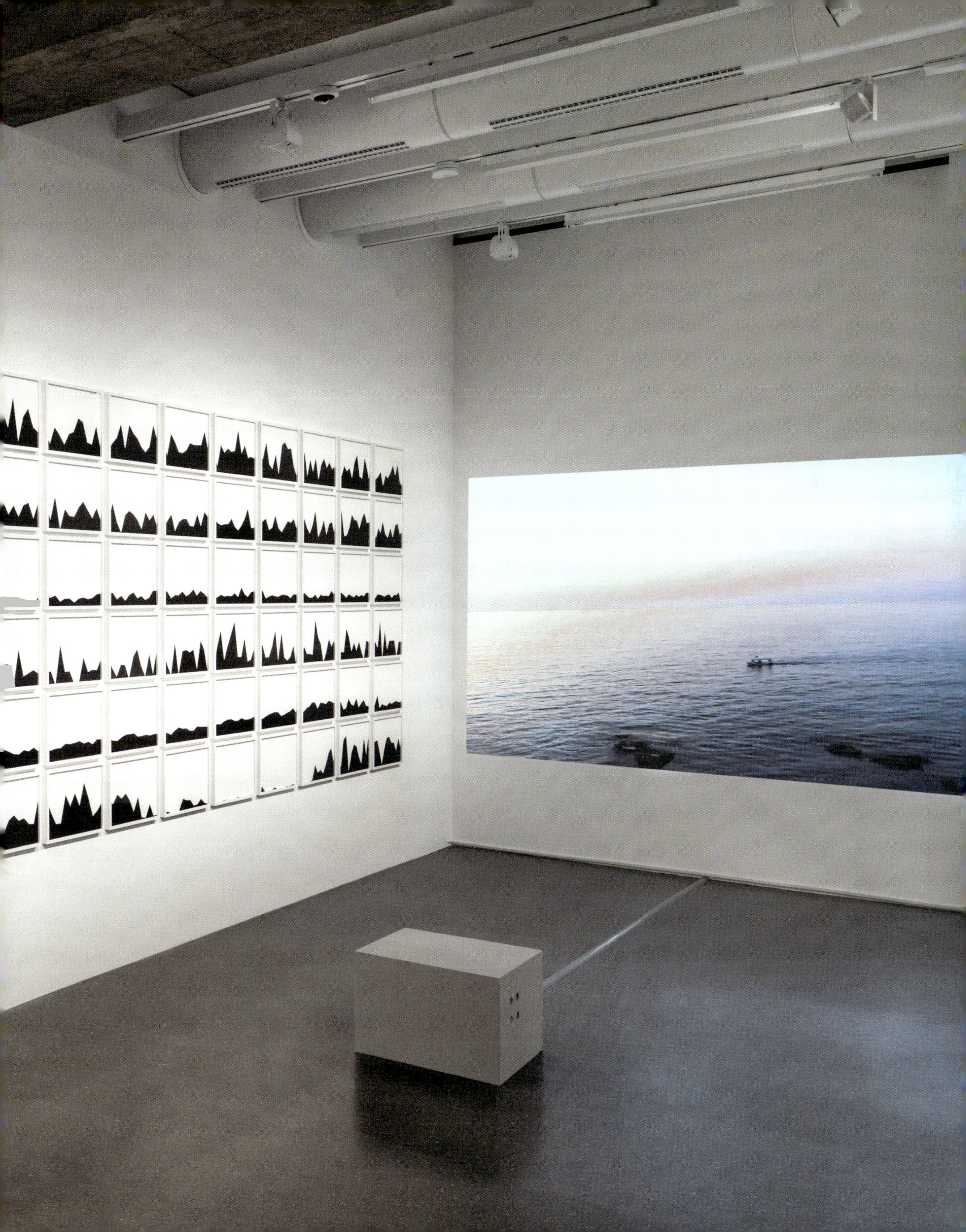

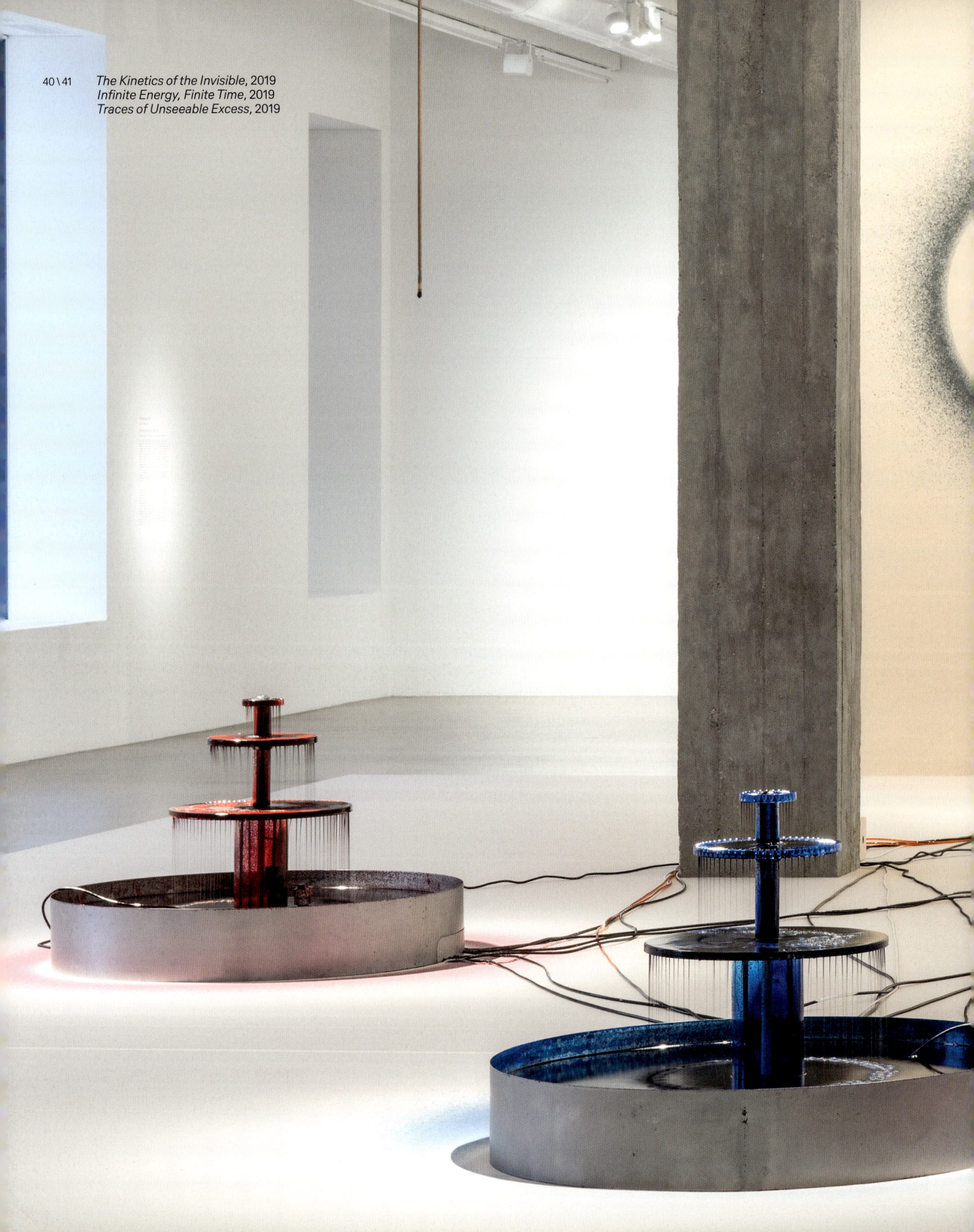

The Kinetics of the Invisible, 2019
Infinite Energy, Finite Time, 2019
Traces of Unseeable Excess, 2019

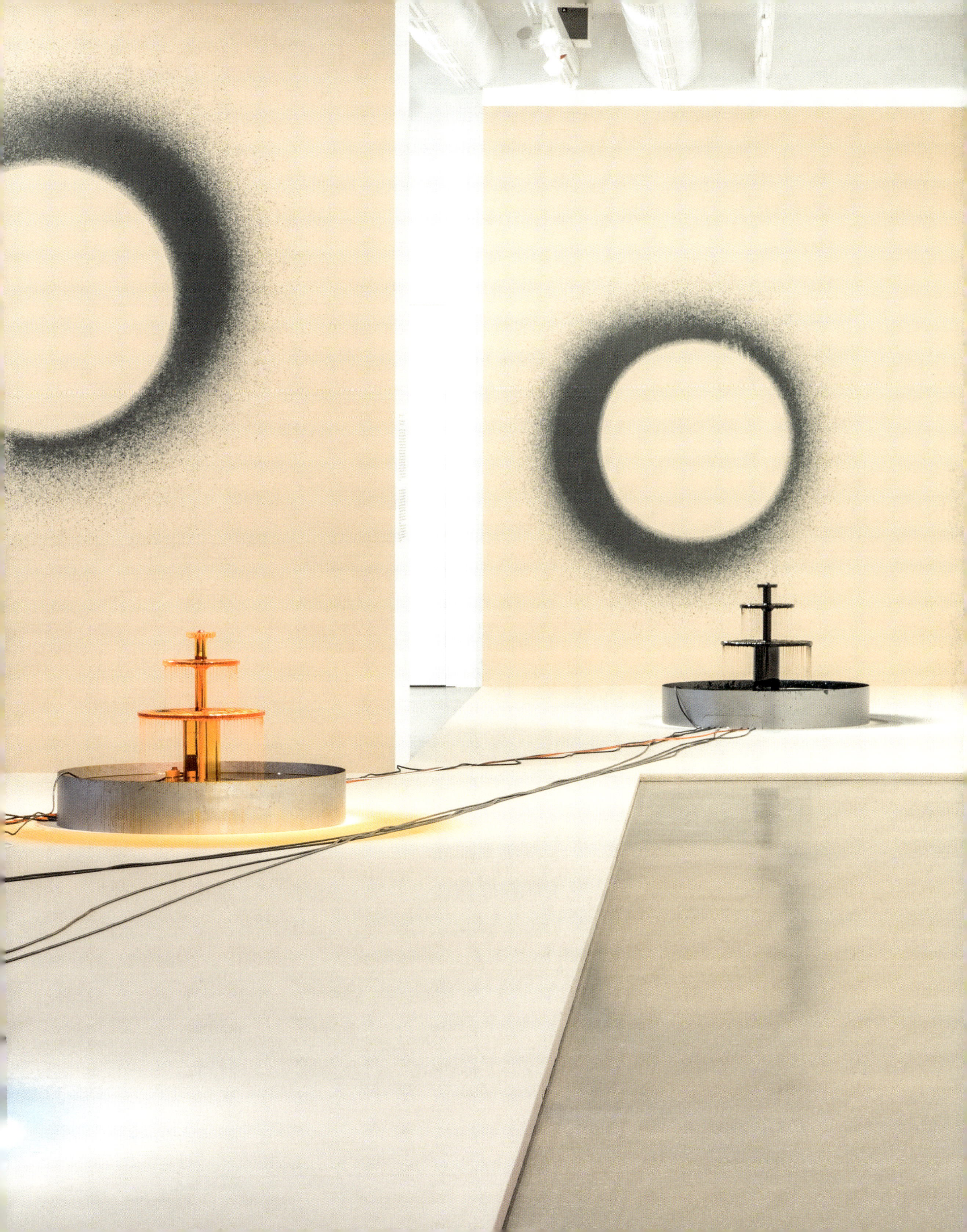

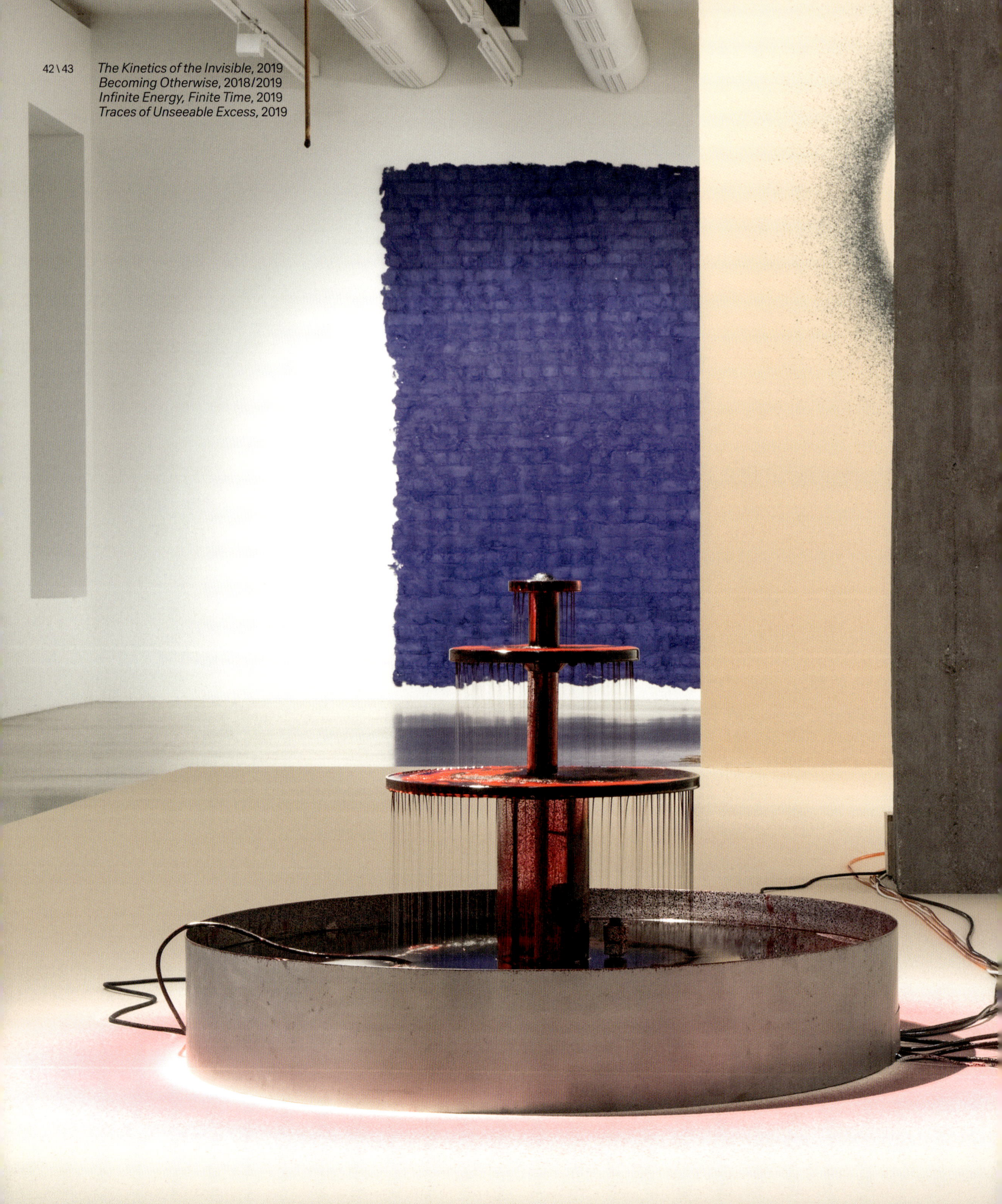

The Kinetics of the Invisible, 2019
Becoming Otherwise, 2018/2019
Infinite Energy, Finite Time, 2019
Traces of Unseeable Excess, 2019

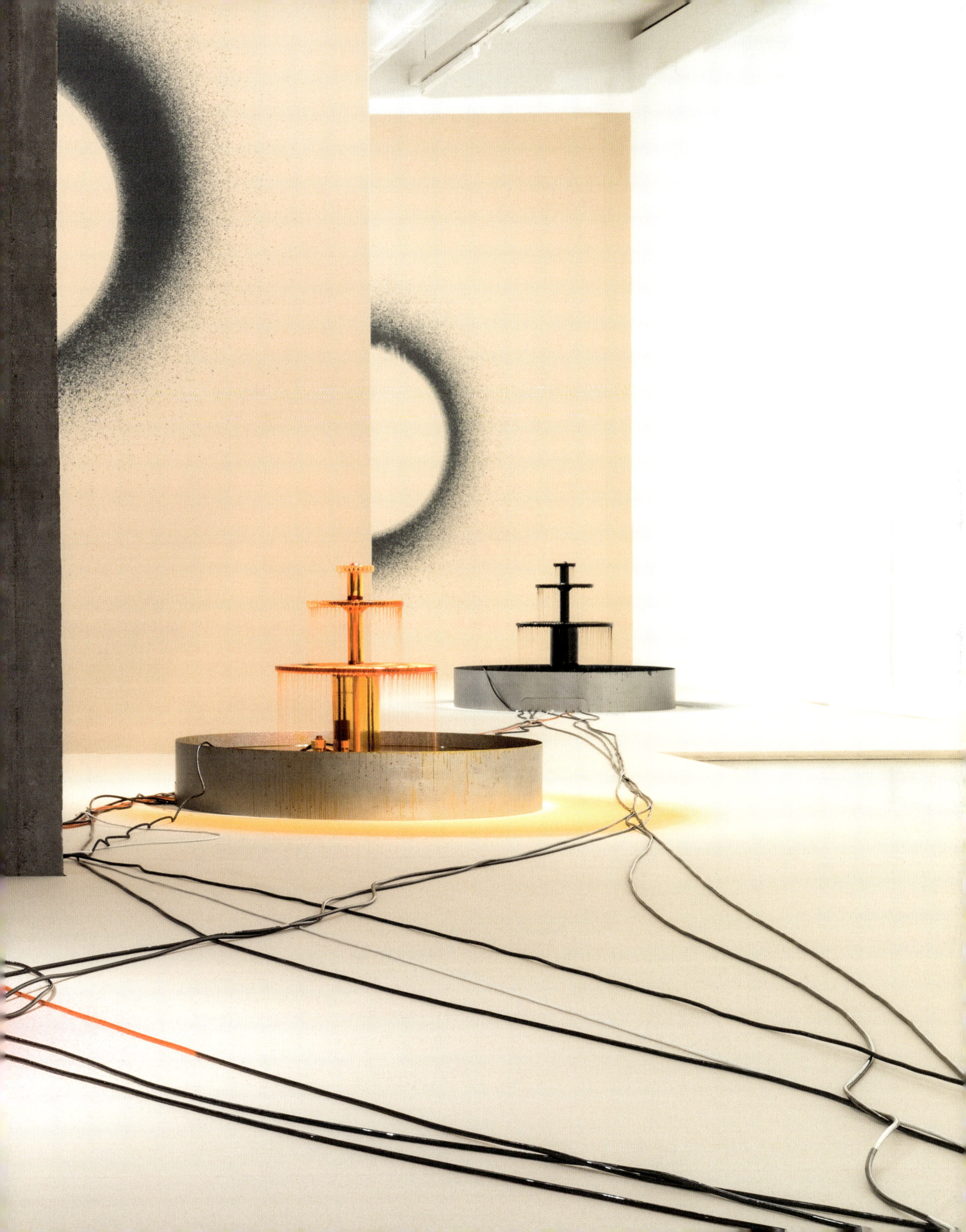

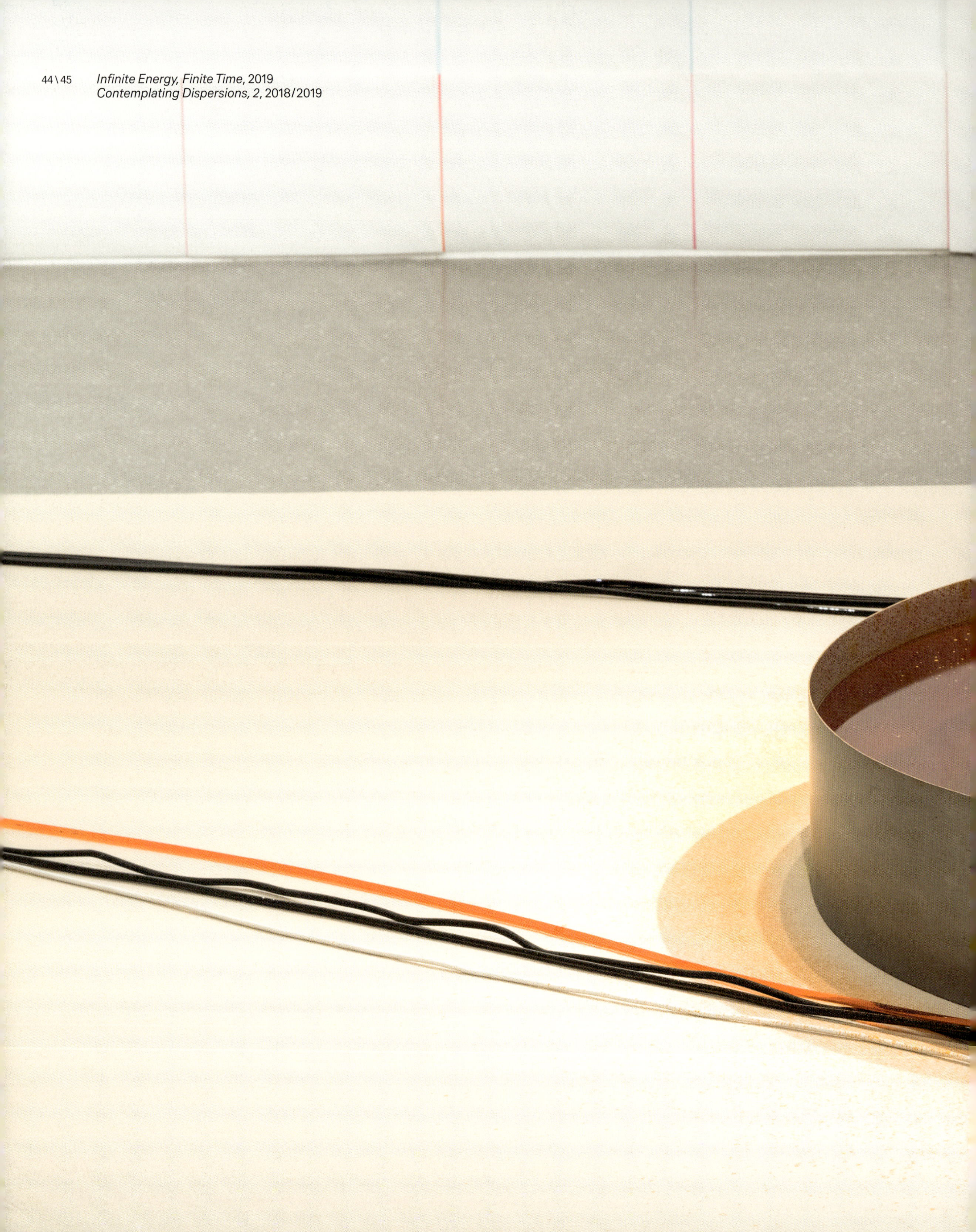

Infinite Energy, Finite Time, 2019
Contemplating Dispersions, 2, 2018/2019

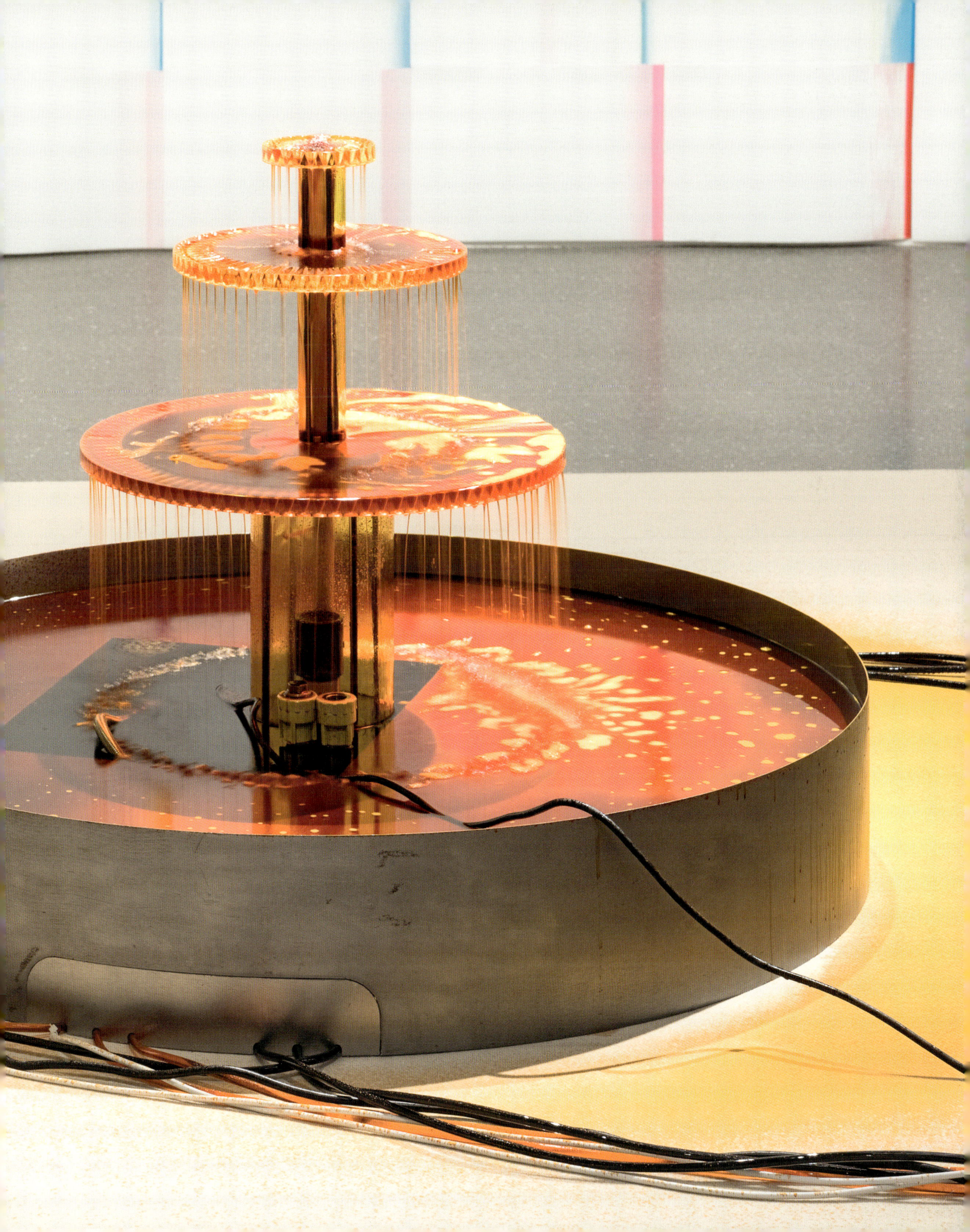

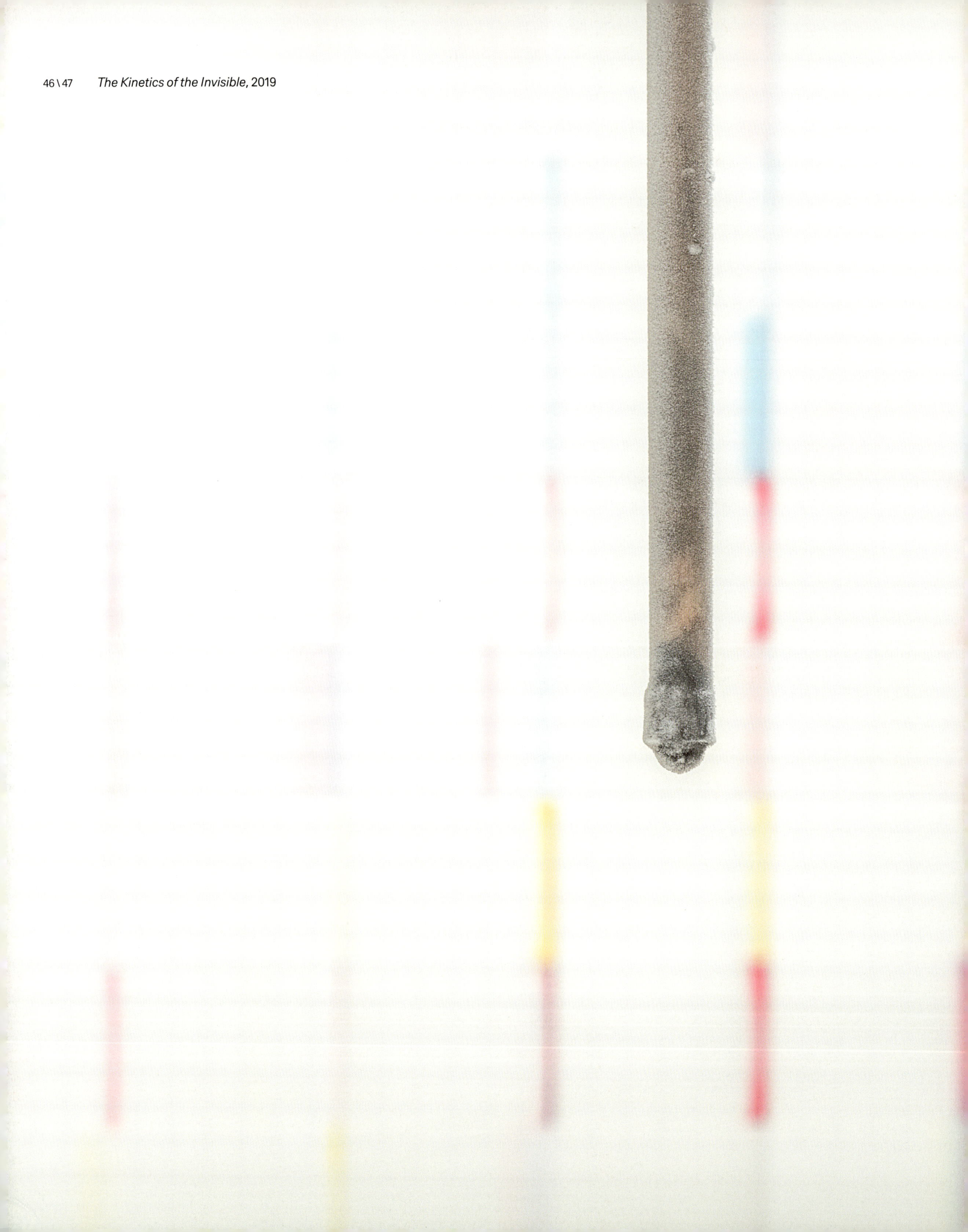

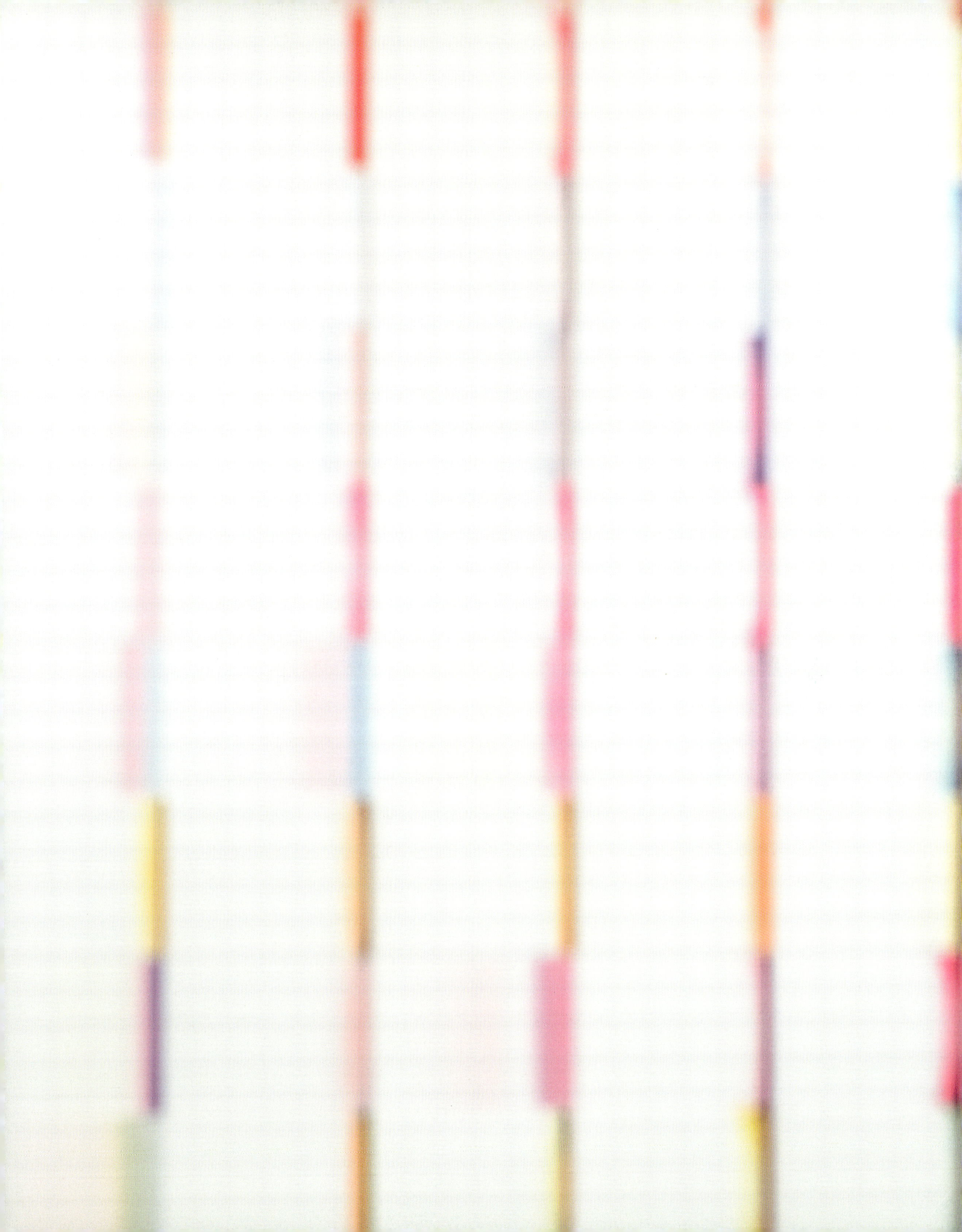

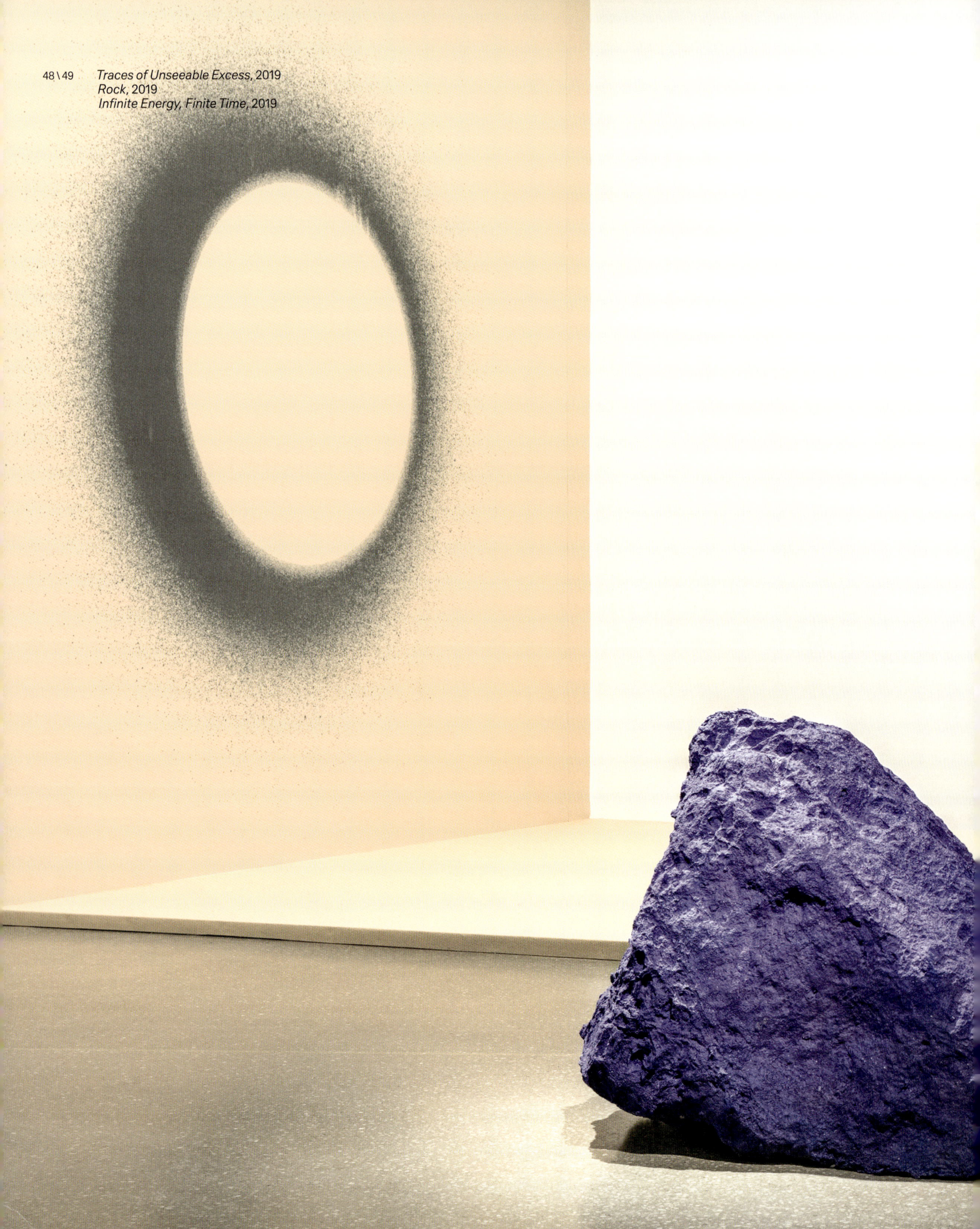

Traces of Unseeable Excess, 2019
Rock, 2019
Infinite Energy, Finite Time, 2019

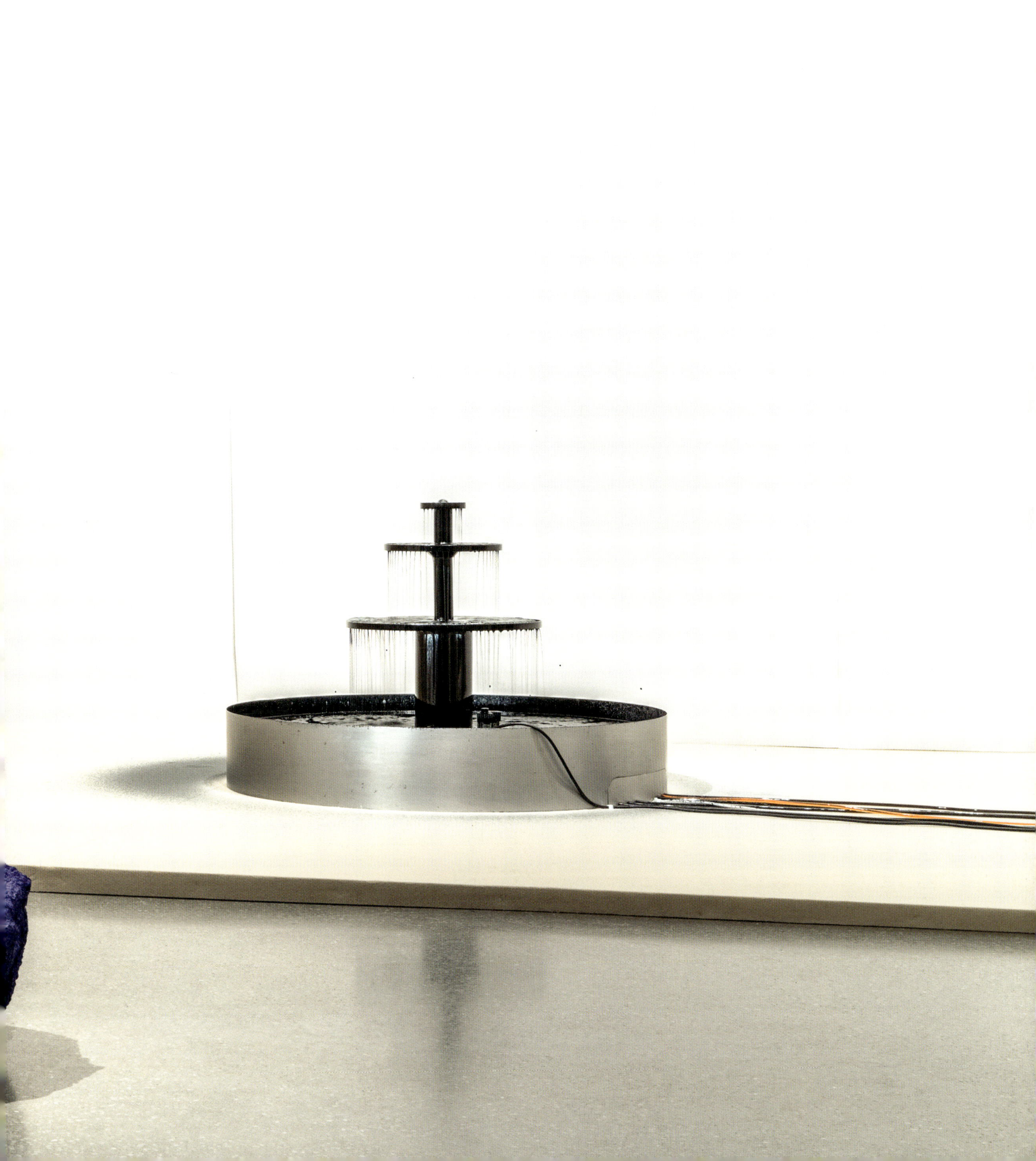

 Paperplane, 2018
MAXXI, Rome 2018

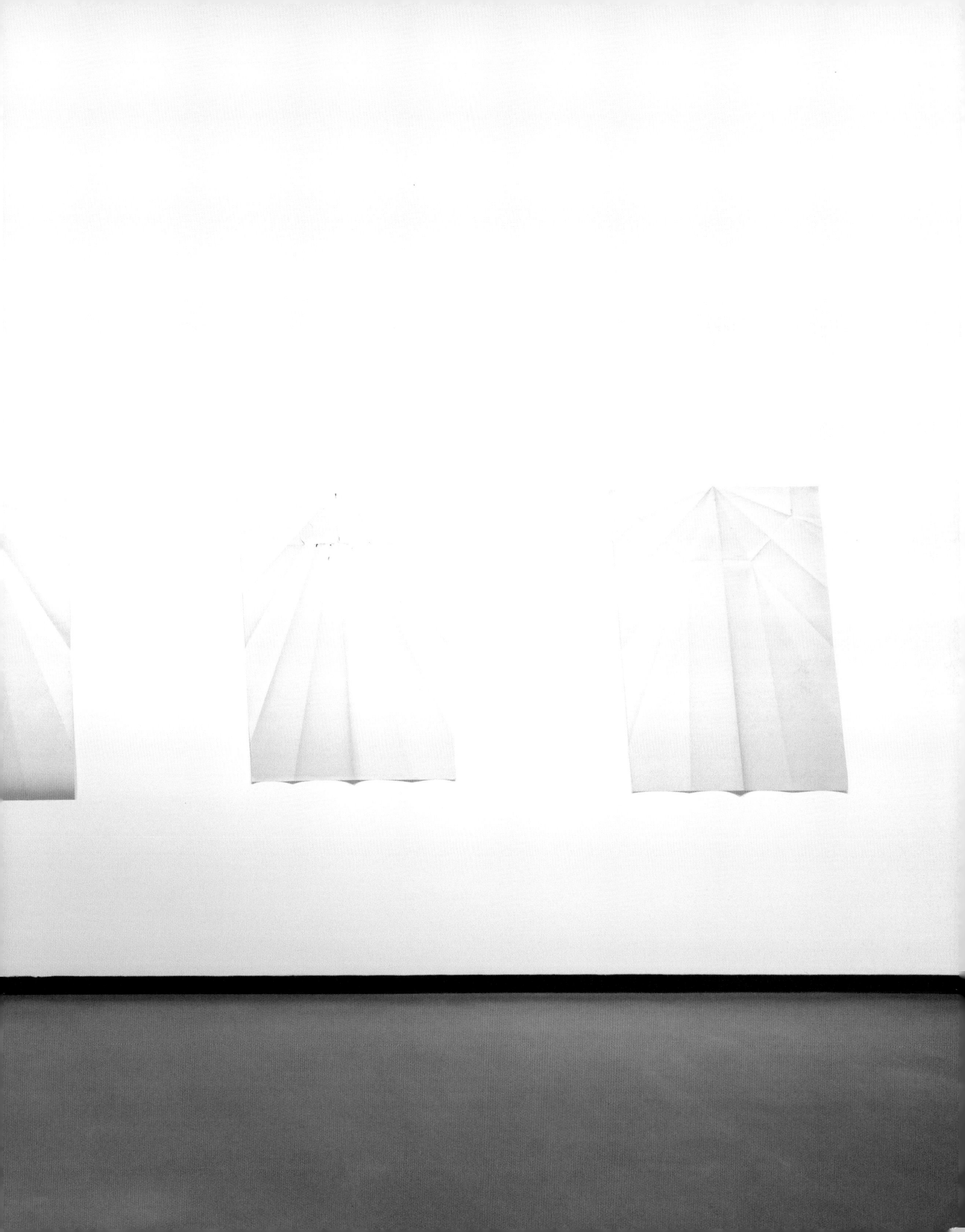

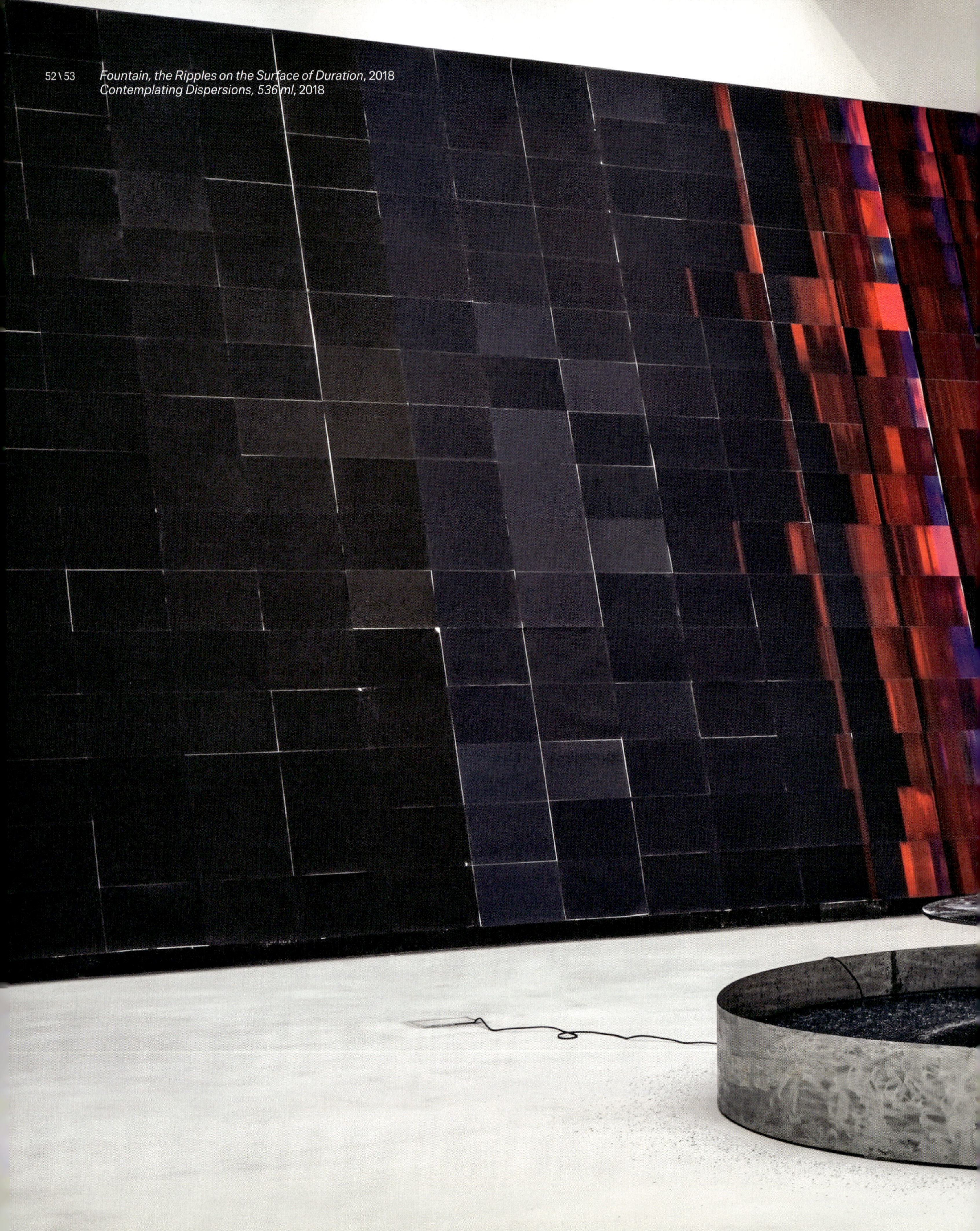

Fountain, the Ripples on the Surface of Duration, 2018
Contemplating Dispersions, 536 ml, 2018

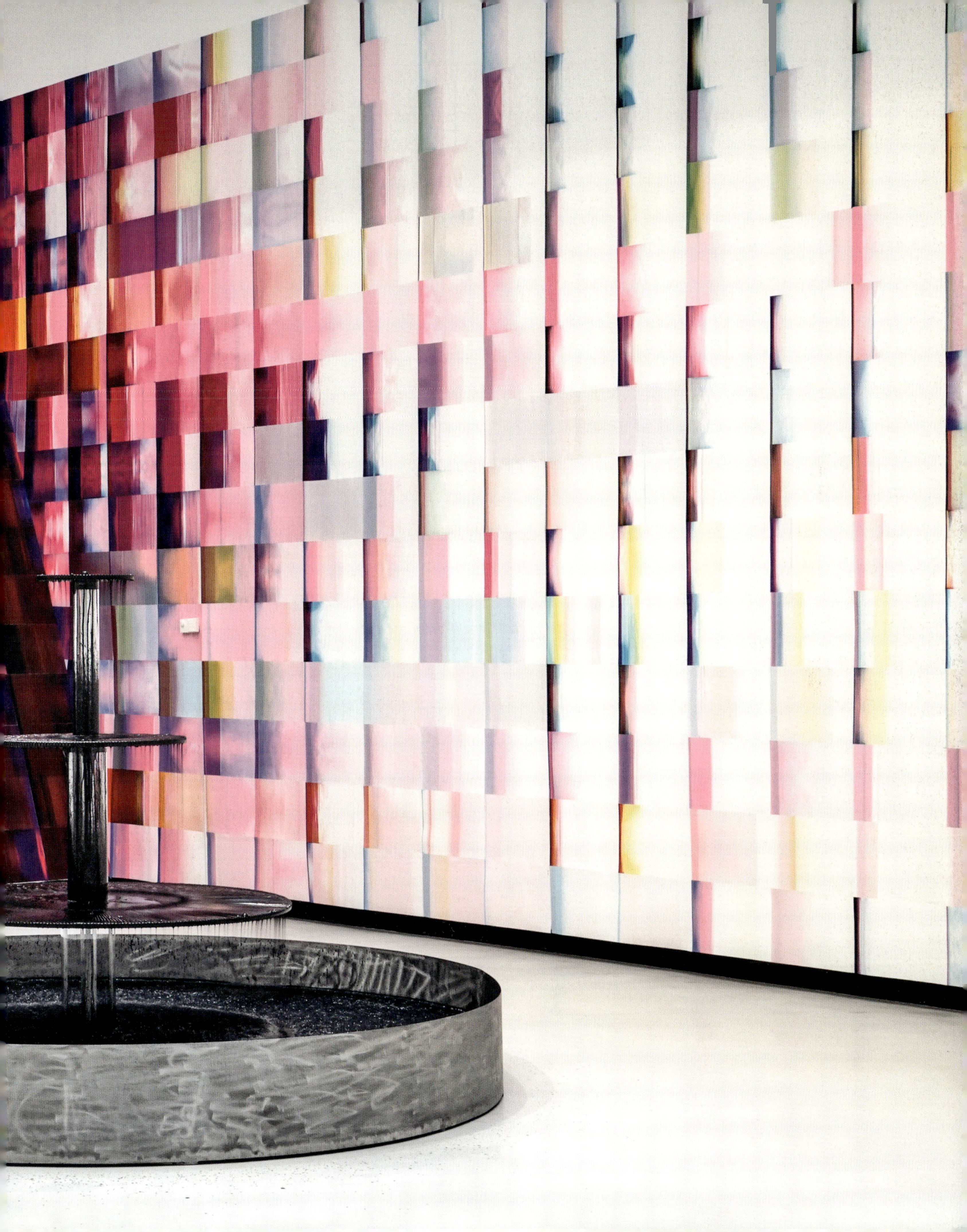

Contemplating Dispersions, 536 ml, 2018
Heavy Duration, Brief Glance, 2018

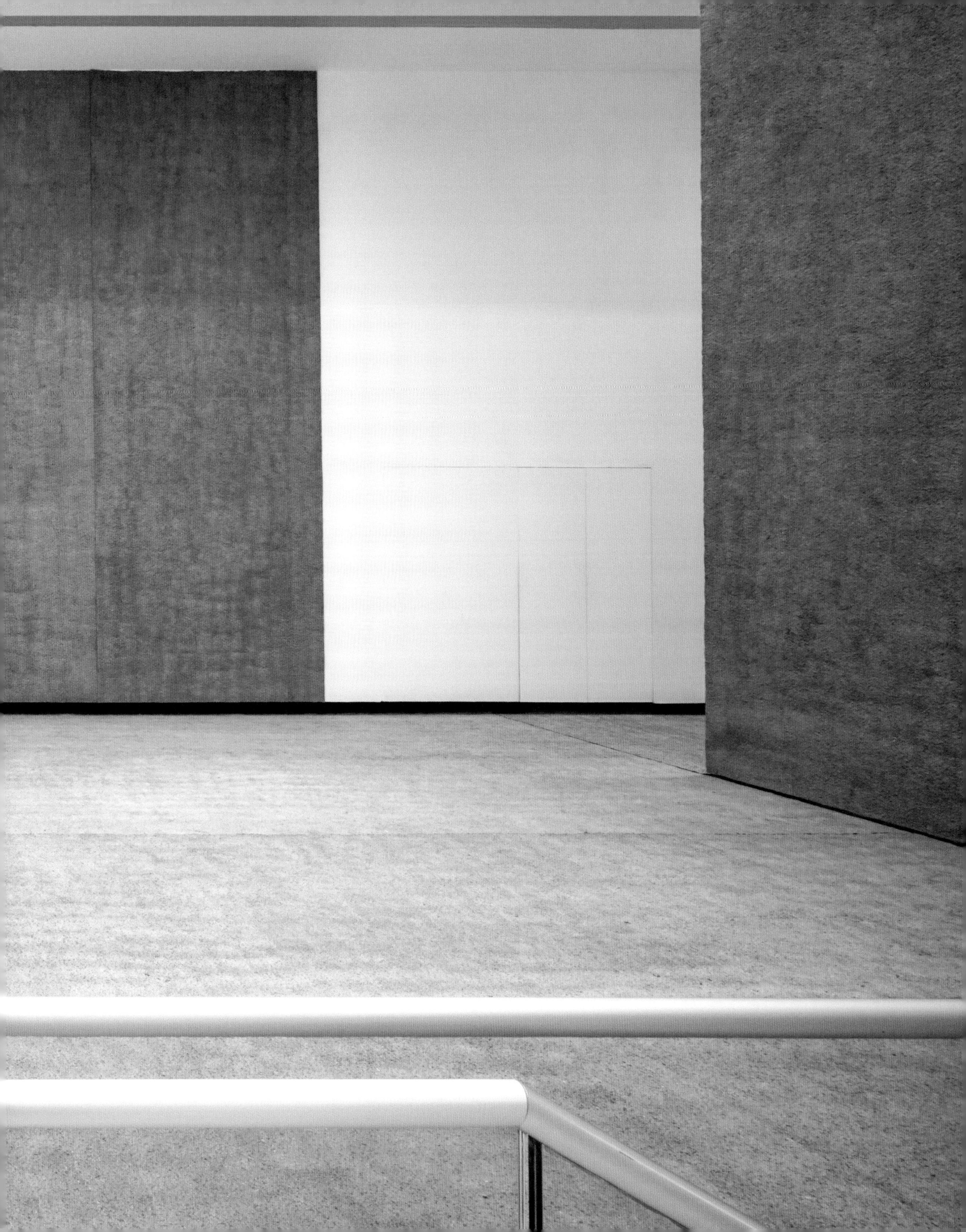

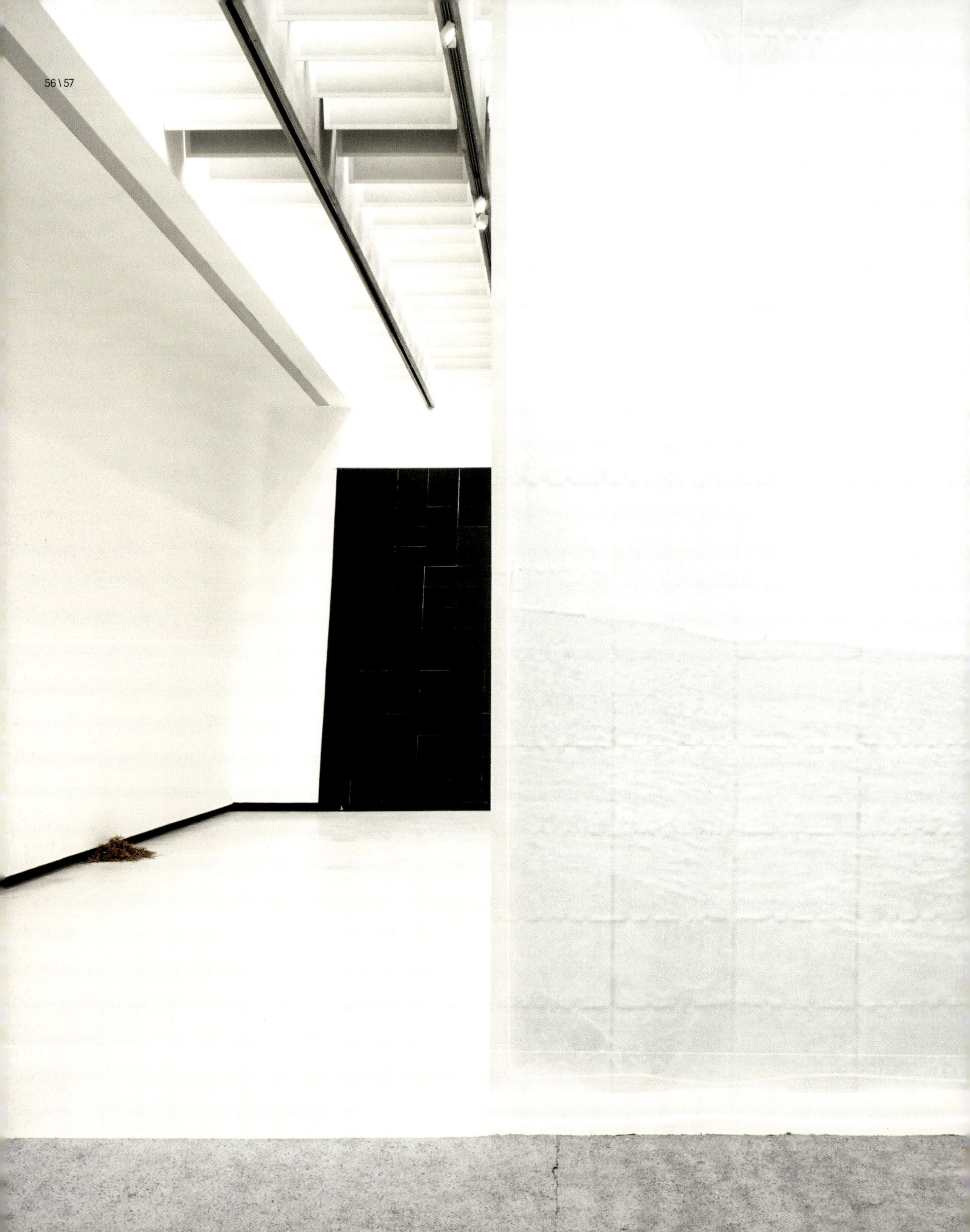

A thin paper "wall" extending the installation *Contemplating Dispersions, 536 ml* created a corridor-like passage moved by the wind of visitors walking past. The floating wall also functioned as a fluid display screen for livestream video of the Mediterranean Sea near Beirut—the camera pointed towards the location of undersea internet cables.

Data translated into ink, water translated into data, water becoming data: The dark and dense matter of the work, as well as that matter which is blank or has since disappeared, offer space for contemplation. They complete a circle that allows us to consider our own role in transforming our environment in all of its convoluted accumulation, in its constant state of flux and movement, in travel and material transport—on the path from saturation to entropy ending in disappearance.

Die Installation *Contemplating Dispersions, 536 ml* wird durch eine dünne Papier-„Wand" um eine Art Korridor ergänzt. Diese schwebende, durch den Luftzug vorbeigehender Besucher sanft bewegte Wand fungiert zudem als Leinwand für einen Livestream, der Bilder vom Mittelmeer nahe Beirut überträgt. Die Kamera ist dabei auf eine Stelle gerichtet, an der unter Wasser Internetkabel verlaufen.

Daten übersetzt in Tinte. Wasser übersetzt in Daten, Wasser verwandelt in Daten: Die dunkle, dichte Materialität des Werkes, aber auch die Leerstellen oder die inzwischen verschwundene Materie, bieten Raum für Kontemplation. Sie schließen einen Kreis, der es uns erlaubt, unsere eigene Rolle bei der Transformation der Welt um uns herum zu betrachten. Einer Welt, die gekennzeichnet ist von komplizierten Akkumulationen, ständigem Wandel und Bewegung, von Reisen und Transport von Material – auf dem Weg von der Sättigung zur Zersetzung, der im Verschwinden endet.

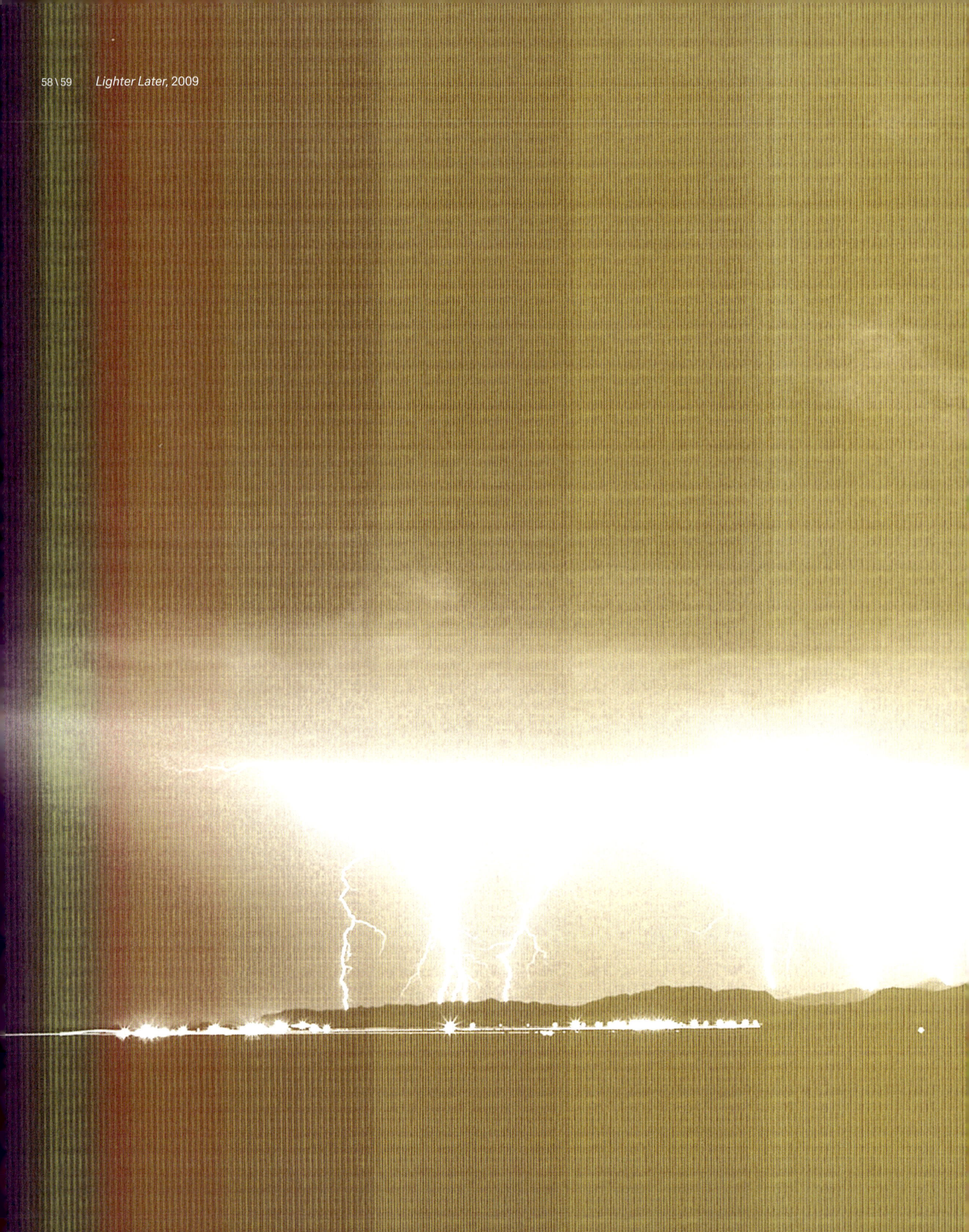

For this project, eight artists produced works to be broadcast live on the internet throughout February 2009. The works were all based on the BBC's traditional broadcast testcard. The internet broadcast, viewable only with dedicated downloadable software, beamed the artists' work to computer desktops, automatically updating and continually projecting new images. At the end of the month, the app automatically uninstalled itself and the broadcast came to an end. *Testcard*, curated by Charles Danby and George Unsworth in collaboration with Rob Smith, was the first initiative undertaken by "Projeckt," a curatorial platform operating internationally across real and virtual sites.

Für dieses Projekt produzierten acht Künstler Werke, die im Februar 2009 live im Internet übertragen wurden. Alle Arbeiten basieren auf dem klassischen Testbild der BBC. Dank einer speziellen Software konnten die Kunstwerke gesehen und aktualisiert werden. Am Monatsende sorgte sie auch für das Ende der Übertragung. *Testcard* wurde von Charles Danby und George Unsworth in Zusammenarbeit mit Rob Smith kuratiert und war die erste Initiative von „Projekt", einer kuratorischen Plattform, die international über reale und virtuelle Standorte hinweg operiert hat.

Brighter Beams, 2010
Sliding Gazes, 2010
Paperplane, exhibition at
Occupy Space, Limerick City 2010

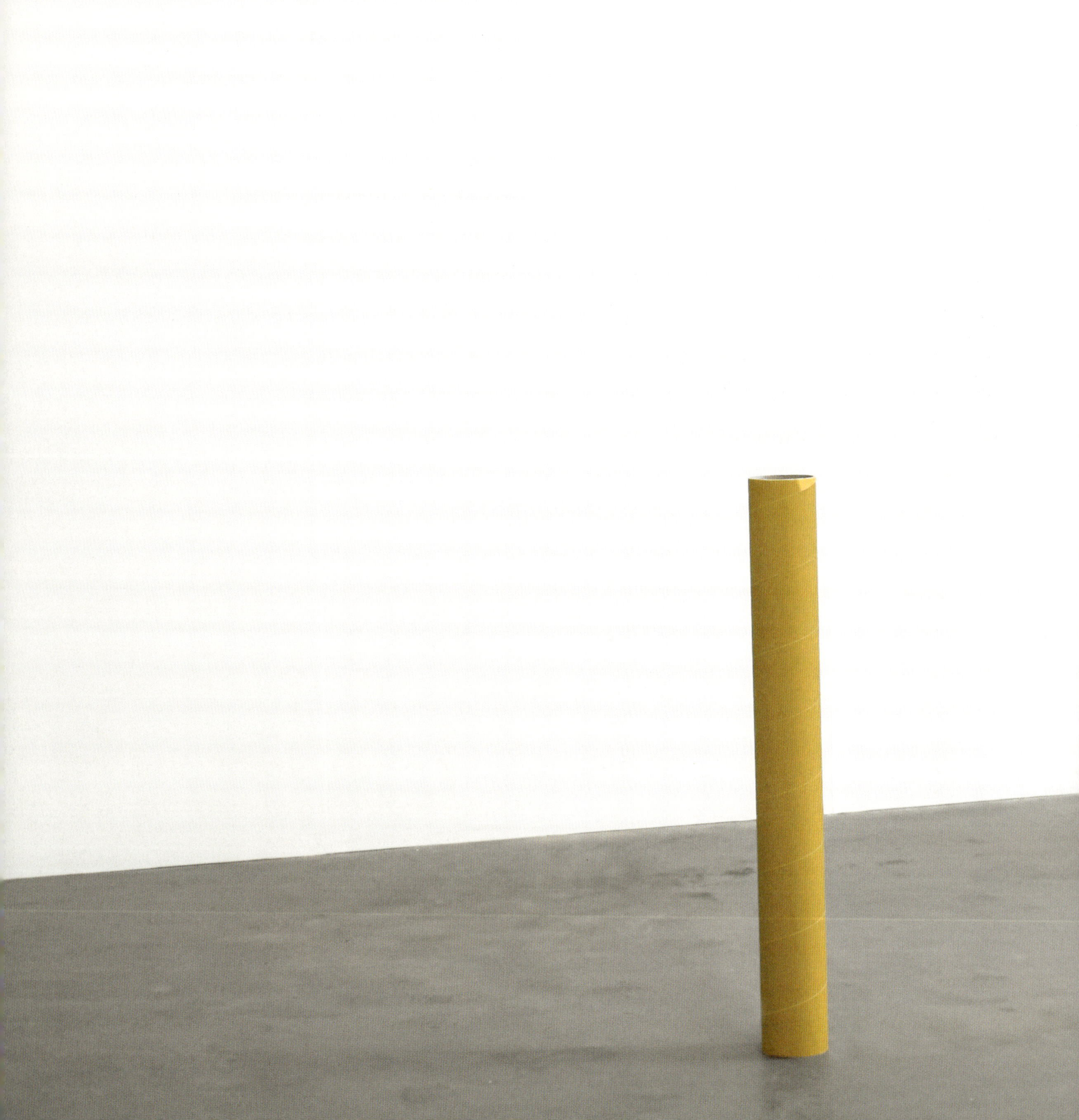

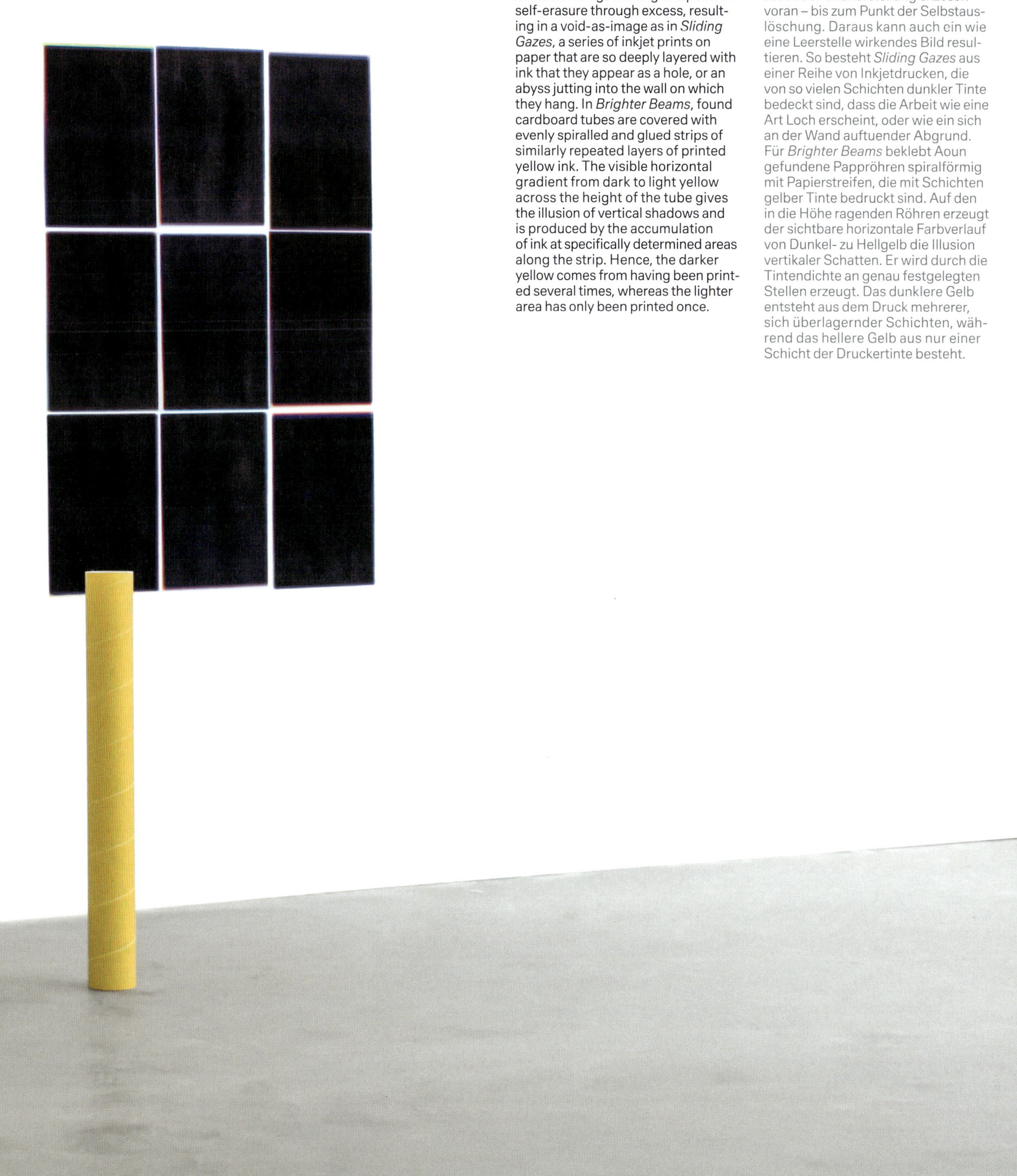

Aoun pushes the mechanical pro-cesses of image making to a point of self-erasure through excess, result-ing in a void-as-image as in *Sliding Gazes*, a series of inkjet prints on paper that are so deeply layered with ink that they appear as a hole, or an abyss jutting into the wall on which they hang. In *Brighter Beams*, found cardboard tubes are covered with evenly spiralled and glued strips of similarly repeated layers of printed yellow ink. The visible horizontal gradient from dark to light yellow across the height of the tube gives the illusion of vertical shadows and is produced by the accumulation of ink at specifically determined areas along the strip. Hence, the darker yellow comes from having been print-ed several times, whereas the lighter area has only been printed once.

Aoun treibt die mechanischen Pro-zesse der Bildherstellung exzessiv voran – bis zum Punkt der Selbstaus-löschung. Daraus kann auch ein wie eine Leerstelle wirkendes Bild resul-tieren. So besteht *Sliding Gazes* aus einer Reihe von Inkjetdrucken, die von so vielen Schichten dunkler Tinte bedeckt sind, dass die Arbeit wie eine Art Loch erscheint, oder wie ein sich an der Wand auftuender Abgrund. Für *Brighter Beams* beklebt Aoun gefundene Pappröhren spiralförmig mit Papierstreifen, die mit Schichten gelber Tinte bedruckt sind. Auf den in die Höhe ragenden Röhren erzeugt der sichtbare horizontale Farbverlauf von Dunkel- zu Hellgelb die Illusion vertikaler Schatten. Er wird durch die Tintendichte an genau festgelegten Stellen erzeugt. Das dunklere Gelb entsteht aus dem Druck mehrerer, sich überlagernder Schichten, wäh-rend das hellere Gelb aus nur einer Schicht der Druckertinte besteht.

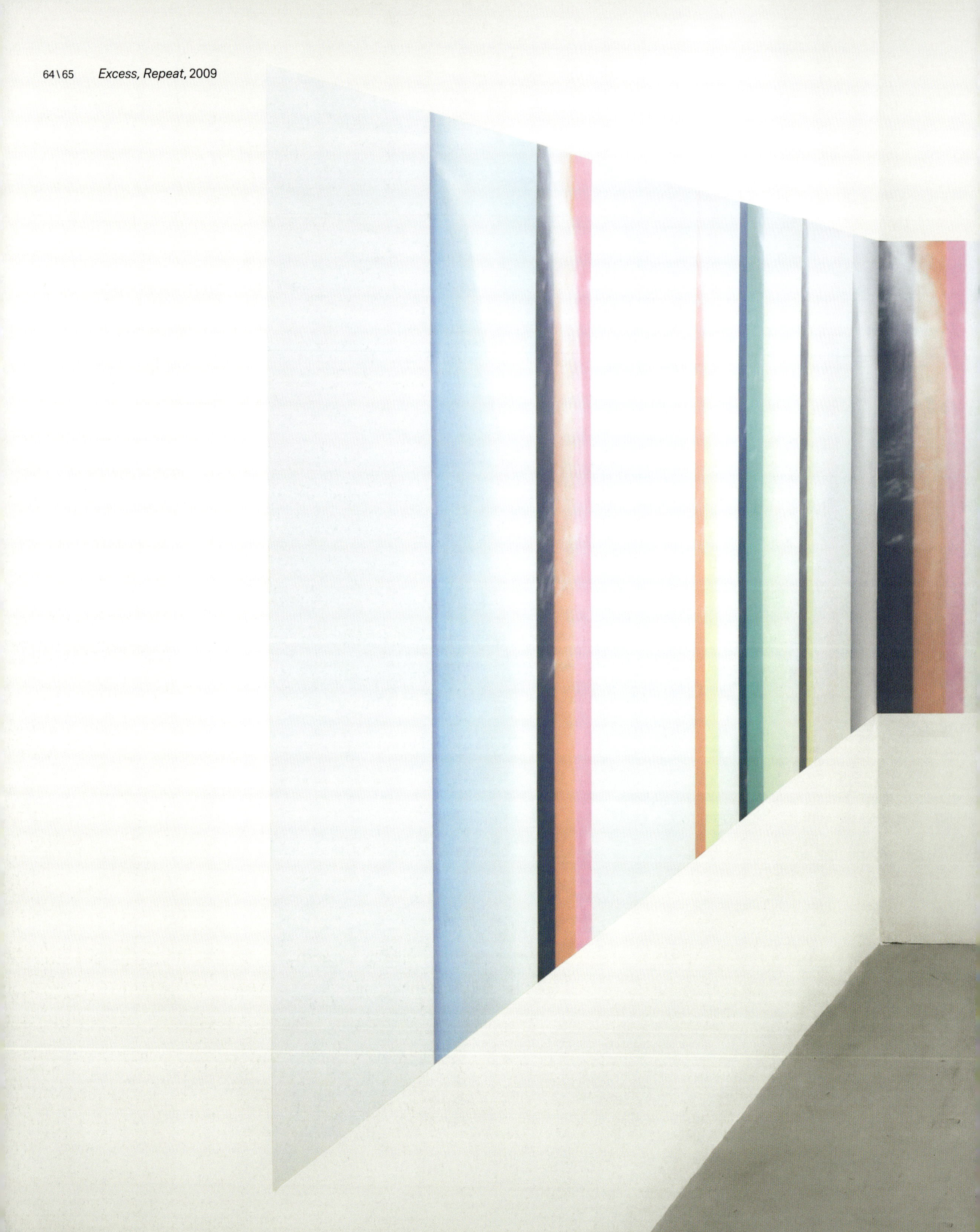

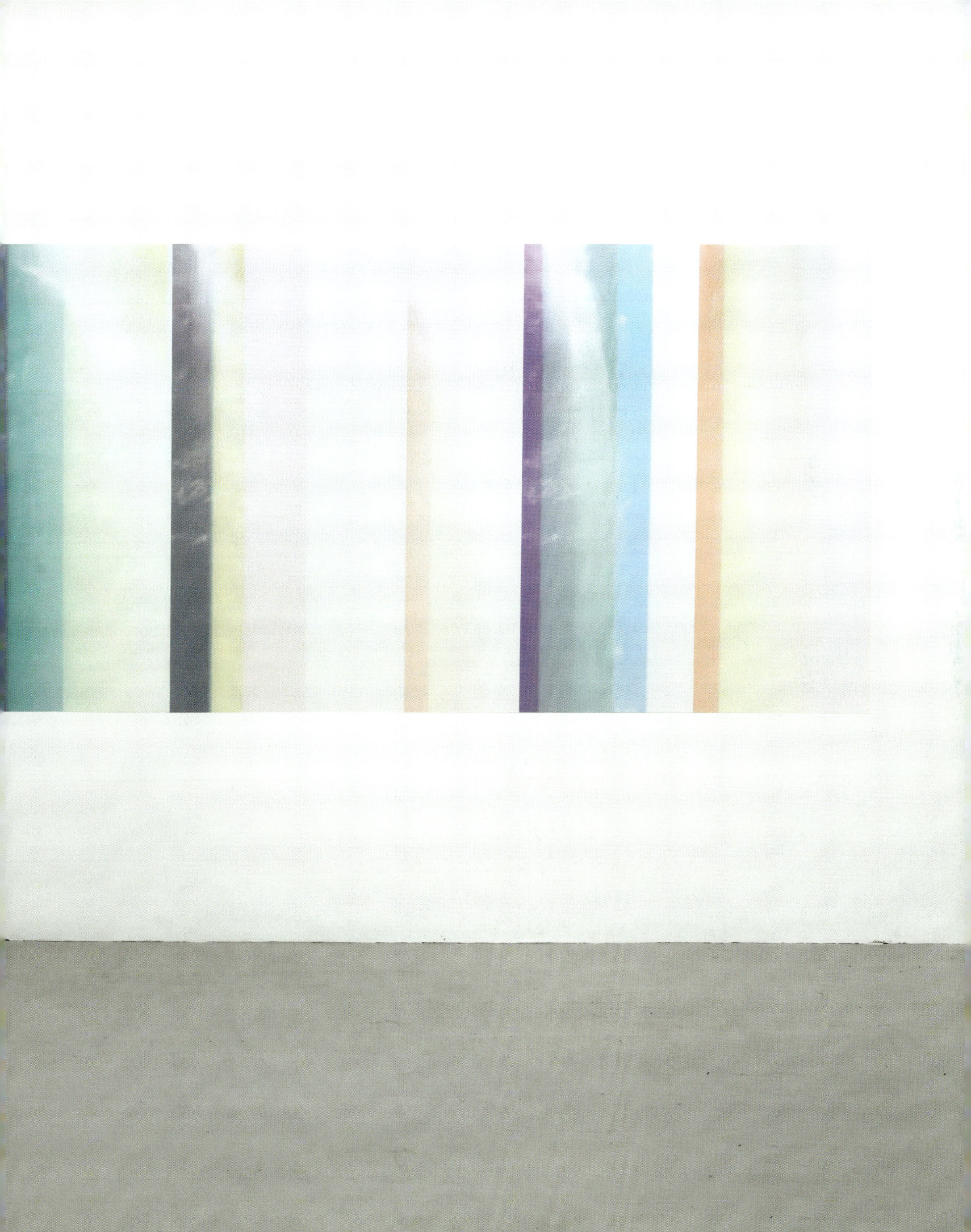

Excess, Repeat, 2009
Detail

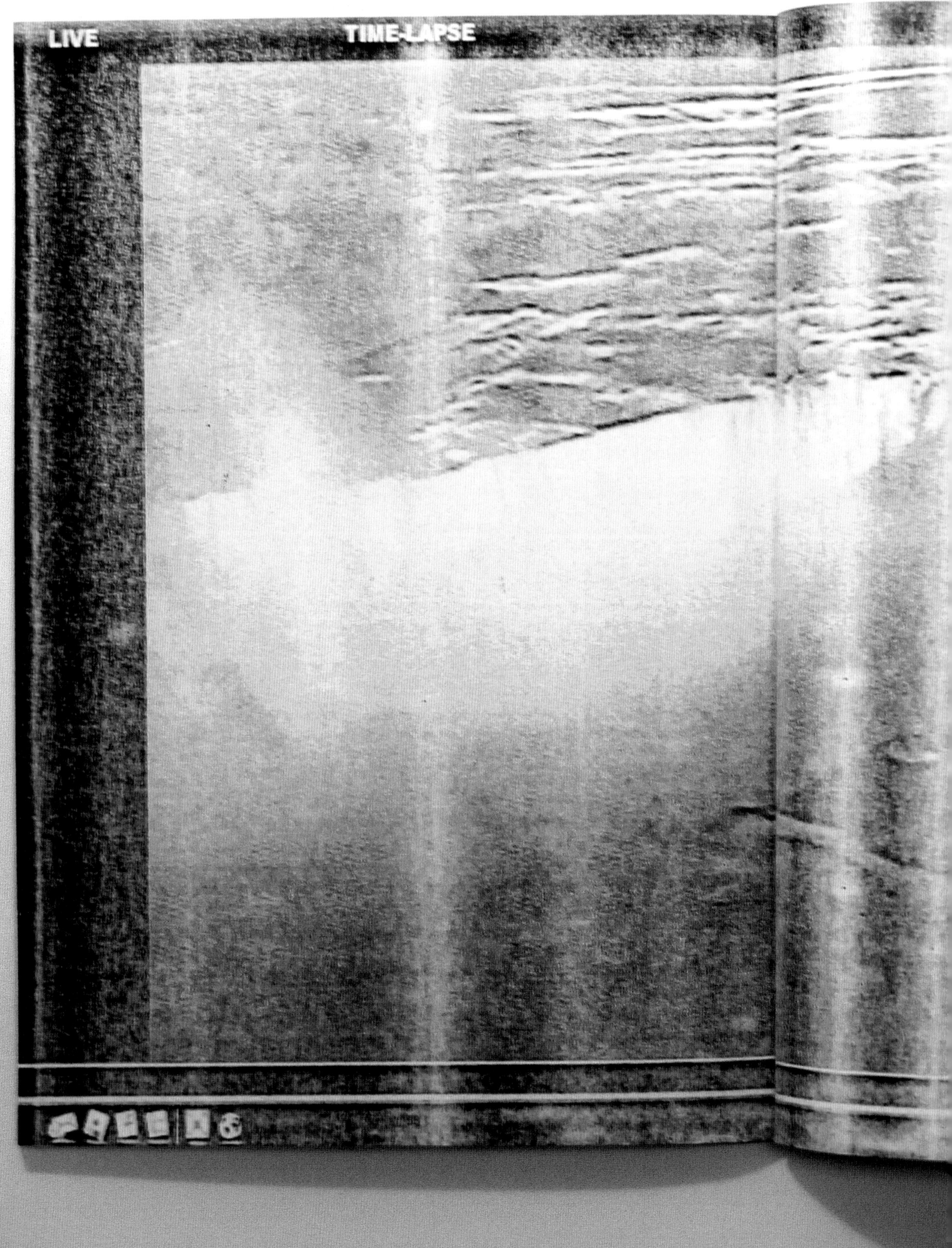

LIVE
TIME-LAPSE

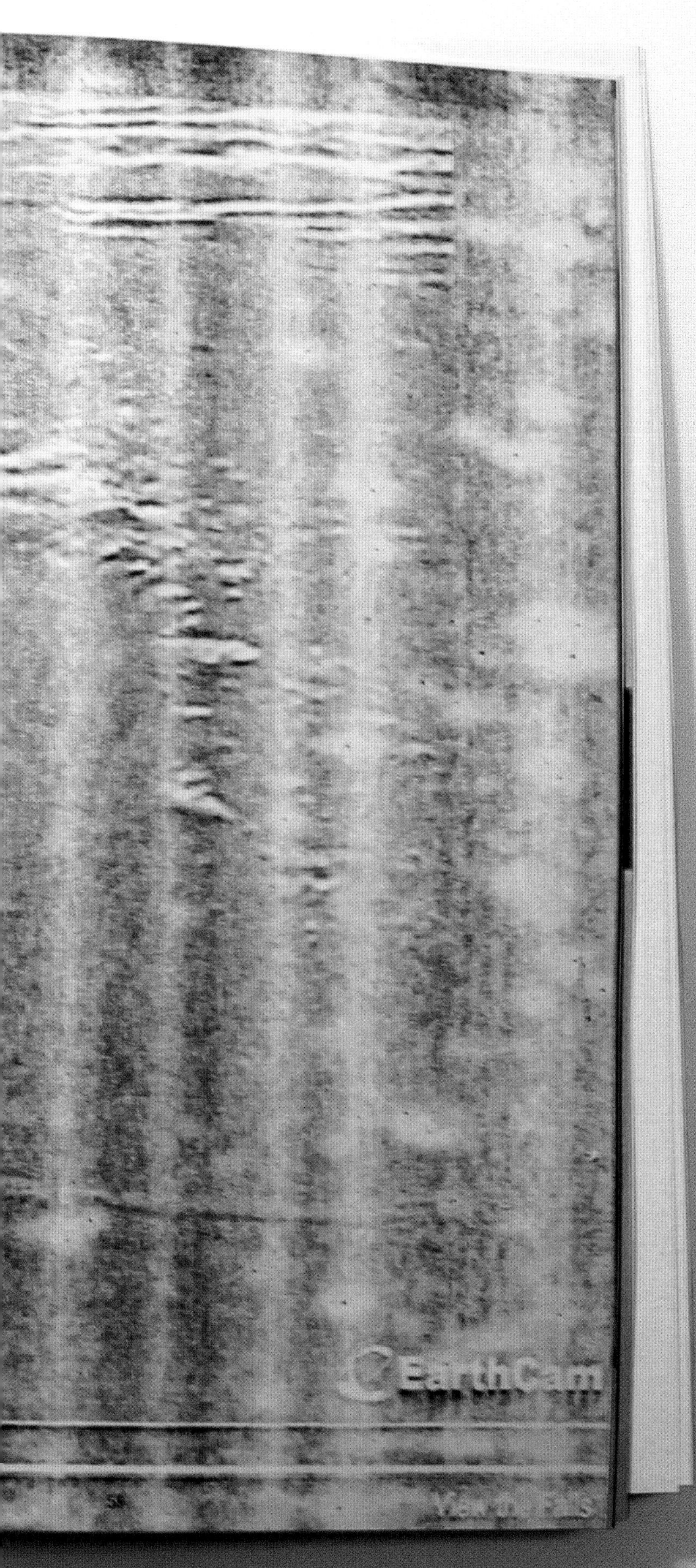

Water is a recurring motif in which the image is often washed or eroded, symbolizing a cleansing, or a return. *Niagara Falls Realtime Webcam, February 25, 2012, 16:36* is a video still pulled from a live feed of Niagara Falls and printed with a printer low on ink. The unchanging yet perpetually animated image of the most famous waterfall in the world is both frozen and threatens to disappear as ink cartridges run dry.

Visiting Niagara Falls as a child, Aoun remembers being "sprayed with water although we were really, really far away." Back then, the image, so familiar on postcards and television, was disrupted by its own material excess—a misting, spraying sensation. Here the image is once again overridden and determined by its materiality. The ink, having run dry, evaporates, leaving the paper's surface an exposed ground.

Wasser ist in Caline Aouns Werk ein häufig wiederkehrendes Motiv. Das Bild wird gewaschen oder verwaschen, Reinigung oder Rückkehr symbolisierend. *Niagara Falls Realtime Webcam, 25. Februar 2012, 16:36 Uhr* ist ein Videostill aus einem Livefeed der Niagarafälle, ausgedruckt von einem Drucker, der nur noch wenig Tinte hatte. Das unveränderliche und doch ständig bewegte Bild des berühmtesten Wasserfalls der Welt ist eingefroren und droht zugleich wegen der austrocknenden Tintenpatronen zu verschwinden.

Als Kind besuchte Aoun die Niagarafälle und sie erinnert, dass sie „mit Wasser besprüht wurde, obwohl wir wirklich weit entfernt waren". Das durch unzählige Postkarten und Fernsehberichte vertraute Bild der Niagarafälle wird durch die sinnliche Erfahrung des sprühenden Nebels, seinen eigentlichen „materiellen Exzess", unterbrochen. Hier wird das Bild zugleich überwunden und durch seine Materialität bestimmt. Die Tinte trocknet ein, verdunstet und hinterlässt auf dem Papier eine belichtete Fläche.

Portal, 2015
Dust, exhibition at
Ujazdowski Castle,
Centre for Contemporary Art,
Warsaw 2015

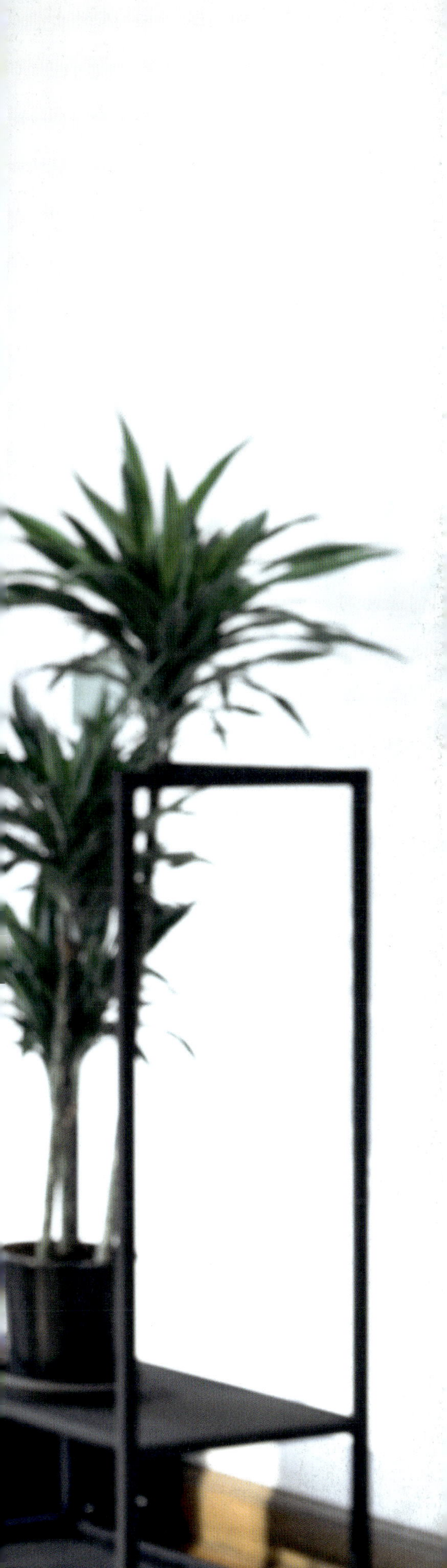

Beirut Art Center Square Meters (2012), deals with the notion of an artwork's response to its exhibition space. It is a by-product of the long history of the center's formal and architectural relationship with the furniture factory that previously occupied the building. The installation is the result of casting recycled paper pulp into silicone molds—made from impressions of large sections of the rough floor surface at the BAC—and then subsequently mounting them on the wall. The casts draw attention to incidental details and textures created during the space's many transformations over the years—questioning synchronicity and materiality, and the relationship between form and space.

Beirut Art Center Square Meters (2012) setzt sich mit der Vorstellung auseinander, dass ein Kunstwerk auf seinen Ausstellungsort reagiert. Es ist ein Nebenprodukt der langjährigen Geschichte der formalen und architektonischen Verbindungen zwischen dem Beirut Art Center und der früher hier ansässigen Möbelfabrik. Für die Installation wurde Pulpe aus Recyclingpapier in Silikonformen gegeben, die zuvor von großen Teilen des groben Bodens des BAC abgenommen wurden. Die Stücke wurden schließlich an der Wand befestigt. Sie zeigen zufällige Details ebenso wie Spuren der frü-Synchronizität, Materialität und die Beziehung von Form und Raum.

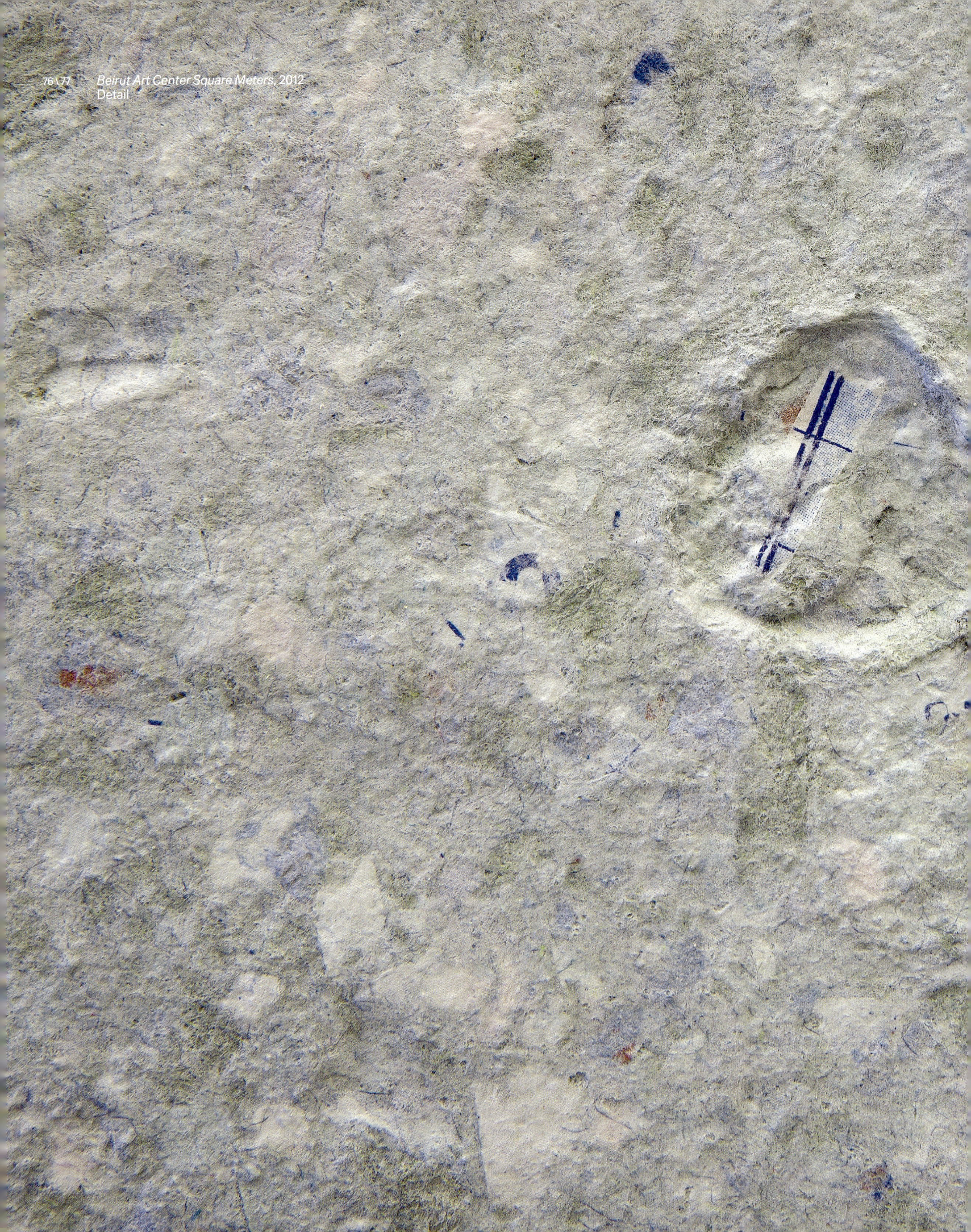

Beirut Art Center Square Meters, 2012
Detail

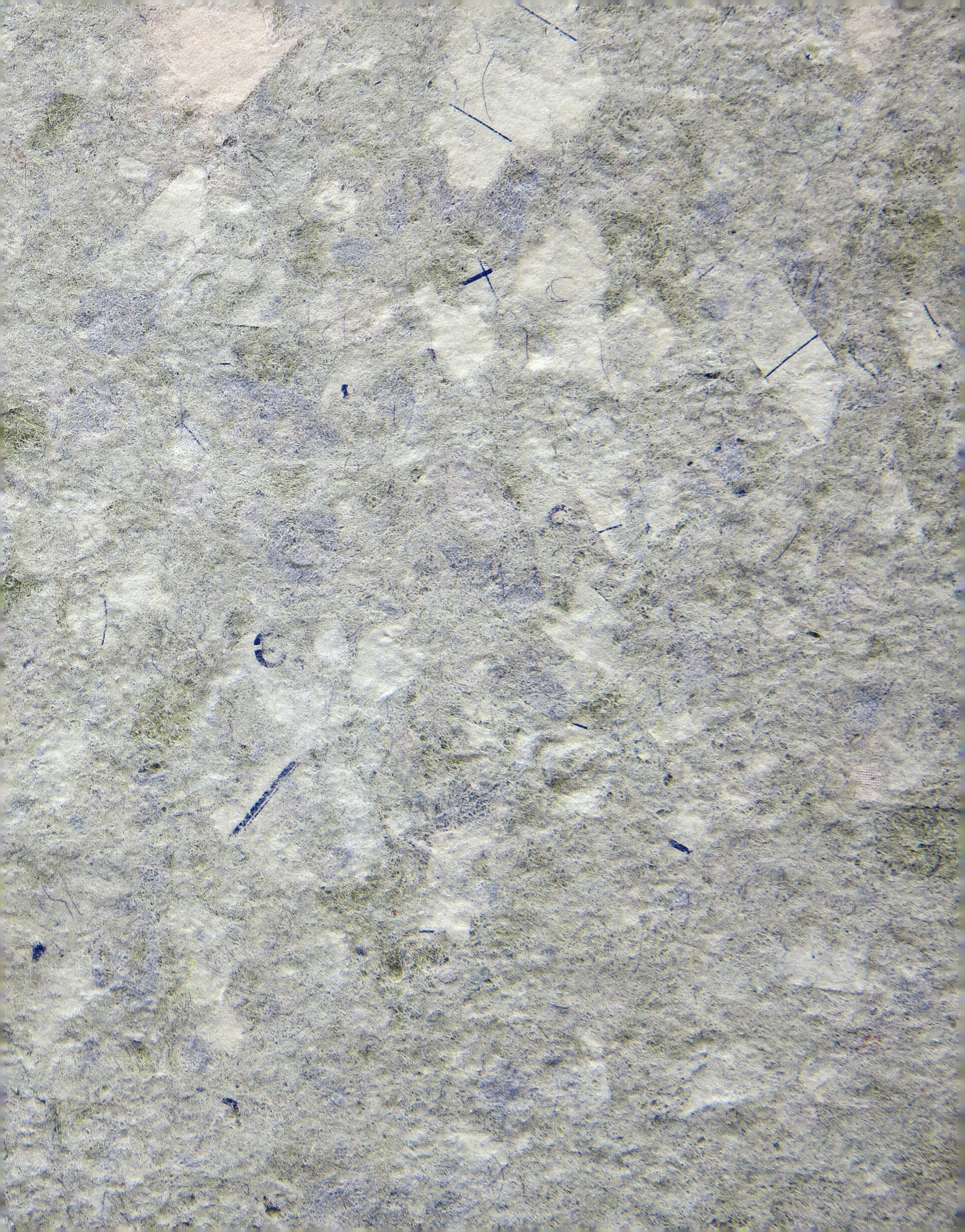

   Untitled, 2013

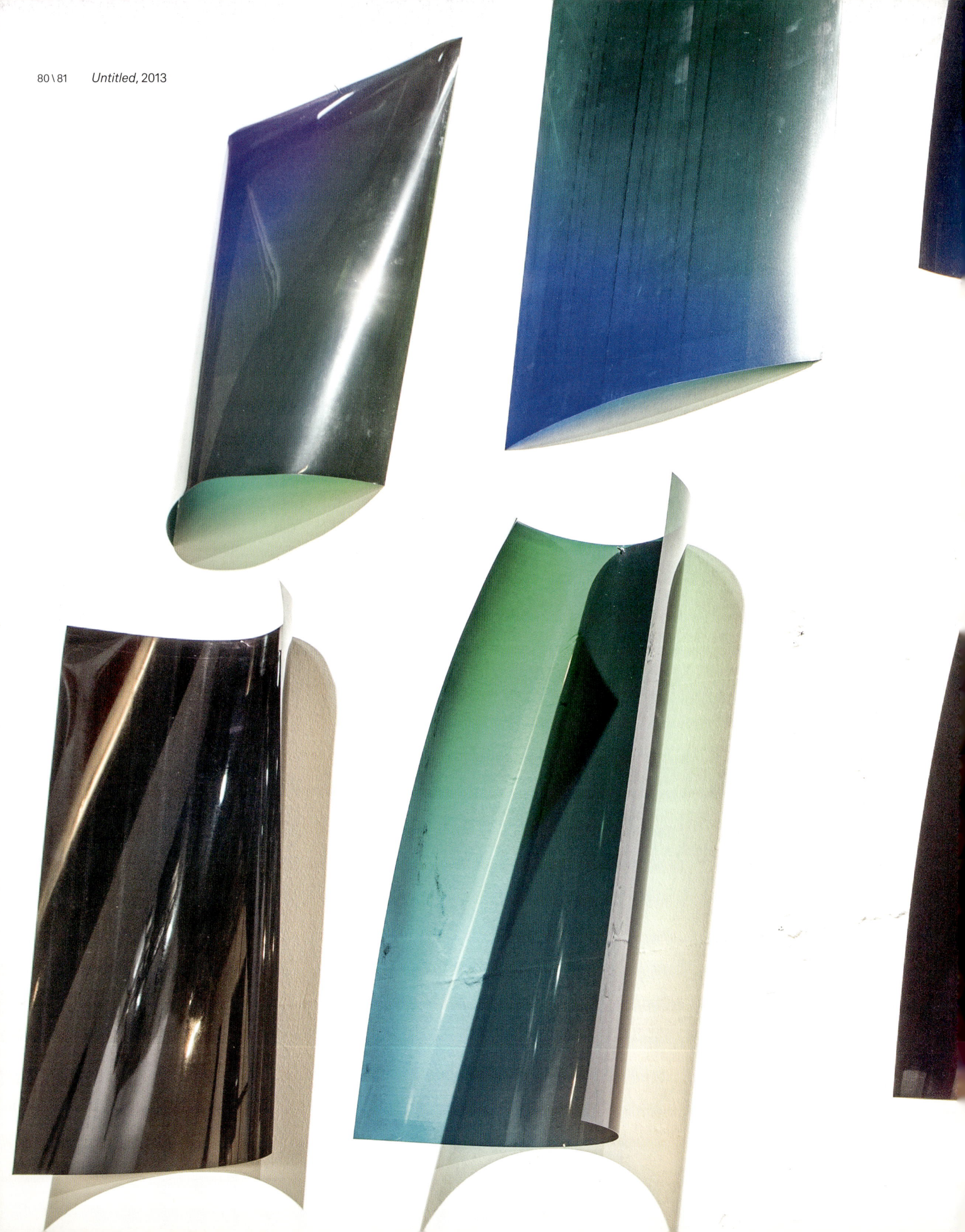

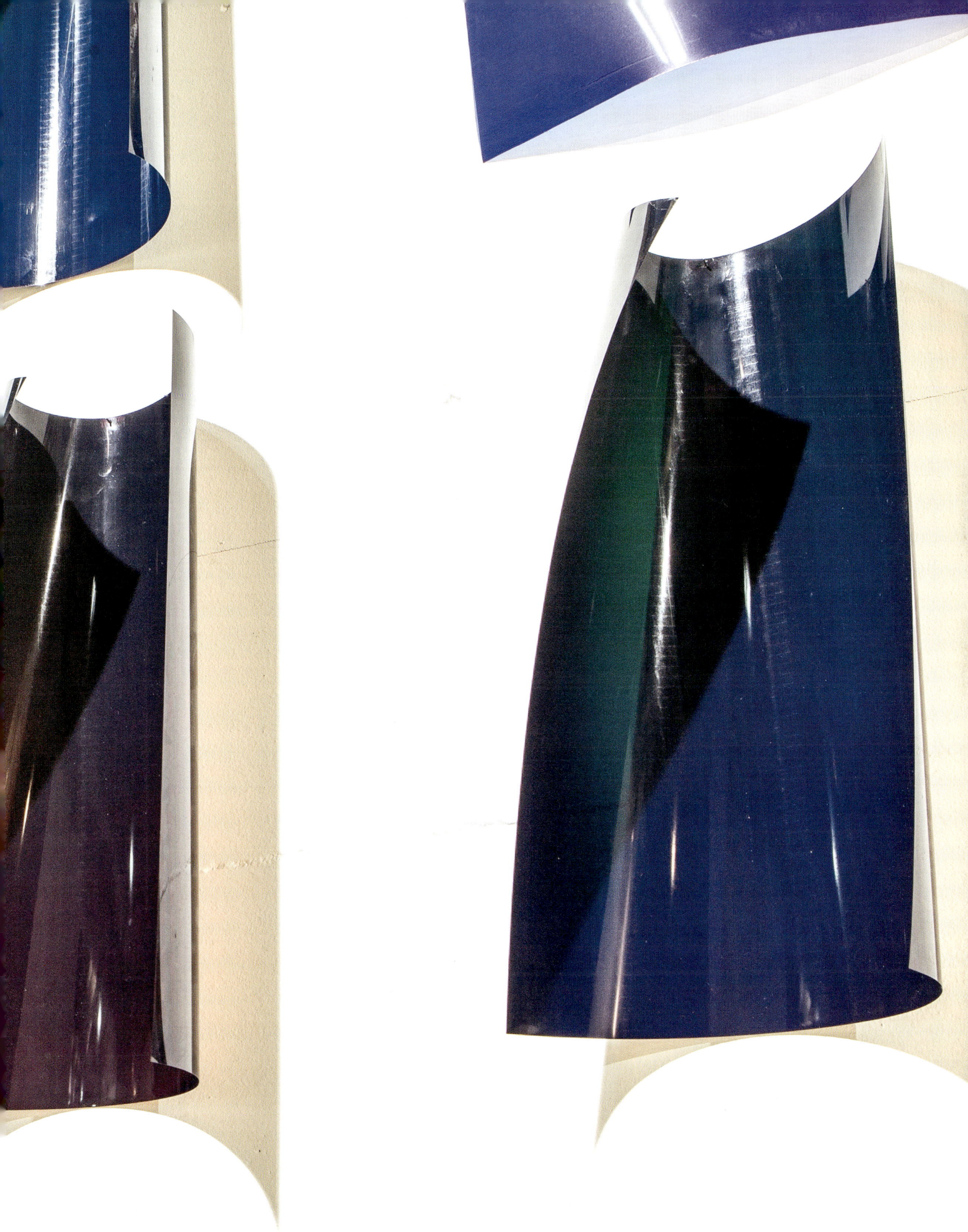

 Untitled, 2013

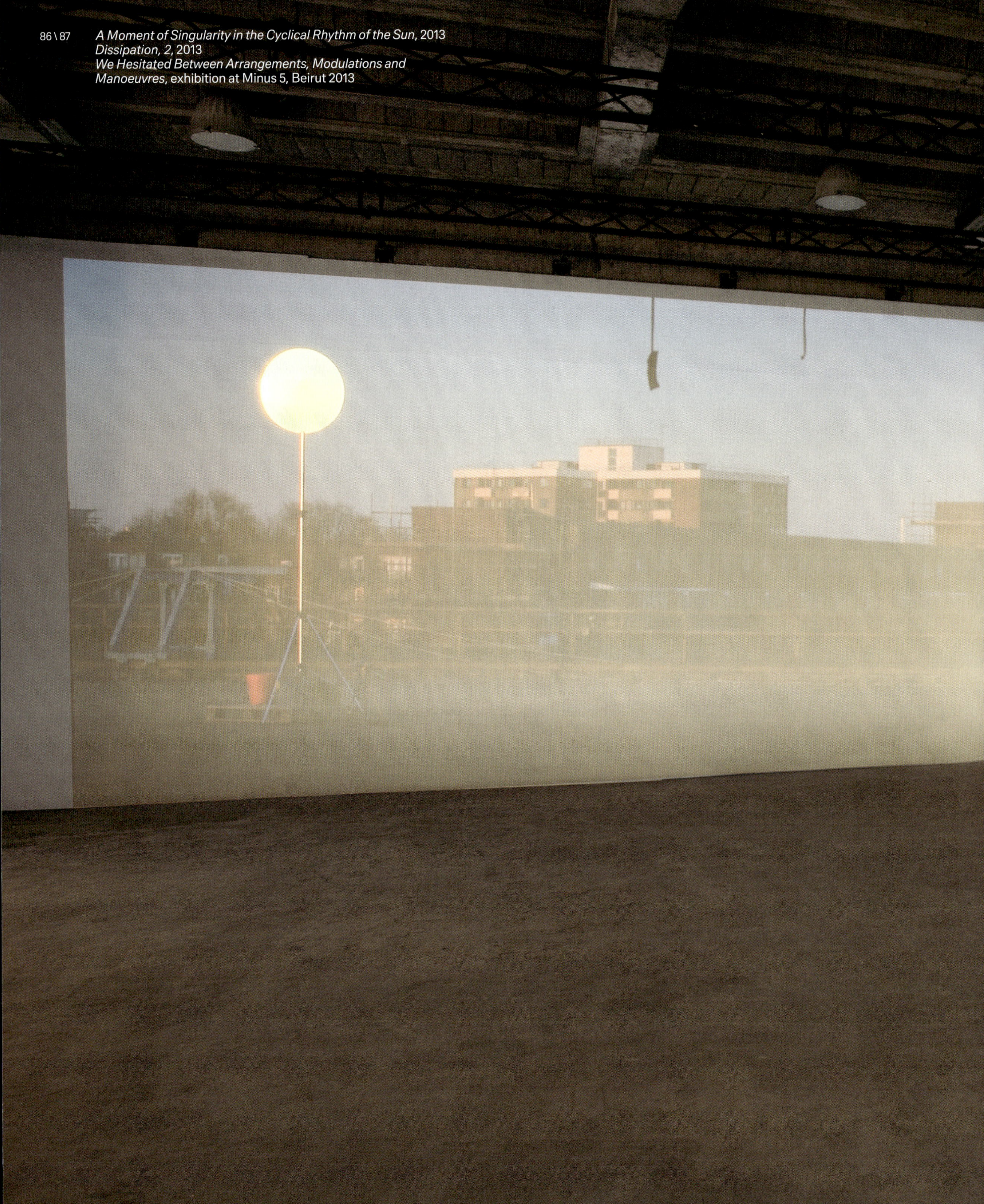

A Moment of Singularity in the Cyclical Rhythm of the Sun, 2013
Dissipation, 2, 2013
*We Hesitated Between Arrangements, Modulations and
Manoeuvres*, exhibition at Minus 5, Beirut 2013

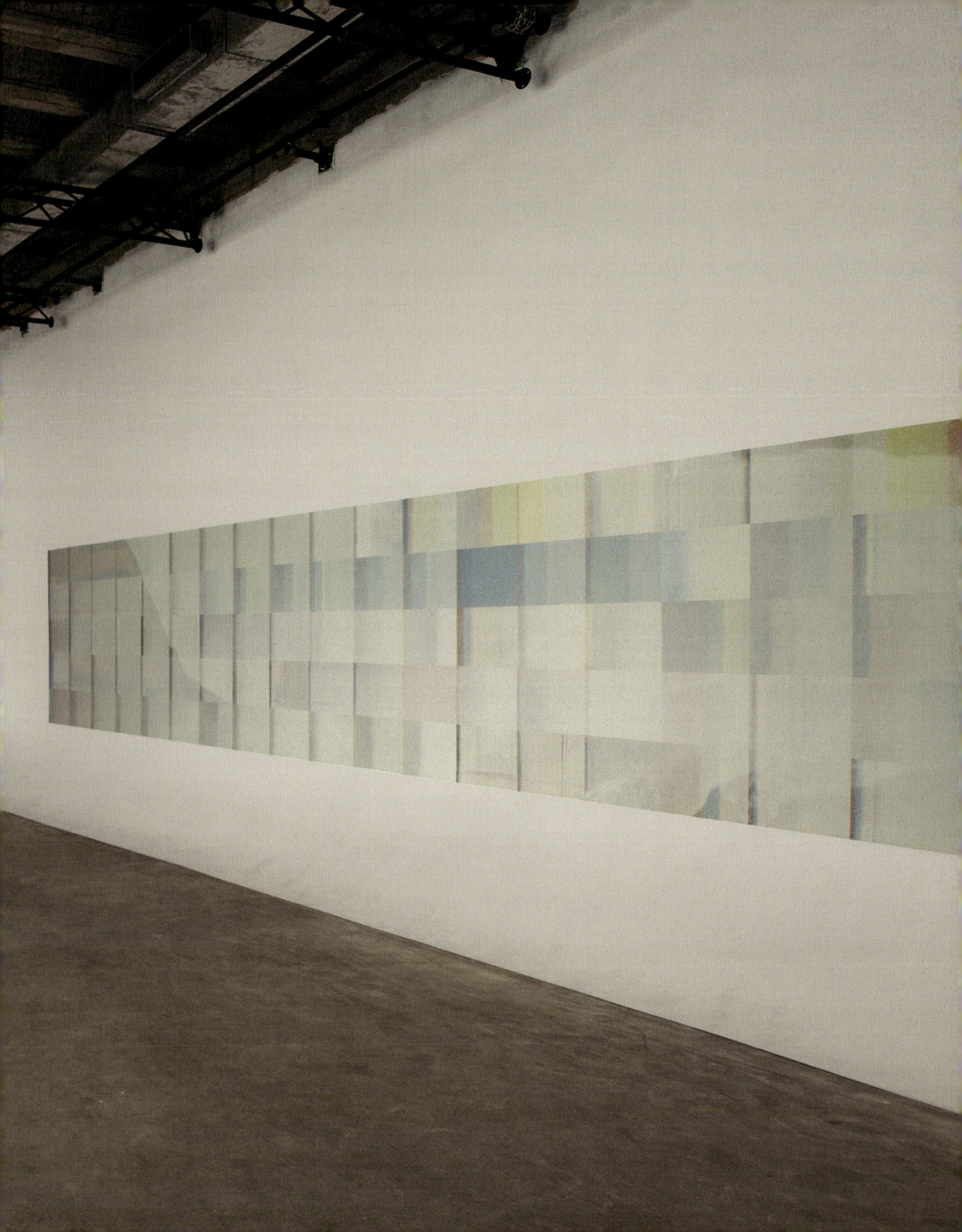

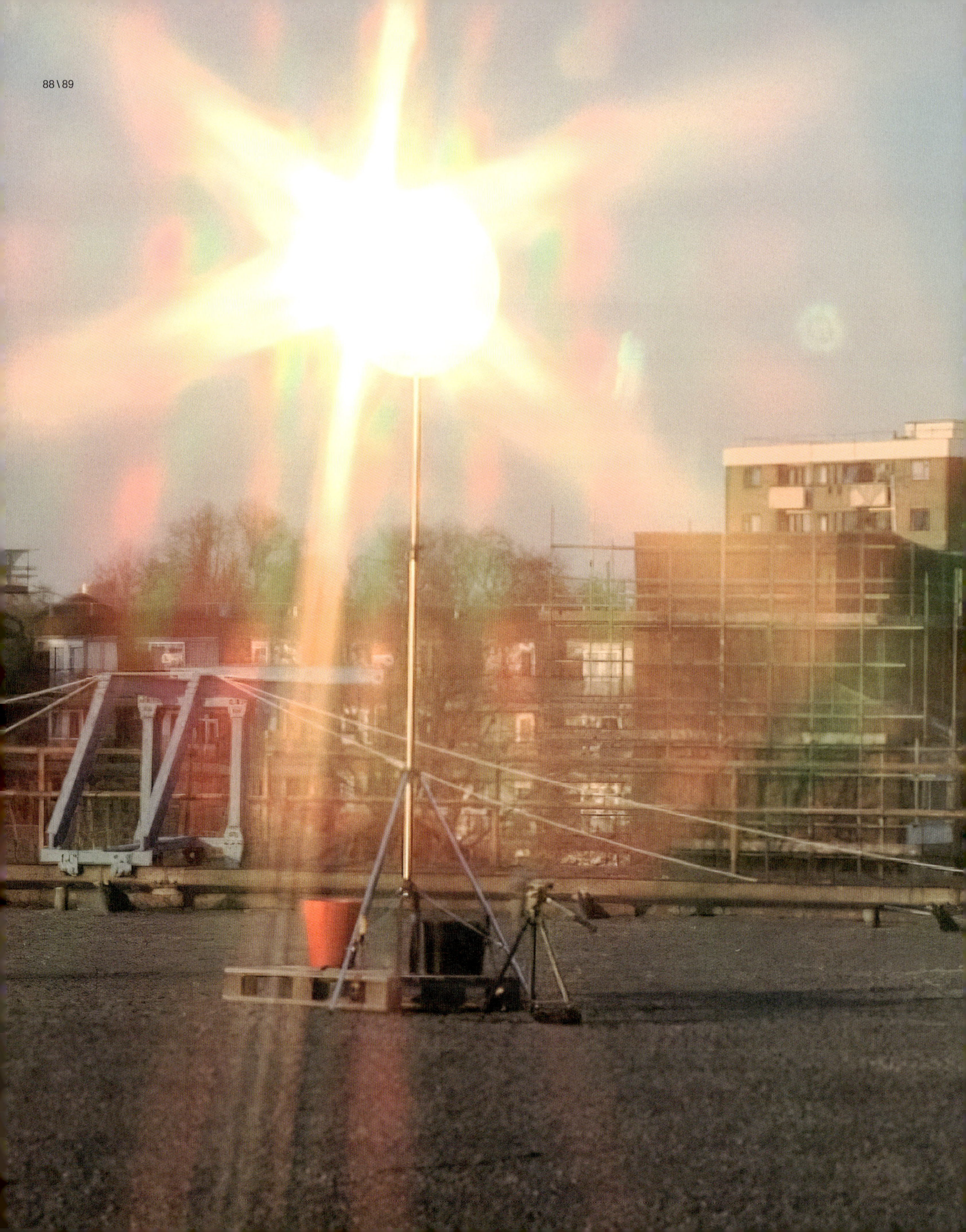

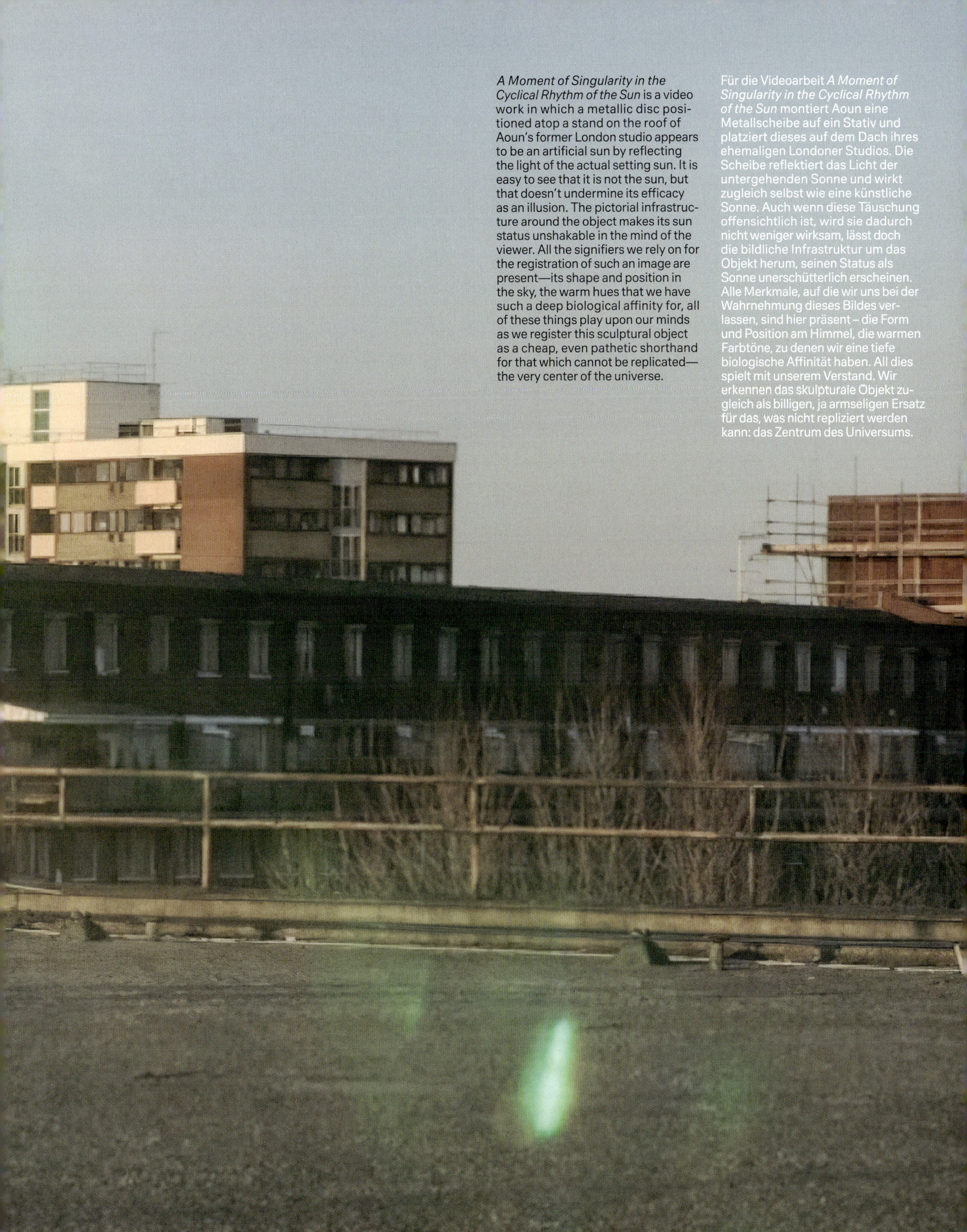

A Moment of Singularity in the Cyclical Rhythm of the Sun is a video work in which a metallic disc positioned atop a stand on the roof of Aoun's former London studio appears to be an artificial sun by reflecting the light of the actual setting sun. It is easy to see that it is not the sun, but that doesn't undermine its efficacy as an illusion. The pictorial infrastructure around the object makes its sun status unshakable in the mind of the viewer. All the signifiers we rely on for the registration of such an image are present—its shape and position in the sky, the warm hues that we have such a deep biological affinity for, all of these things play upon our minds as we register this sculptural object as a cheap, even pathetic shorthand for that which cannot be replicated— the very center of the universe.

Für die Videoarbeit *A Moment of Singularity in the Cyclical Rhythm of the Sun* montiert Aoun eine Metallscheibe auf ein Stativ und platziert dieses auf dem Dach ihres ehemaligen Londoner Studios. Die Scheibe reflektiert das Licht der untergehenden Sonne und wirkt zugleich selbst wie eine künstliche Sonne. Auch wenn diese Täuschung offensichtlich ist, wird sie dadurch nicht weniger wirksam, lässt doch die bildliche Infrastruktur um das Objekt herum, seinen Status als Sonne unerschütterlich erscheinen. Alle Merkmale, auf die wir uns bei der Wahrnehmung dieses Bildes verlassen, sind hier präsent – die Form und Position am Himmel, die warmen Farbtöne, zu denen wir eine tiefe biologische Affinität haben. All dies spielt mit unserem Verstand. Wir erkennen das skulpturale Objekt zugleich als billigen, ja armseligen Ersatz für das, was nicht repliziert werden kann: das Zentrum des Universums.

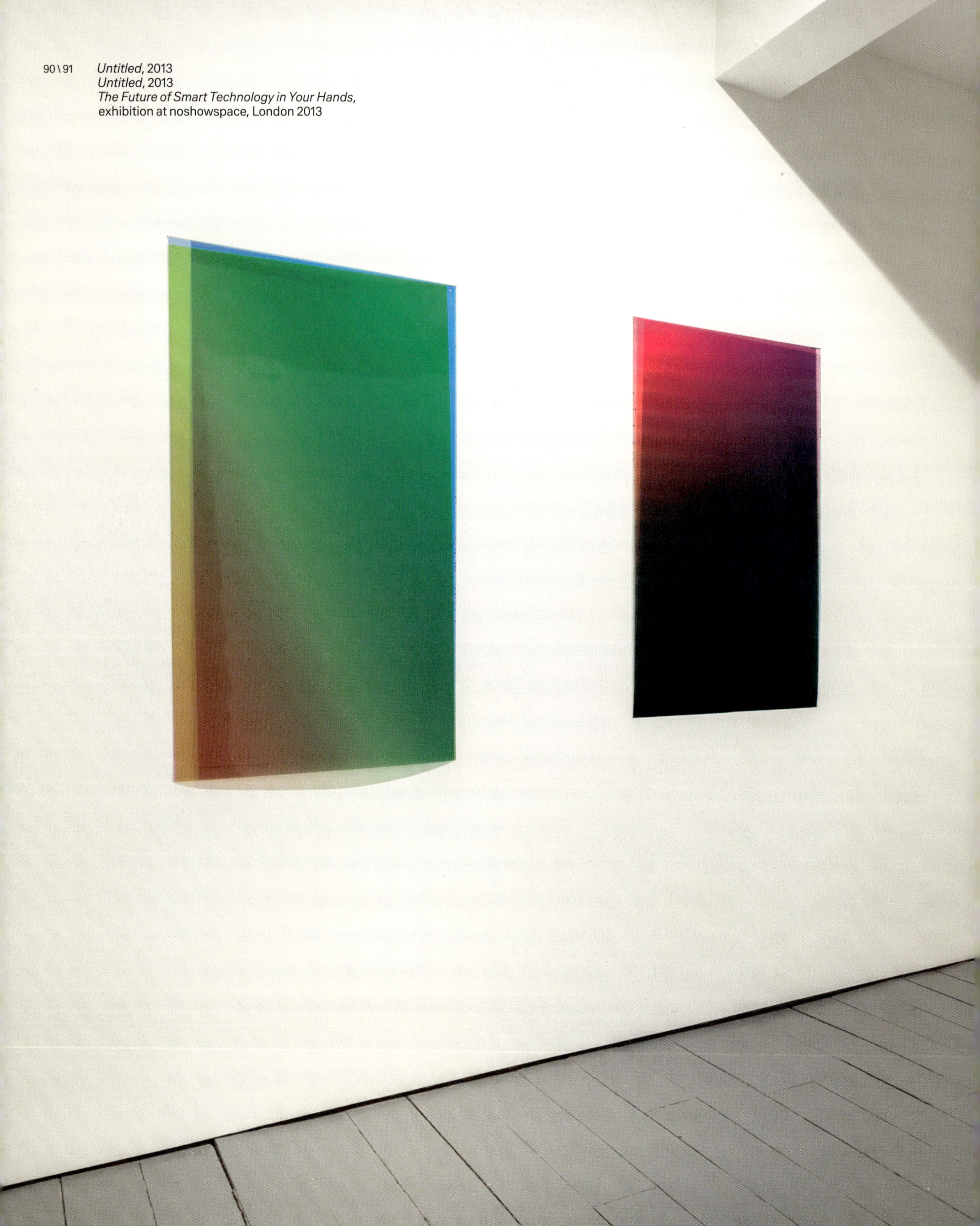

Untitled, 2013
Untitled, 2013
The Future of Smart Technology in Your Hands,
exhibition at noshowspace, London 2013

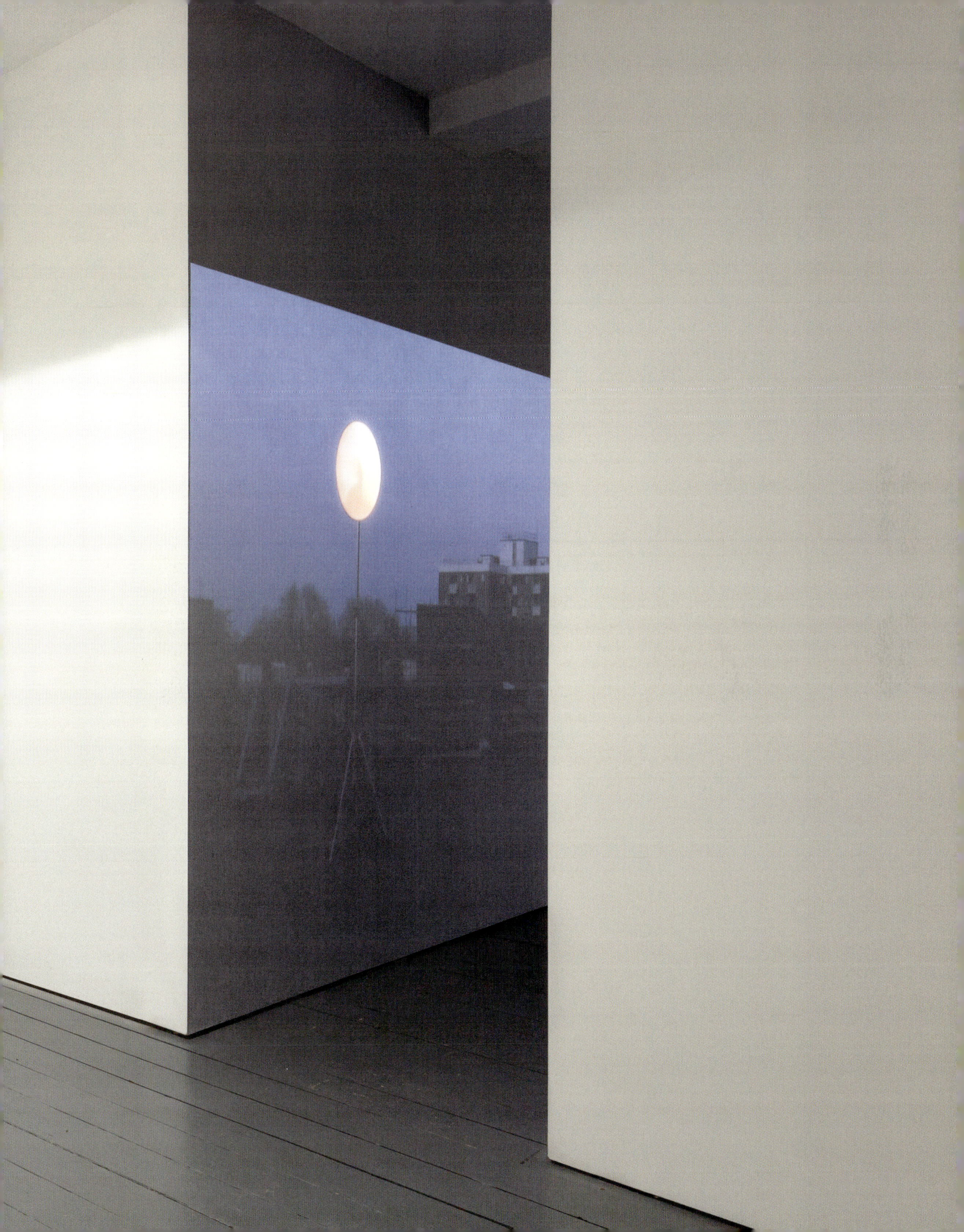

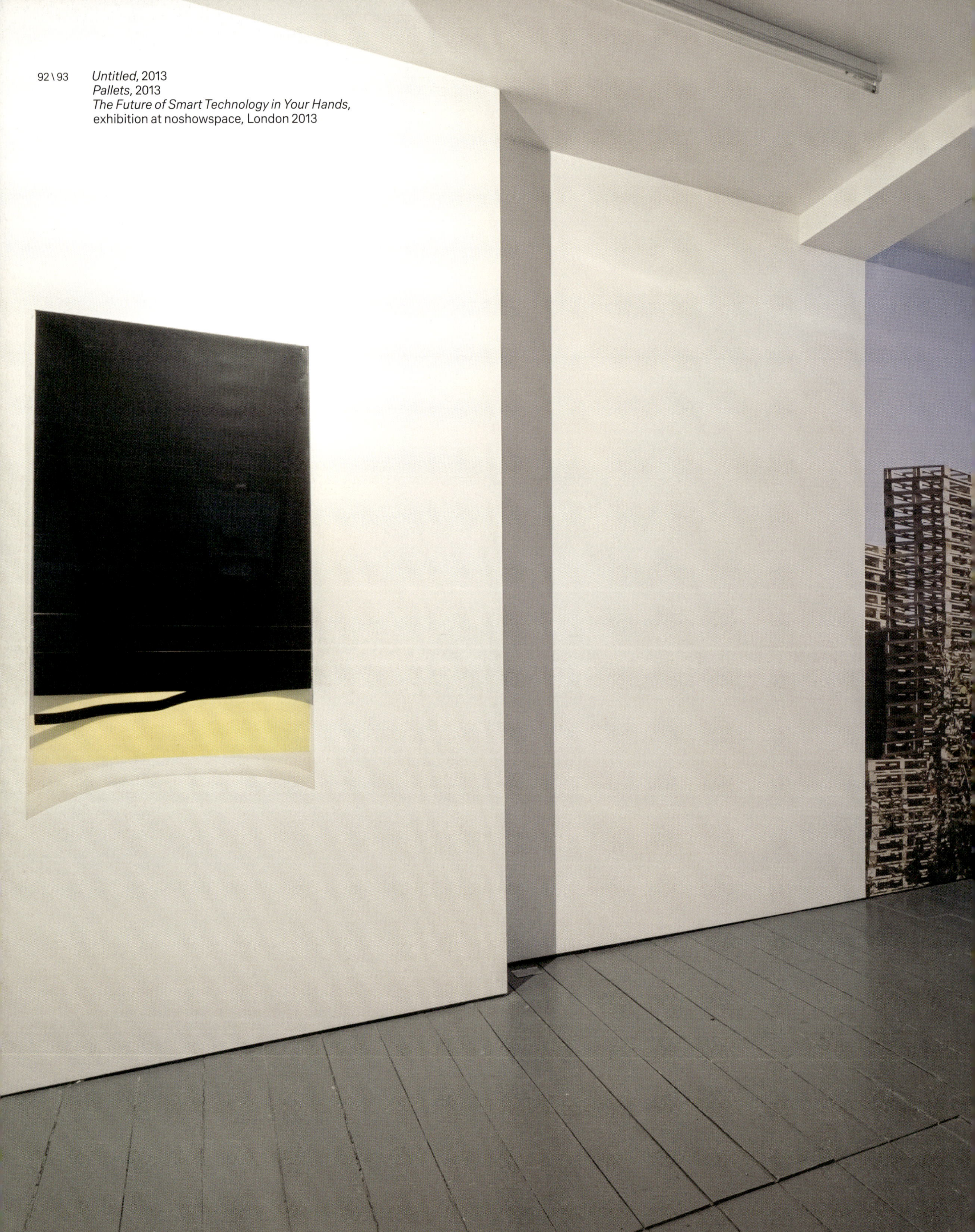

Untitled, 2013
Pallets, 2013
The Future of Smart Technology in Your Hands,
exhibition at noshowspace, London 2013

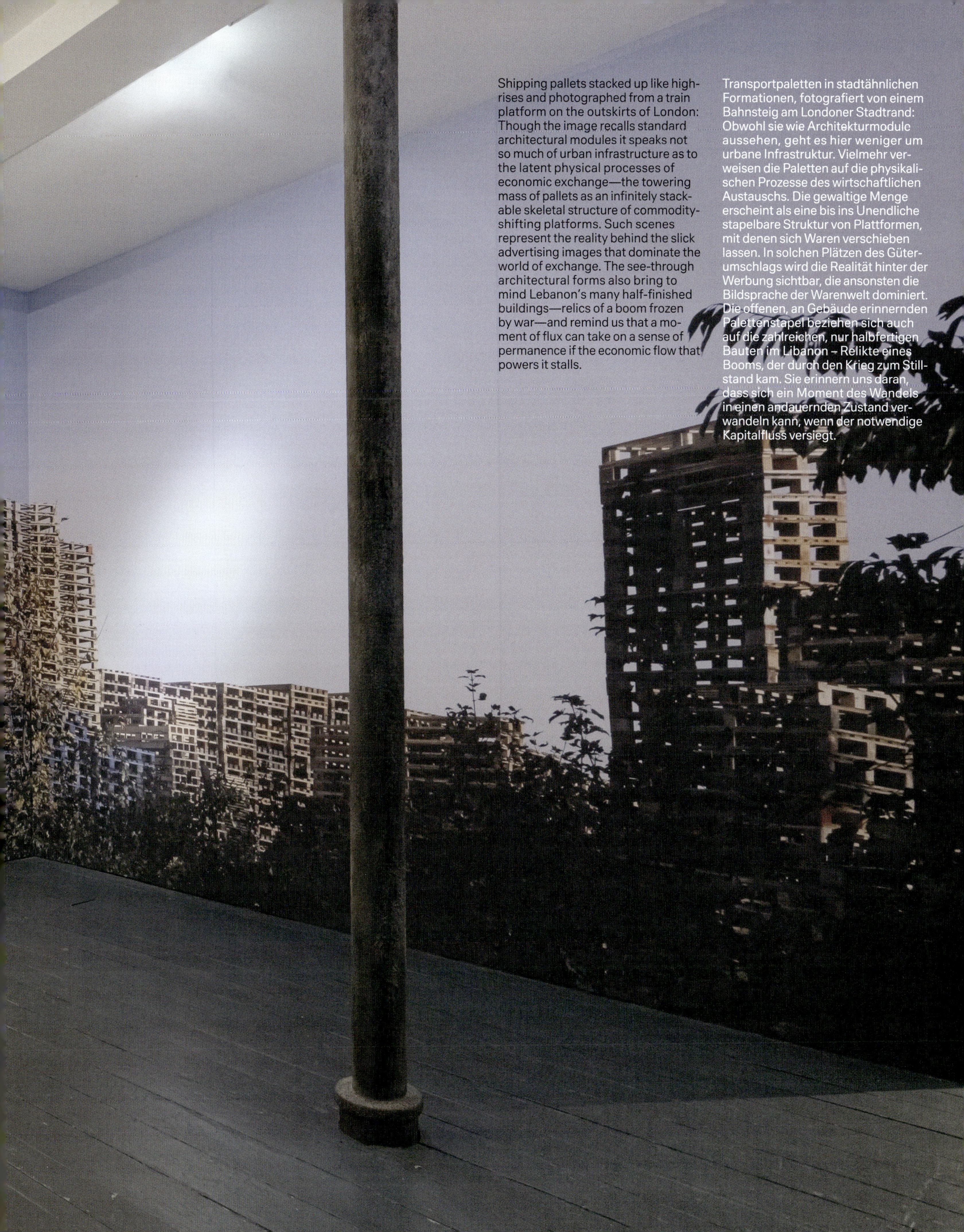

Shipping pallets stacked up like high-rises and photographed from a train platform on the outskirts of London: Though the image recalls standard architectural modules it speaks not so much of urban infrastructure as to the latent physical processes of economic exchange—the towering mass of pallets as an infinitely stackable skeletal structure of commodity-shifting platforms. Such scenes represent the reality behind the slick advertising images that dominate the world of exchange. The see-through architectural forms also bring to mind Lebanon's many half-finished buildings—relics of a boom frozen by war—and remind us that a moment of flux can take on a sense of permanence if the economic flow that powers it stalls.

Transportpaletten in stadtähnlichen Formationen, fotografiert von einem Bahnsteig am Londoner Stadtrand: Obwohl sie wie Architekturmodule aussehen, geht es hier weniger um urbane Infrastruktur. Vielmehr verweisen die Paletten auf die physikalischen Prozesse des wirtschaftlichen Austauschs. Die gewaltige Menge erscheint als eine bis ins Unendliche stapelbare Struktur von Plattformen, mit denen sich Waren verschieben lassen. In solchen Plätzen des Güterumschlags wird die Realität hinter der Werbung sichtbar, die ansonsten die Bildsprache der Warenwelt dominiert. Die offenen, an Gebäude erinnernden Palettenstapel beziehen sich auch auf die zahlreichen, nur halbfertigen Bauten im Libanon – Relikte eines Booms, der durch den Krieg zum Stillstand kam. Sie erinnern uns daran, dass sich ein Moment des Wandels in einen andauernden Zustand verwandeln kann, wenn der notwendige Kapitalfluss versiegt.

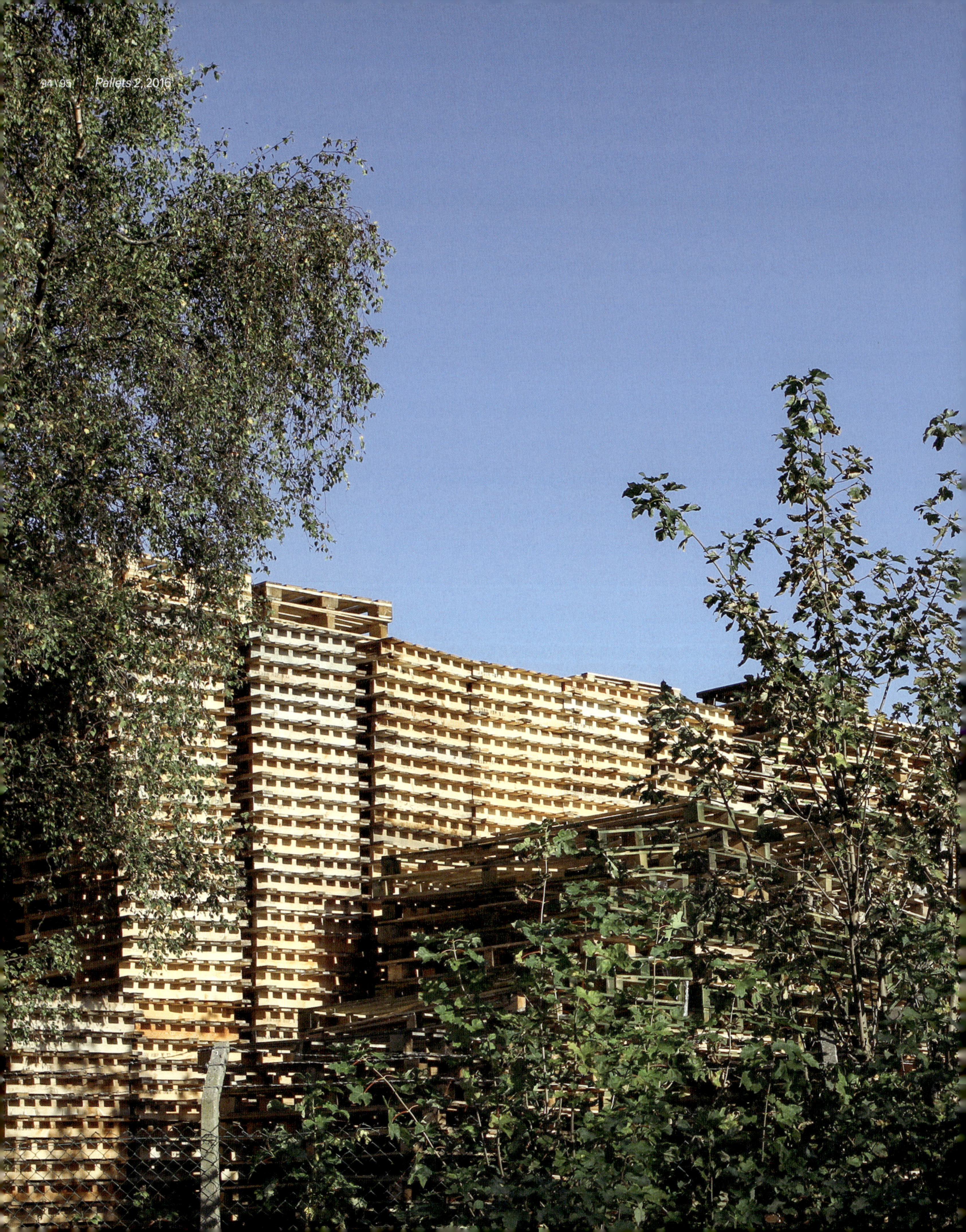

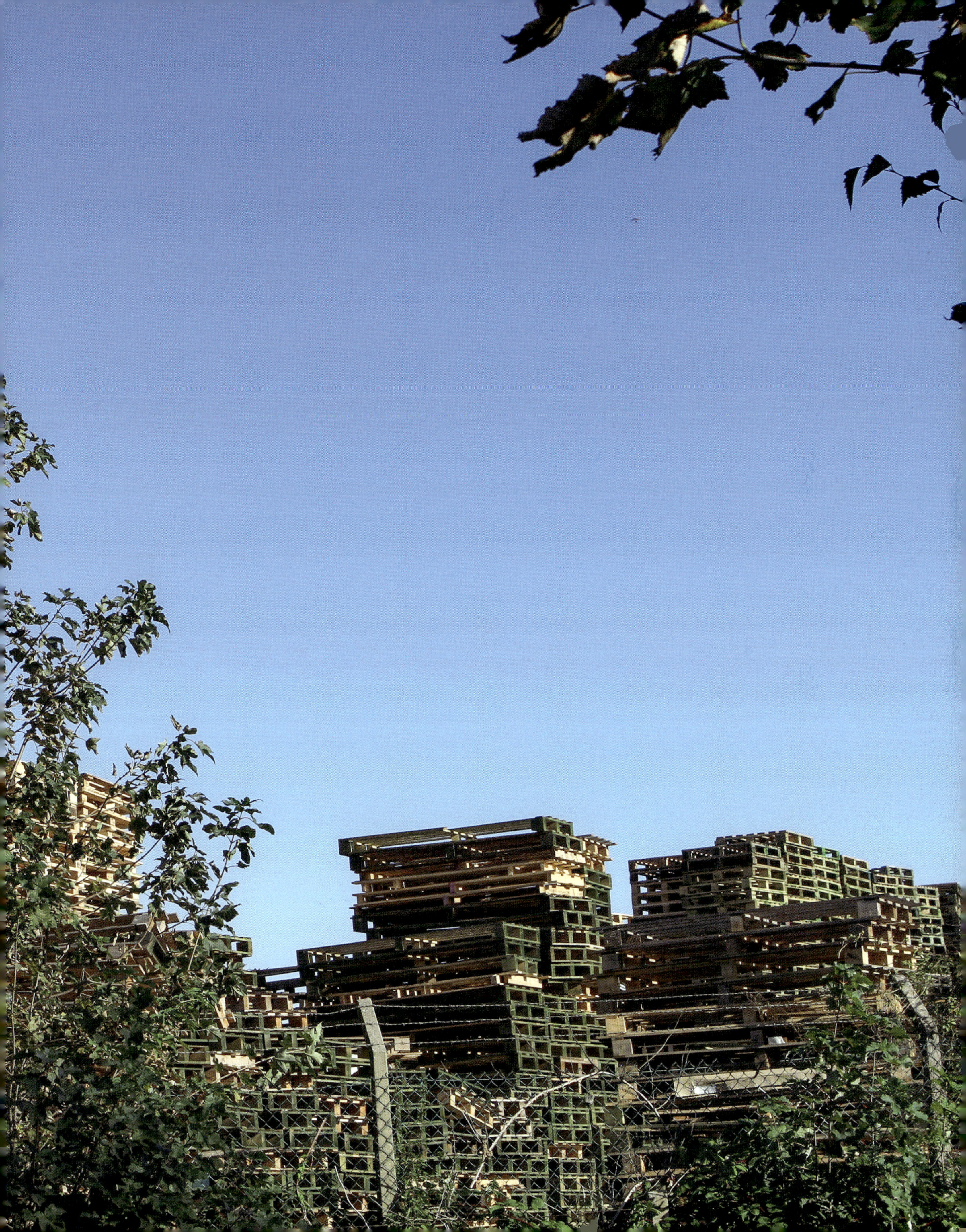

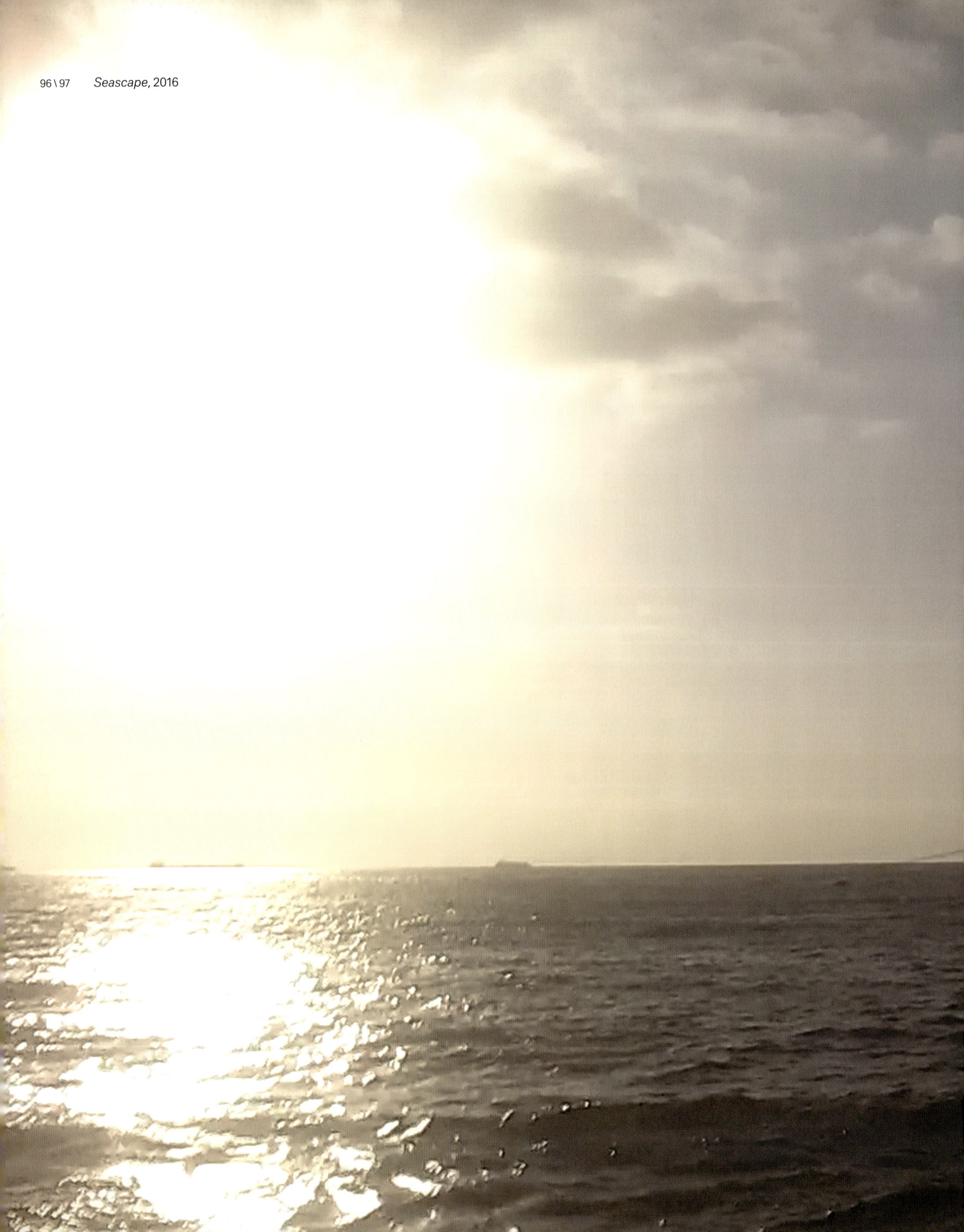

 Seascape, 2016

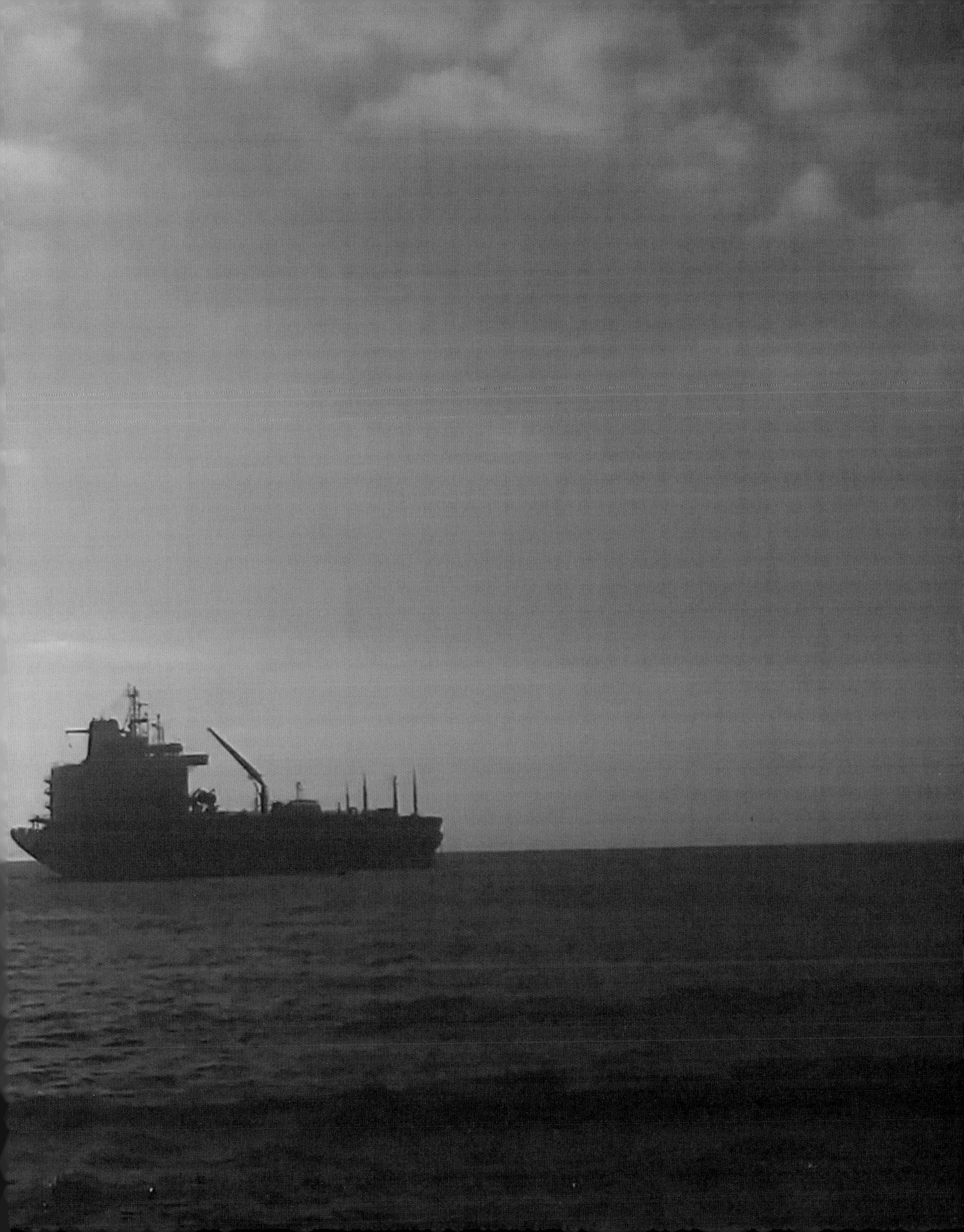

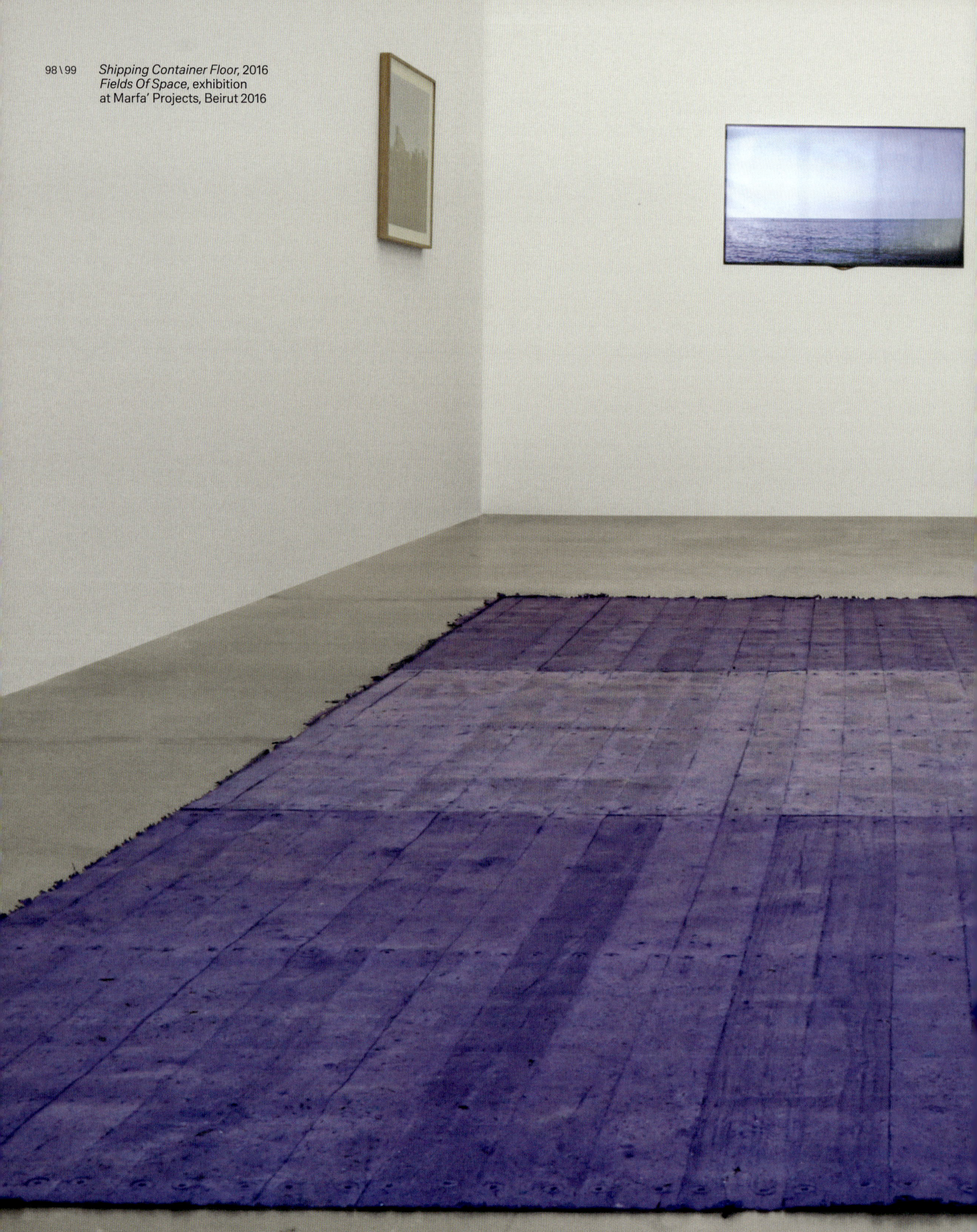

Shipping Container Floor, 2016
Fields Of Space, exhibition
at Marfa' Projects, Beirut 2016

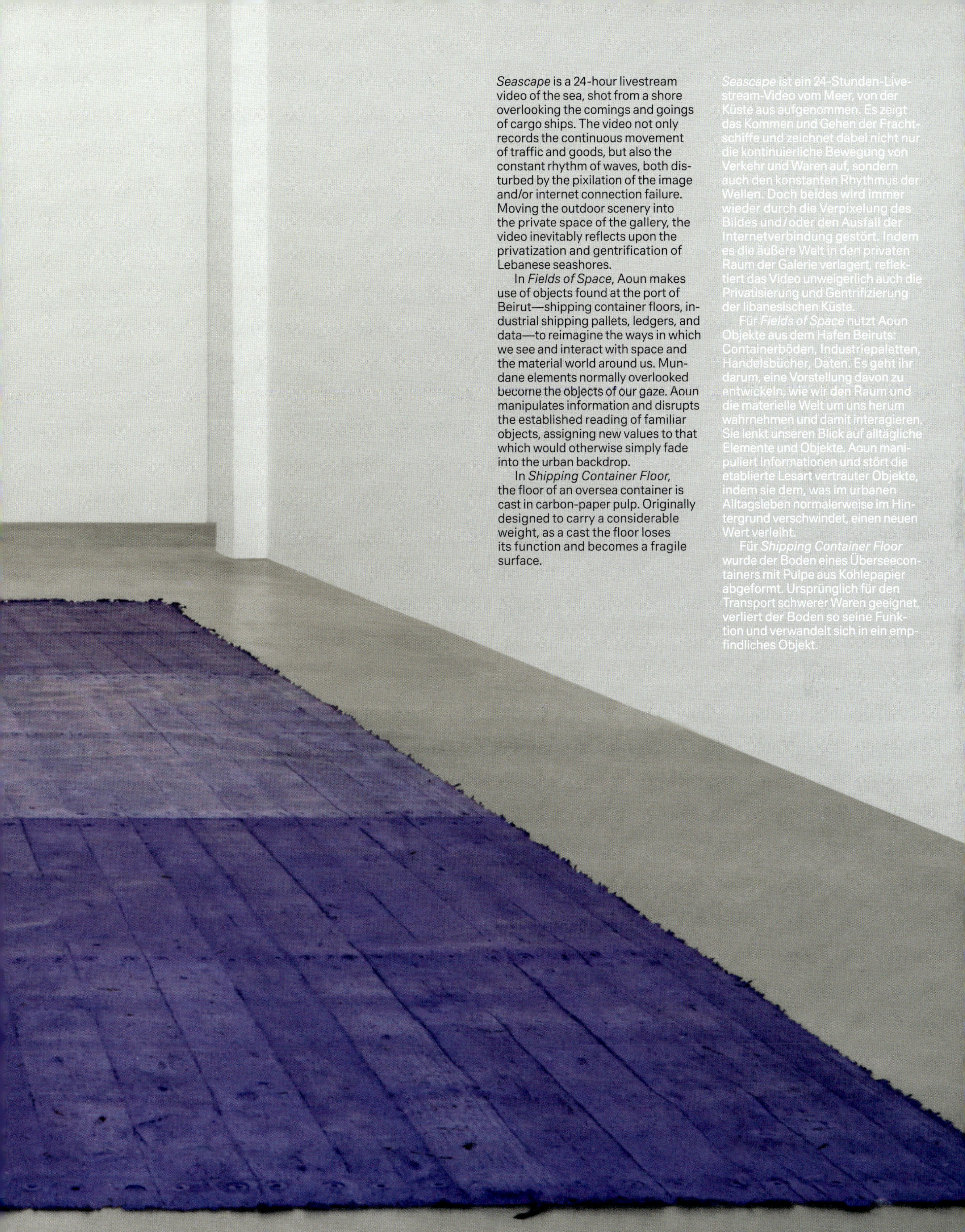

Seascape is a 24-hour livestream video of the sea, shot from a shore overlooking the comings and goings of cargo ships. The video not only records the continuous movement of traffic and goods, but also the constant rhythm of waves, both disturbed by the pixilation of the image and/or internet connection failure. Moving the outdoor scenery into the private space of the gallery, the video inevitably reflects upon the privatization and gentrification of Lebanese seashores.

In *Fields of Space*, Aoun makes use of objects found at the port of Beirut—shipping container floors, industrial shipping pallets, ledgers, and data—to reimagine the ways in which we see and interact with space and the material world around us. Mundane elements normally overlooked become the objects of our gaze. Aoun manipulates information and disrupts the established reading of familiar objects, assigning new values to that which would otherwise simply fade into the urban backdrop.

In *Shipping Container Floor*, the floor of an oversea container is cast in carbon-paper pulp. Originally designed to carry a considerable weight, as a cast the floor loses its function and becomes a fragile surface.

Seascape ist ein 24-Stunden-Livestream-Video vom Meer, von der Küste aus aufgenommen. Es zeigt das Kommen und Gehen der Frachtschiffe und zeichnet dabei nicht nur die kontinuierliche Bewegung von Verkehr und Waren auf, sondern auch den konstanten Rhythmus der Wellen. Doch beides wird immer wieder durch die Verpixelung des Bildes und/oder den Ausfall der Internetverbindung gestört. Indem es die äußere Welt in den privaten Raum der Galerie verlagert, reflektiert das Video unweigerlich auch die Privatisierung und Gentrifizierung der libanesischen Küste.

Für *Fields of Space* nutzt Aoun Objekte aus dem Hafen Beiruts: Containerböden, Industriepaletten, Handelsbücher, Daten. Es geht ihr darum, eine Vorstellung davon zu entwickeln, wie wir den Raum und die materielle Welt um uns herum wahrnehmen und damit interagieren. Sie lenkt unseren Blick auf alltägliche Elemente und Objekte. Aoun manipuliert Informationen und stört die etablierte Lesart vertrauter Objekte, indem sie dem, was im urbanen Alltagsleben normalerweise im Hintergrund verschwindet, einen neuen Wert verleiht.

Für *Shipping Container Floor* wurde der Boden eines Überseecontainers mit Pulpe aus Kohlepapier abgeformt. Ursprünglich für den Transport schwerer Waren geeignet, verliert der Boden so seine Funktion und verwandelt sich in ein empfindliches Objekt.

Shipping Container Floor, 2016
Detail

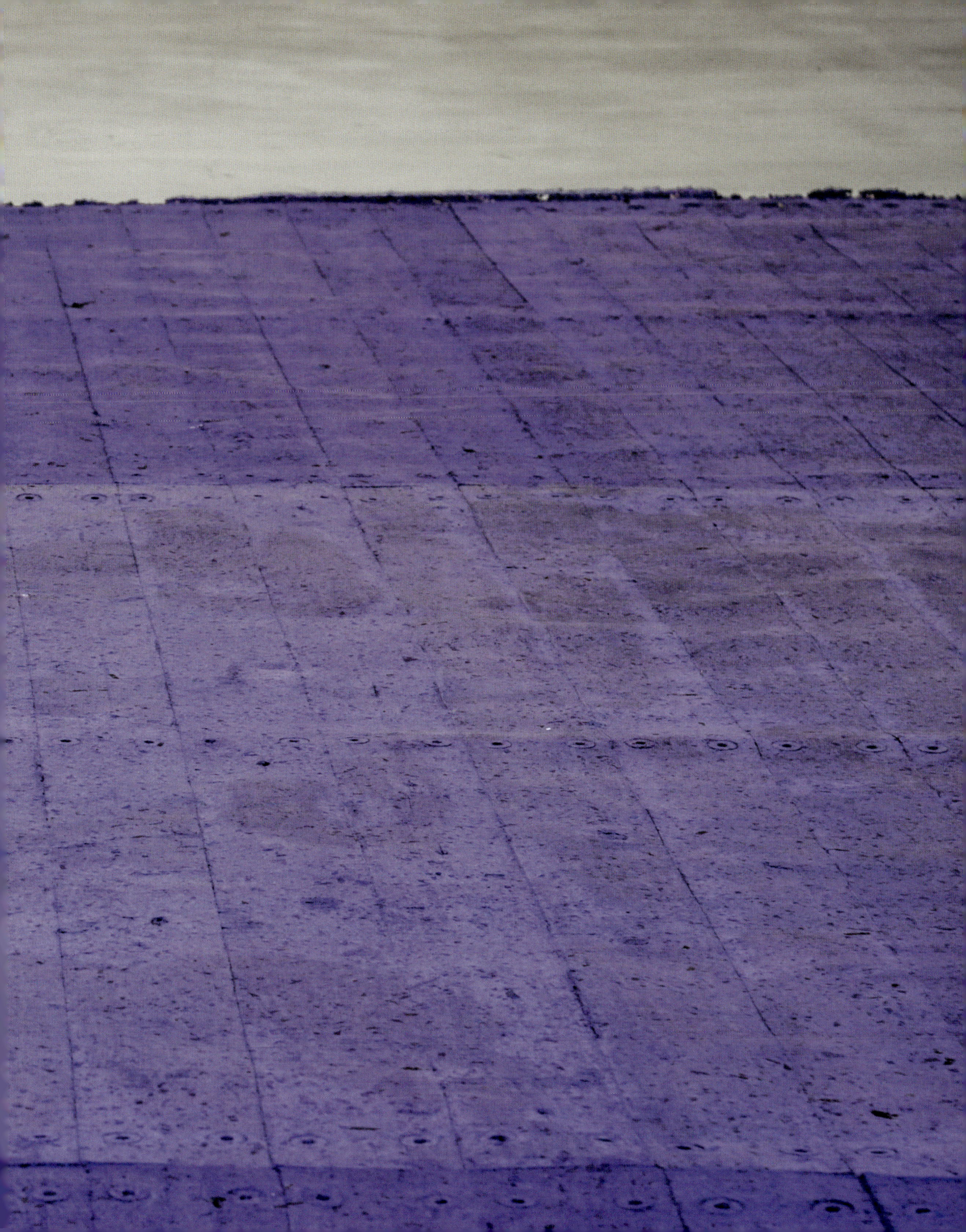

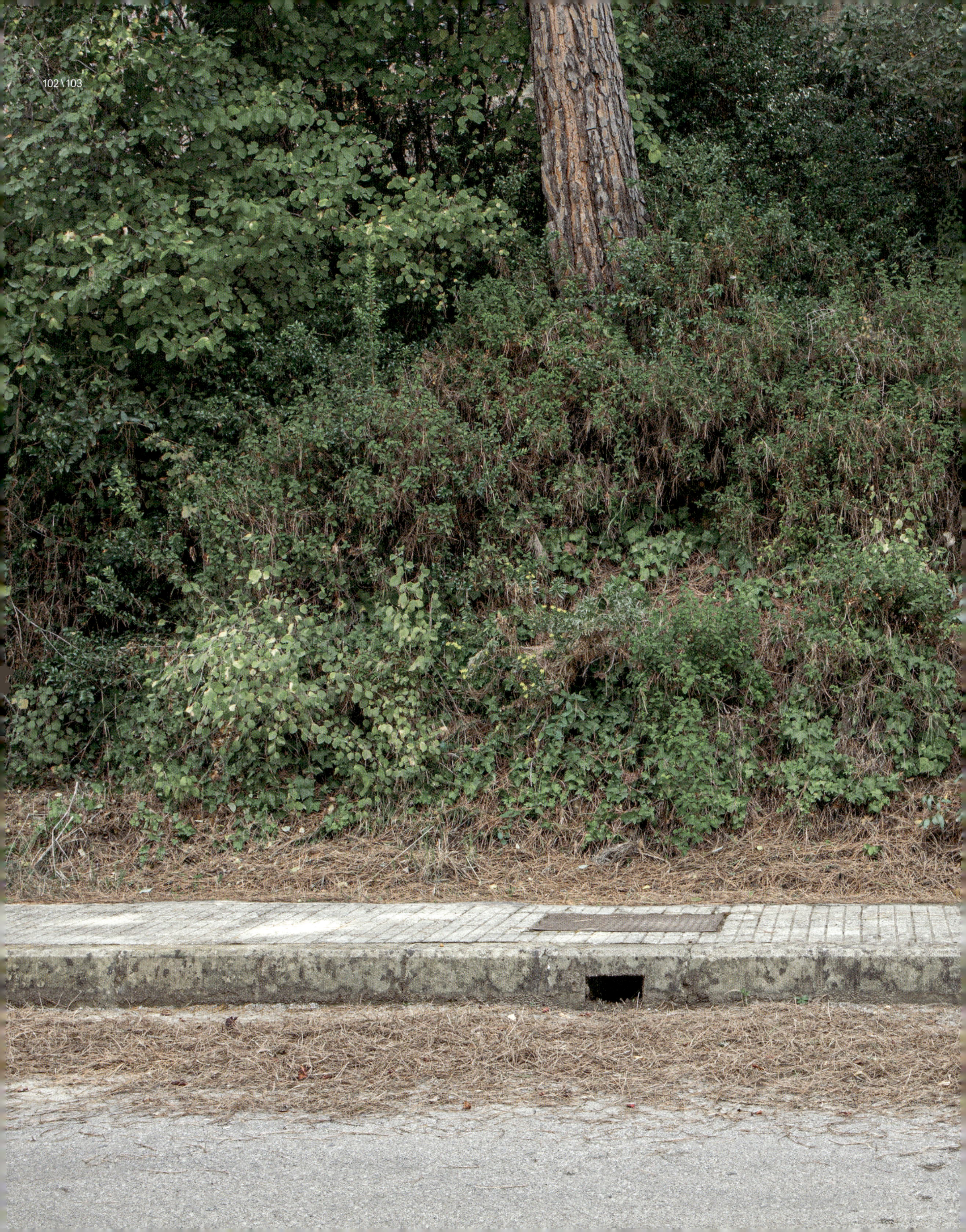

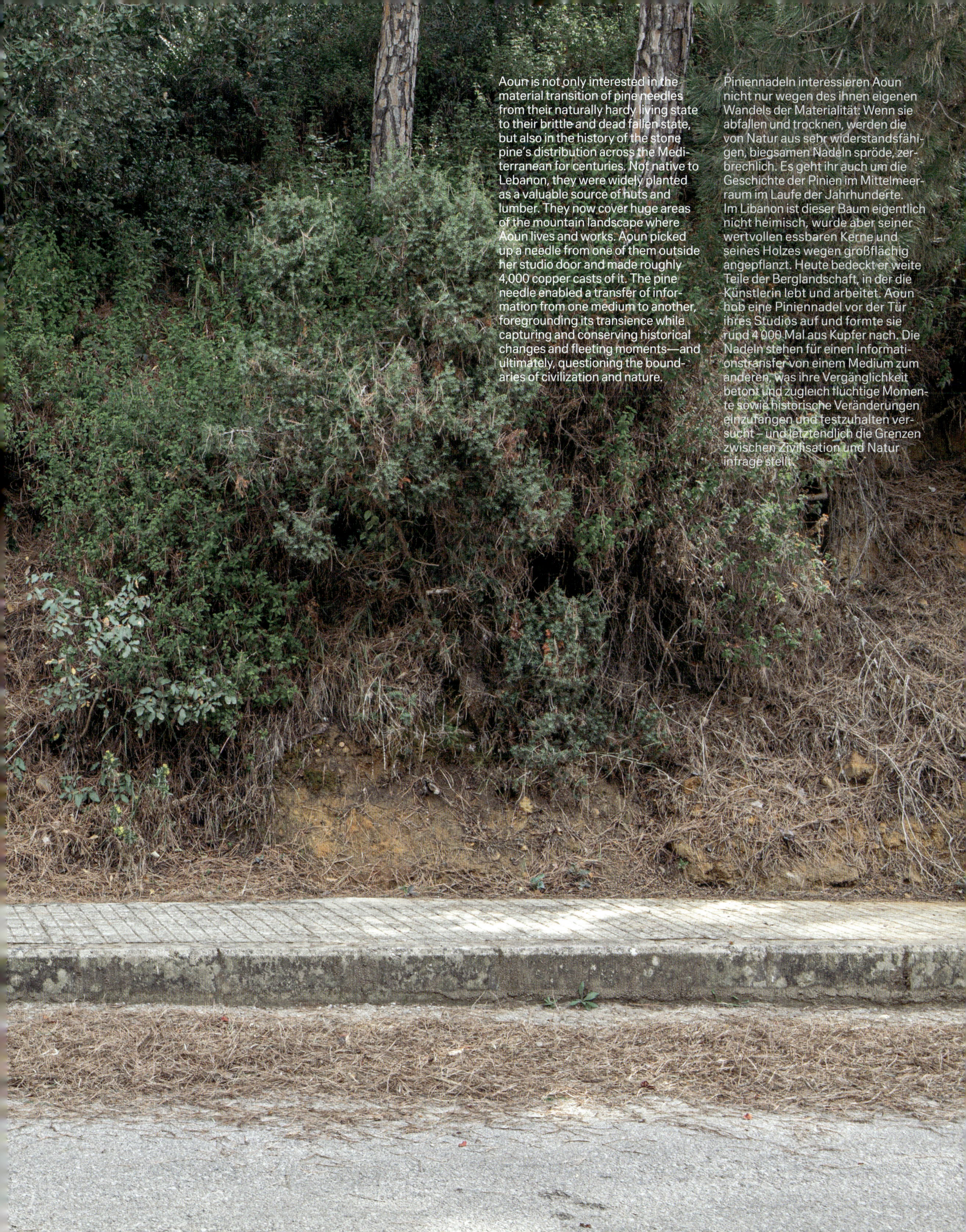
Aoun is not only interested in the material transition of pine needles from their naturally hardy living state to their brittle and dead fallen state, but also in the history of the stone pine's distribution across the Mediterranean for centuries. Not native to Lebanon, they were widely planted as a valuable source of huts and lumber. They now cover huge areas of the mountain landscape where Aoun lives and works. Aoun picked up a needle from one of them outside her studio door and made roughly 4,000 copper casts of it. The pine needle enabled a transfer of information from one medium to another, foregrounding its transience while capturing and conserving historical changes and fleeting moments—and ultimately, questioning the boundaries of civilization and nature.

Piniennadeln interessieren Aoun nicht nur wegen des ihnen eigenen Wandels der Materialität: Wenn sie abfallen und trocknen, werden die von Natur aus sehr widerstandsfähigen, biegsamen Nadeln spröde, zerbrechlich. Es geht ihr auch um die Geschichte der Pinien im Mittelmeerraum im Laufe der Jahrhunderte. Im Libanon ist dieser Baum eigentlich nicht heimisch, wurde aber seiner wertvollen essbaren Kerne und seines Holzes wegen großflächig angepflanzt. Heute bedeckt er weite Teile der Berglandschaft, in der die Künstlerin lebt und arbeitet. Aoun hob eine Piniennadel vor der Tür ihres Studios auf und formte sie rund 4 000 Mal aus Kupfer nach. Die Nadeln stehen für einen Informationstransfer von einem Medium zum anderen, was ihre Vergänglichkeit betont und zugleich flüchtige Momente sowie historische Veränderungen einzufangen und festzuhalten versucht – und letztendlich die Grenzen zwischen Zivilisation und Natur infrage stellt.

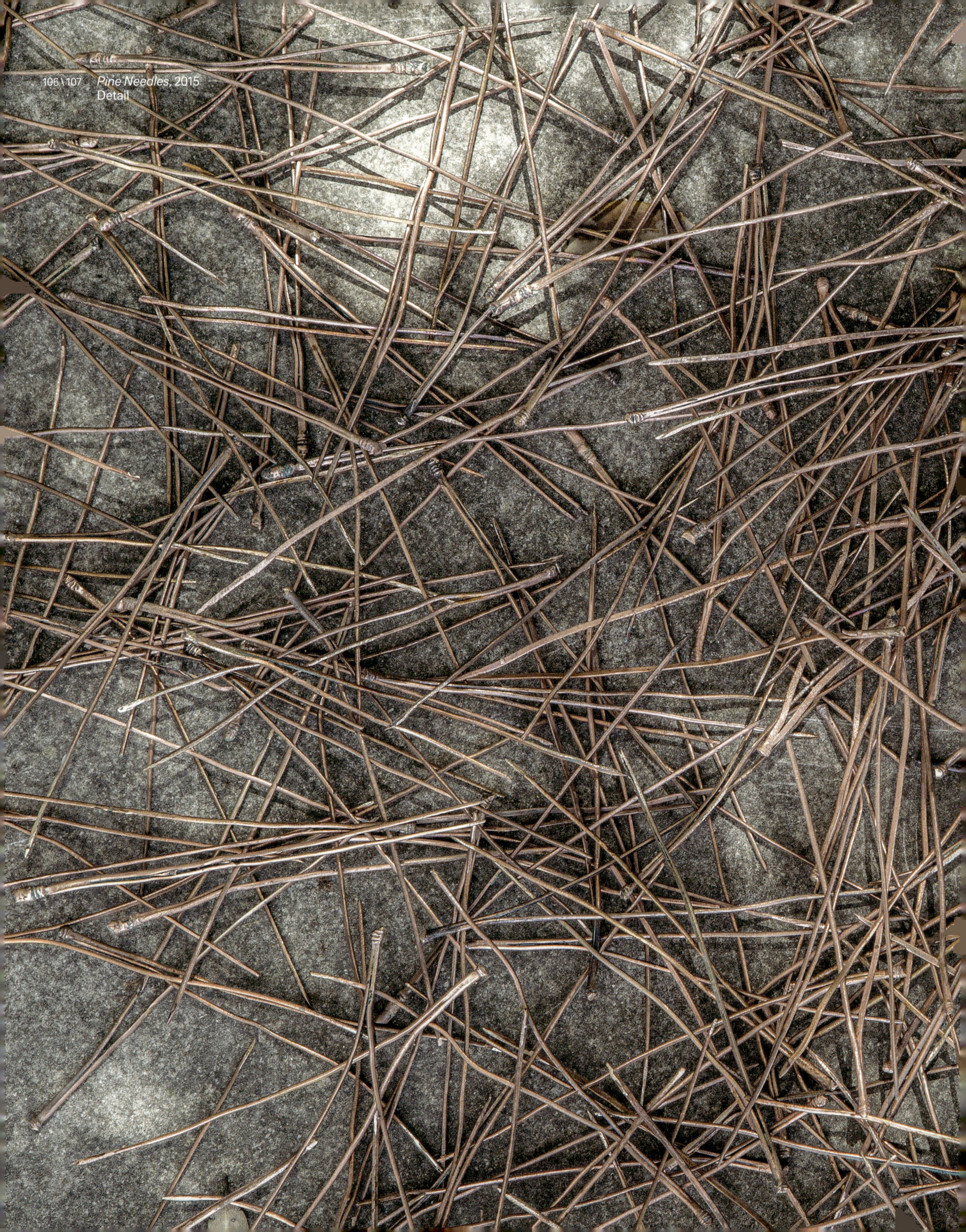

Pine Needles, 2015
Detail

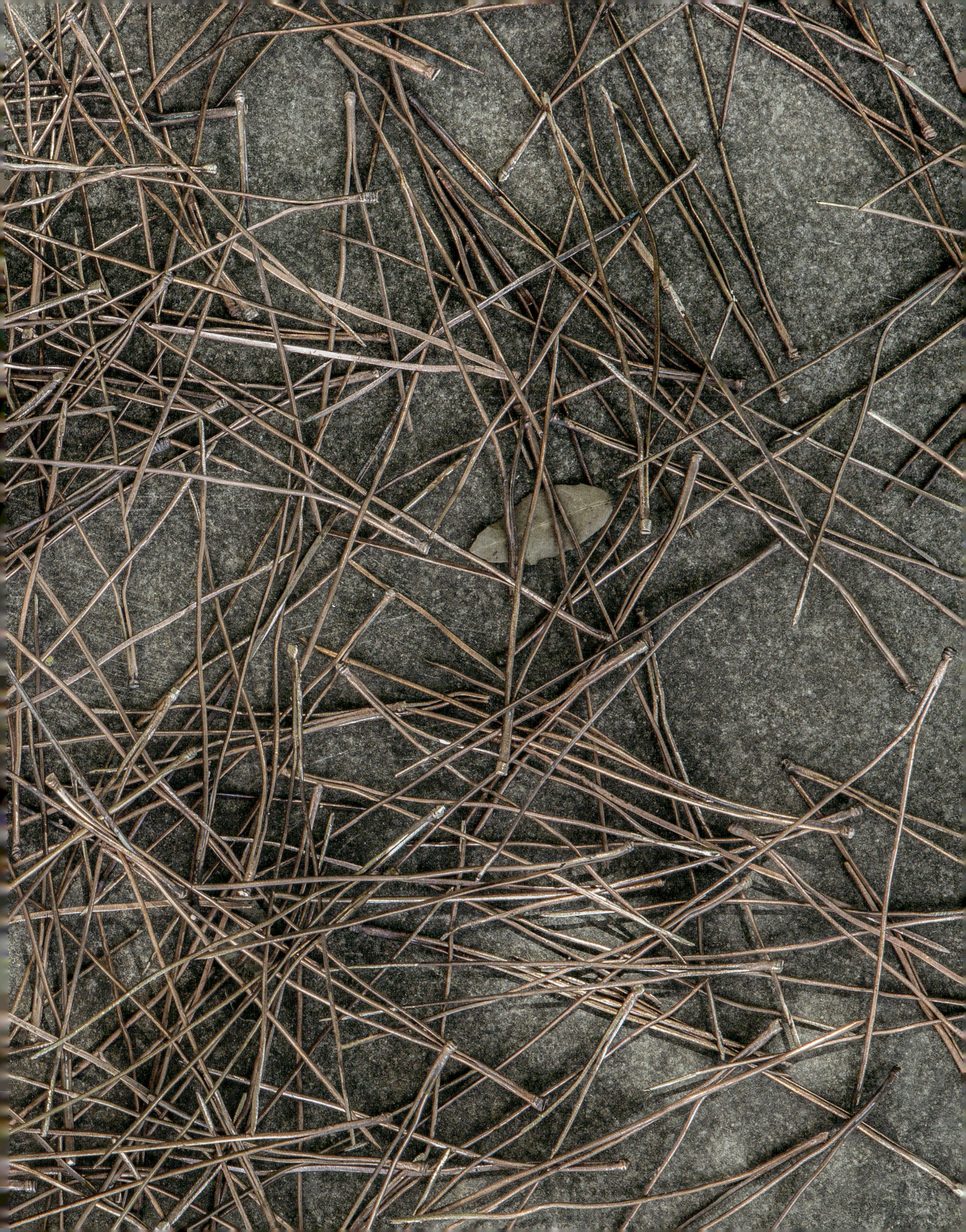

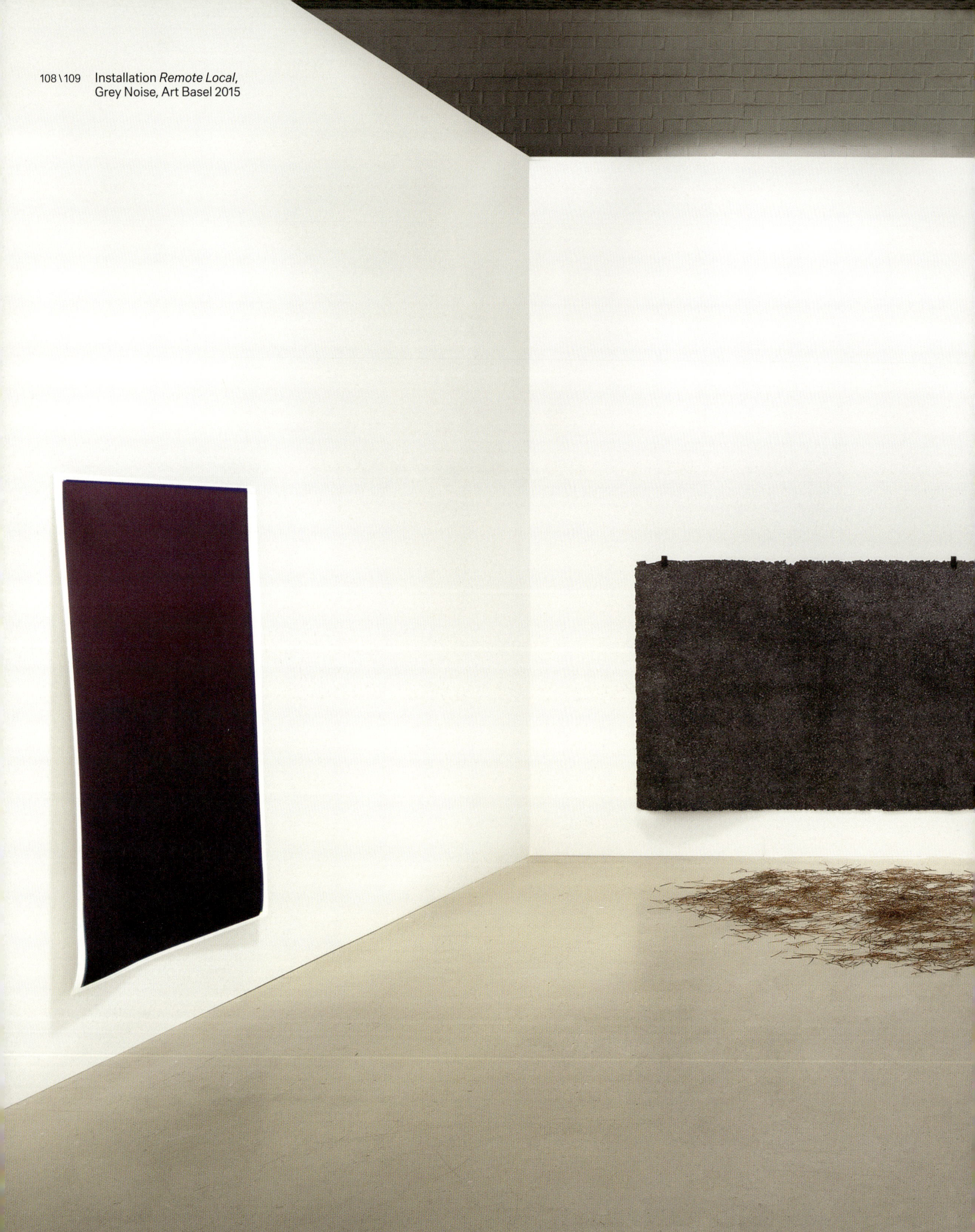

 Installation *Remote Local*,
Grey Noise, Art Basel 2015

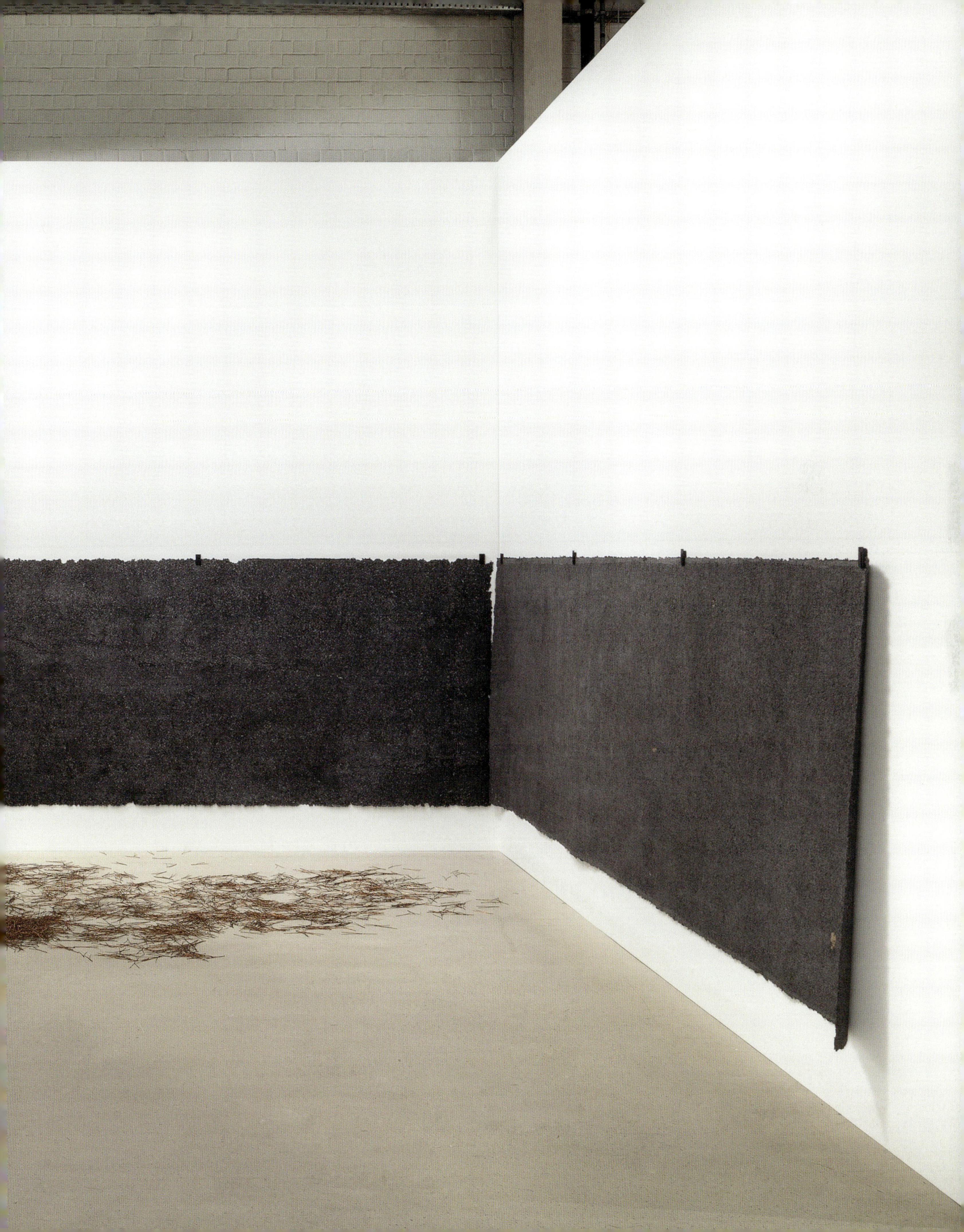

Rhythm Breakers, 2015
Processing Days and Nights 1, 2015
Concrete Layers, exhibition
at Grey Noise, Dubai 2015

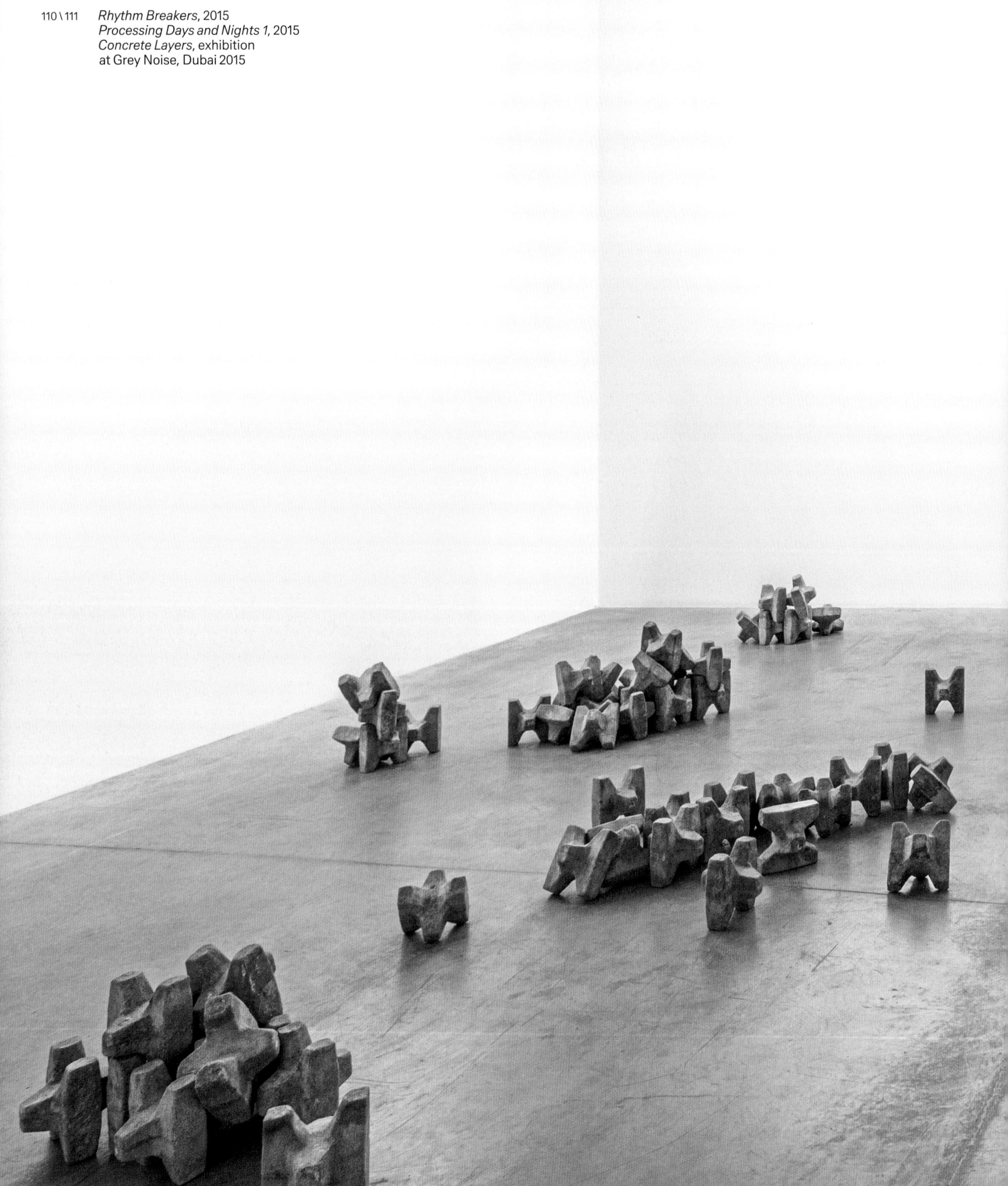

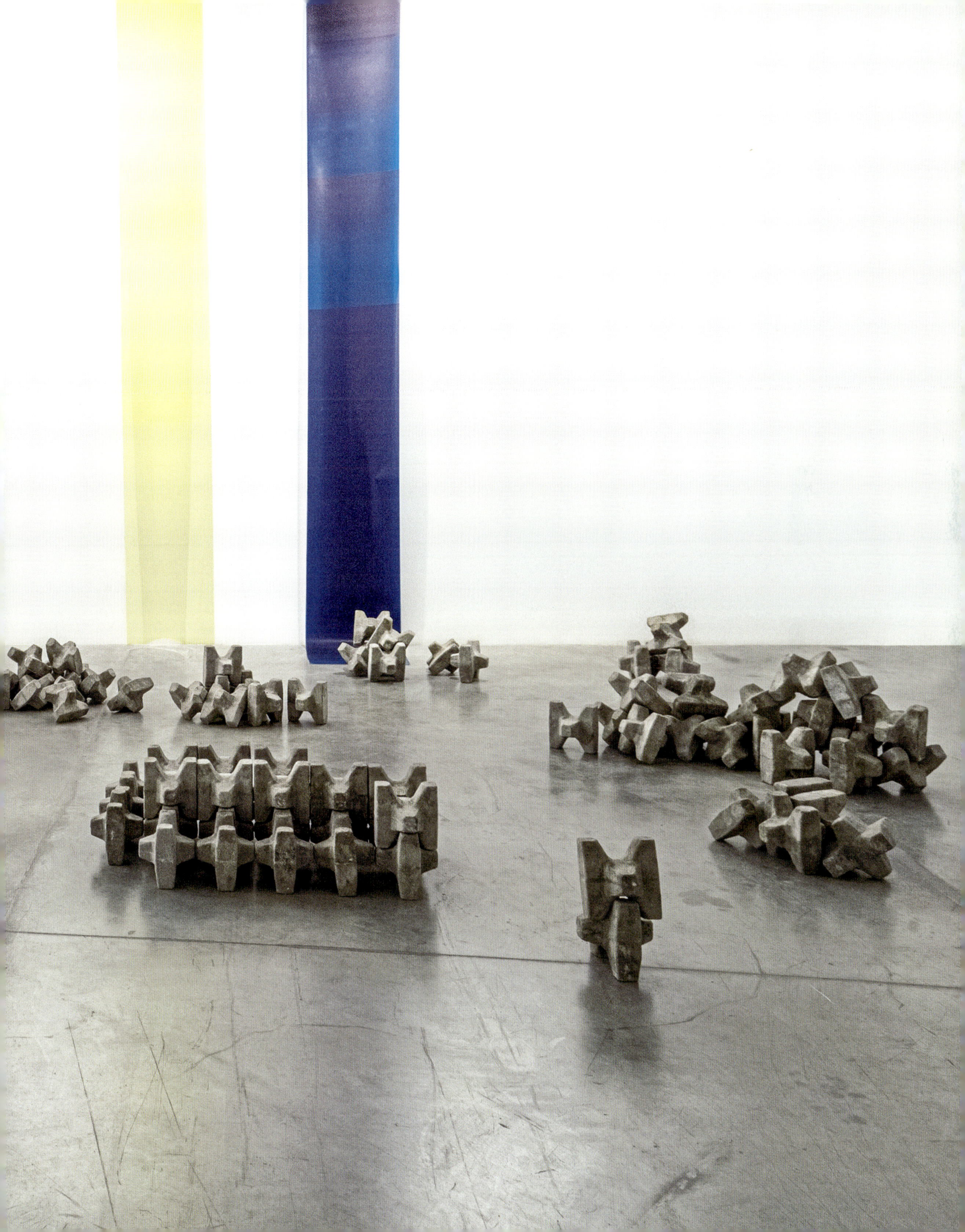

  Rhythm Breakers, 2015

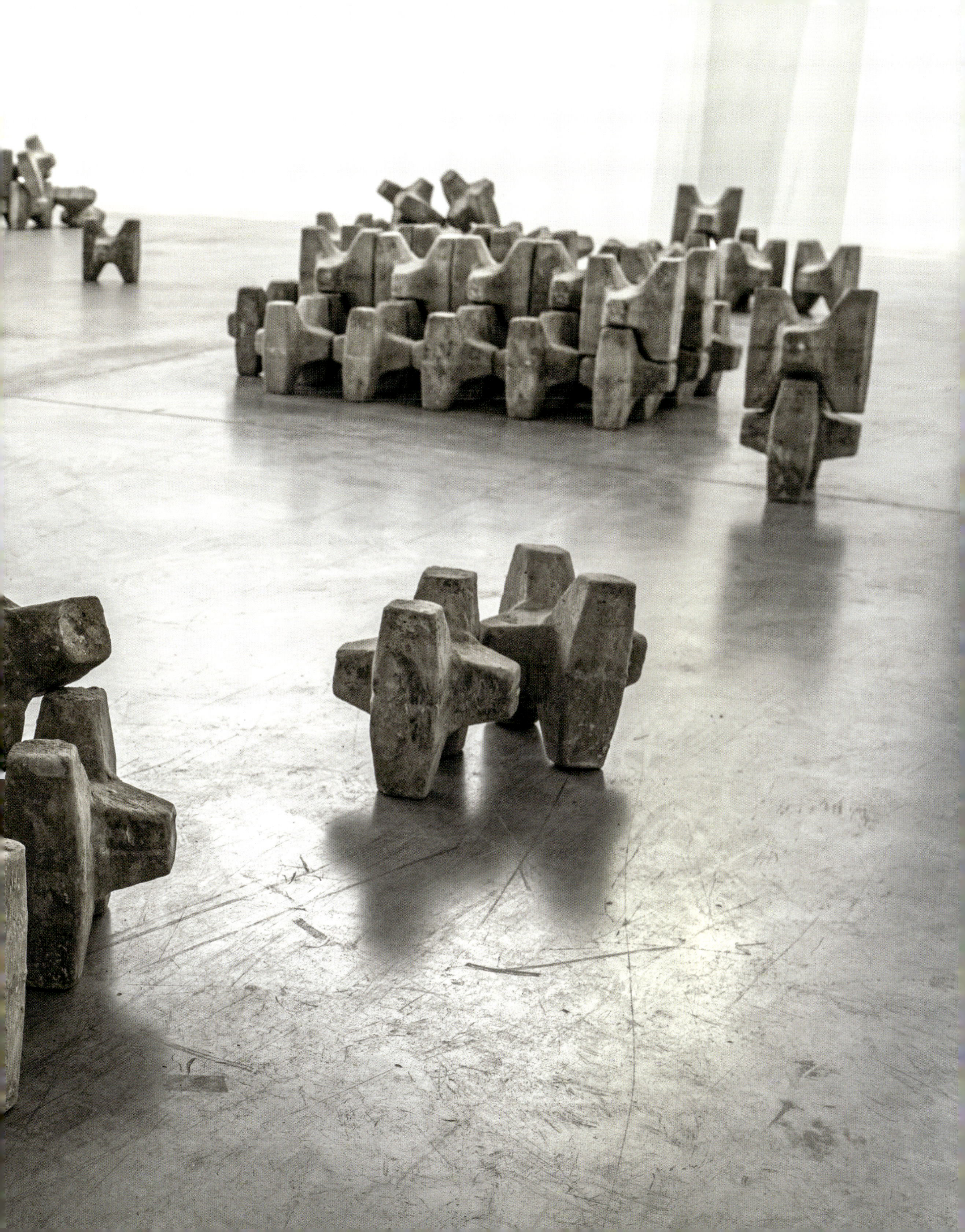

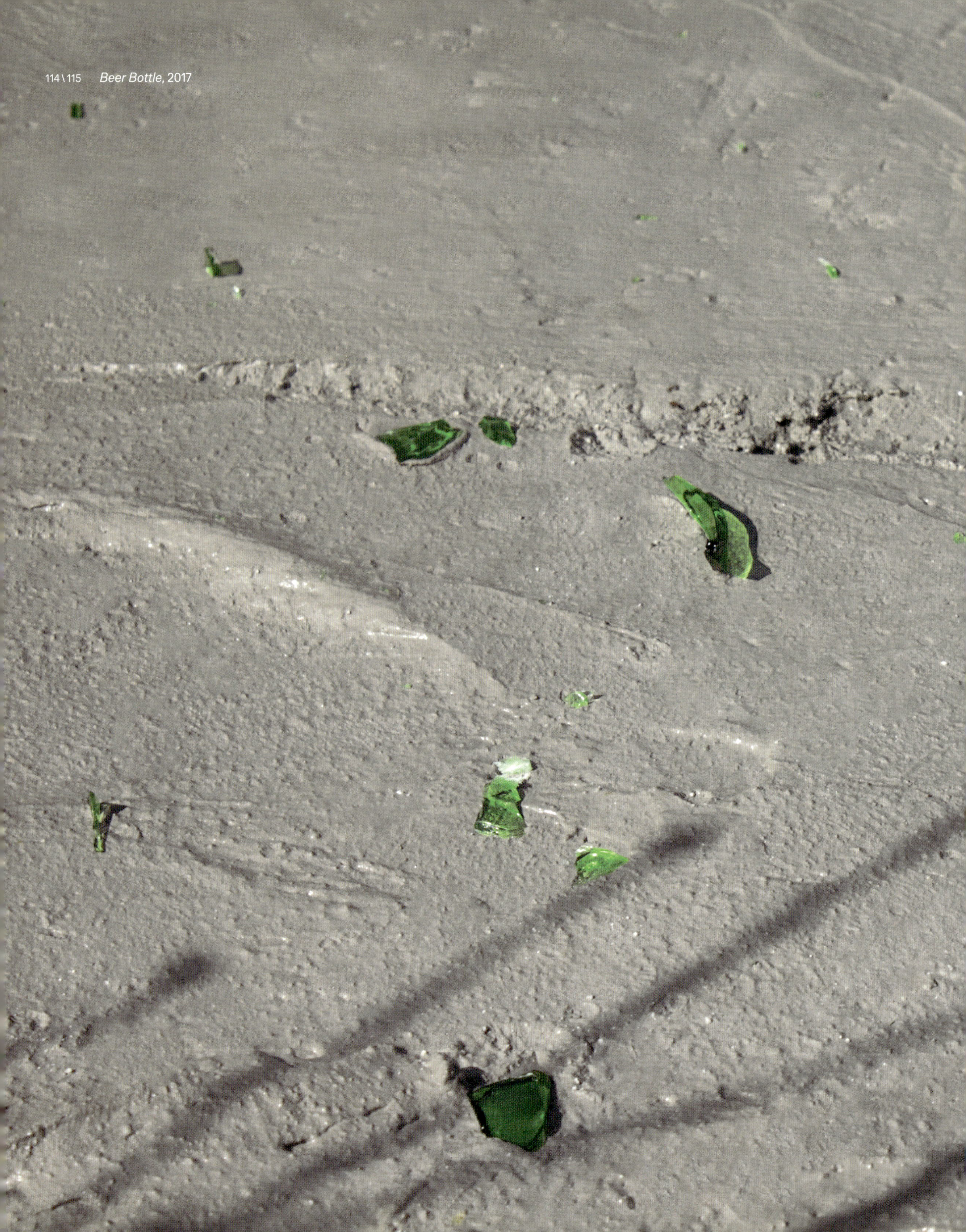

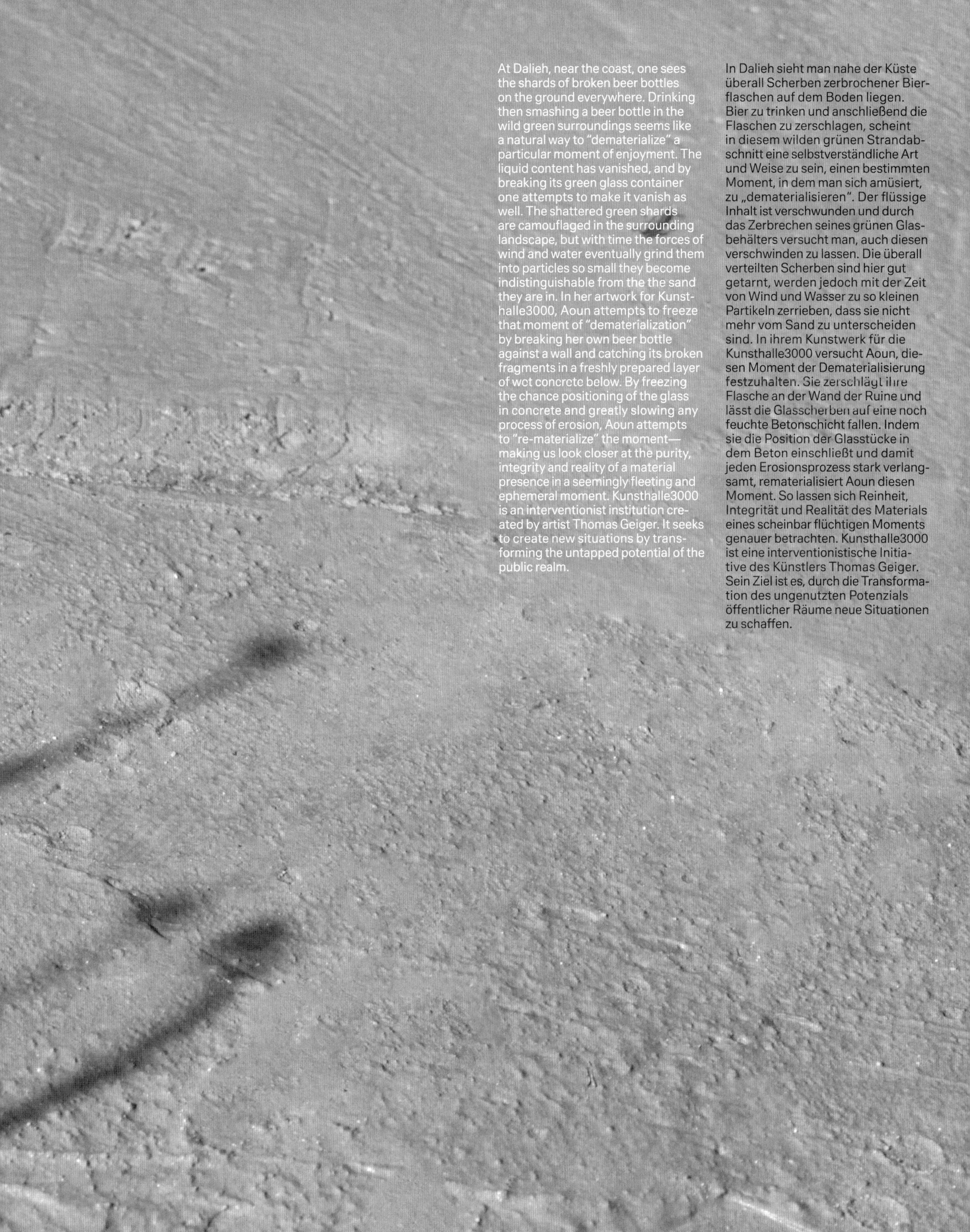

At Dalieh, near the coast, one sees the shards of broken beer bottles on the ground everywhere. Drinking then smashing a beer bottle in the wild green surroundings seems like a natural way to "dematerialize" a particular moment of enjoyment. The liquid content has vanished, and by breaking its green glass container one attempts to make it vanish as well. The shattered green shards are camouflaged in the surrounding landscape, but with time the forces of wind and water eventually grind them into particles so small they become indistinguishable from the the sand they are in. In her artwork for Kunsthalle3000, Aoun attempts to freeze that moment of "dematerialization" by breaking her own beer bottle against a wall and catching its broken fragments in a freshly prepared layer of wet concrete below. By freezing the chance positioning of the glass in concrete and greatly slowing any process of erosion, Aoun attempts to "re-materialize" the moment— making us look closer at the purity, integrity and reality of a material presence in a seemingly fleeting and ephemeral moment. Kunsthalle3000 is an interventionist institution created by artist Thomas Geiger. It seeks to create new situations by transforming the untapped potential of the public realm.

In Dalieh sieht man nahe der Küste überall Scherben zerbrochener Bierflaschen auf dem Boden liegen. Bier zu trinken und anschließend die Flaschen zu zerschlagen, scheint in diesem wilden grünen Strandabschnitt eine selbstverständliche Art und Weise zu sein, einen bestimmten Moment, in dem man sich amüsiert, zu „dematerialisieren". Der flüssige Inhalt ist verschwunden und durch das Zerbrechen seines grünen Glasbehälters versucht man, auch diesen verschwinden zu lassen. Die überall verteilten Scherben sind hier gut getarnt, werden jedoch mit der Zeit von Wind und Wasser zu so kleinen Partikeln zerrieben, dass sie nicht mehr vom Sand zu unterscheiden sind. In ihrem Kunstwerk für die Kunsthalle3000 versucht Aoun, diesen Moment der Dematerialisierung festzuhalten. Sie zerschlägt ihre Flasche an der Wand der Ruine und lässt die Glasscherben auf eine noch feuchte Betonschicht fallen. Indem sie die Position der Glasstücke in dem Beton einschließt und damit jeden Erosionsprozess stark verlangsamt, rematerialisiert Aoun diesen Moment. So lassen sich Reinheit, Integrität und Realität des Materials eines scheinbar flüchtigen Moments genauer betrachten. Kunsthalle3000 ist eine interventionistische Initiative des Künstlers Thomas Geiger. Sein Ziel ist es, durch die Transformation des ungenutzten Potenzials öffentlicher Räume neue Situationen zu schaffen.

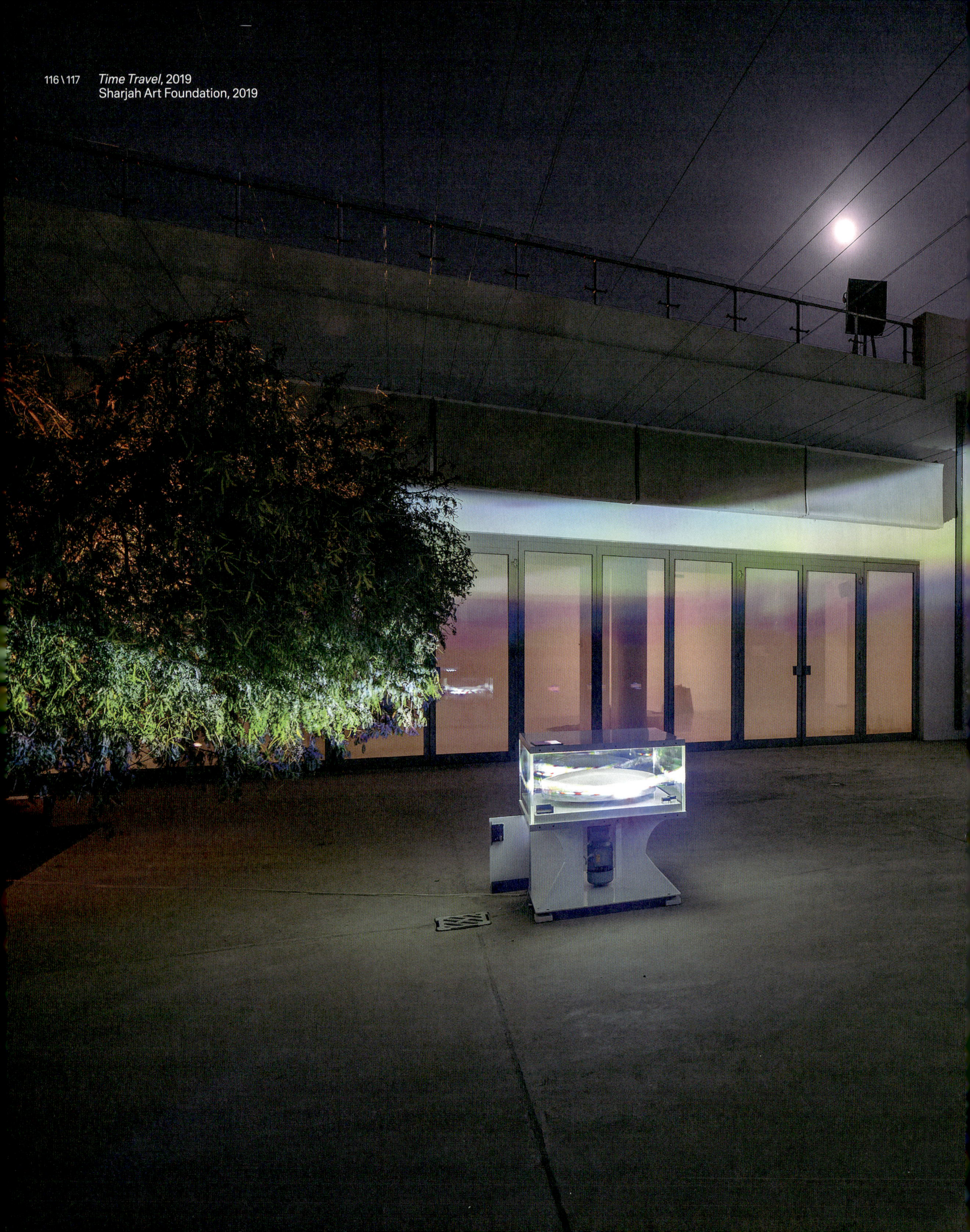

Time Travel, 2019
Sharjah Art Foundation, 2019

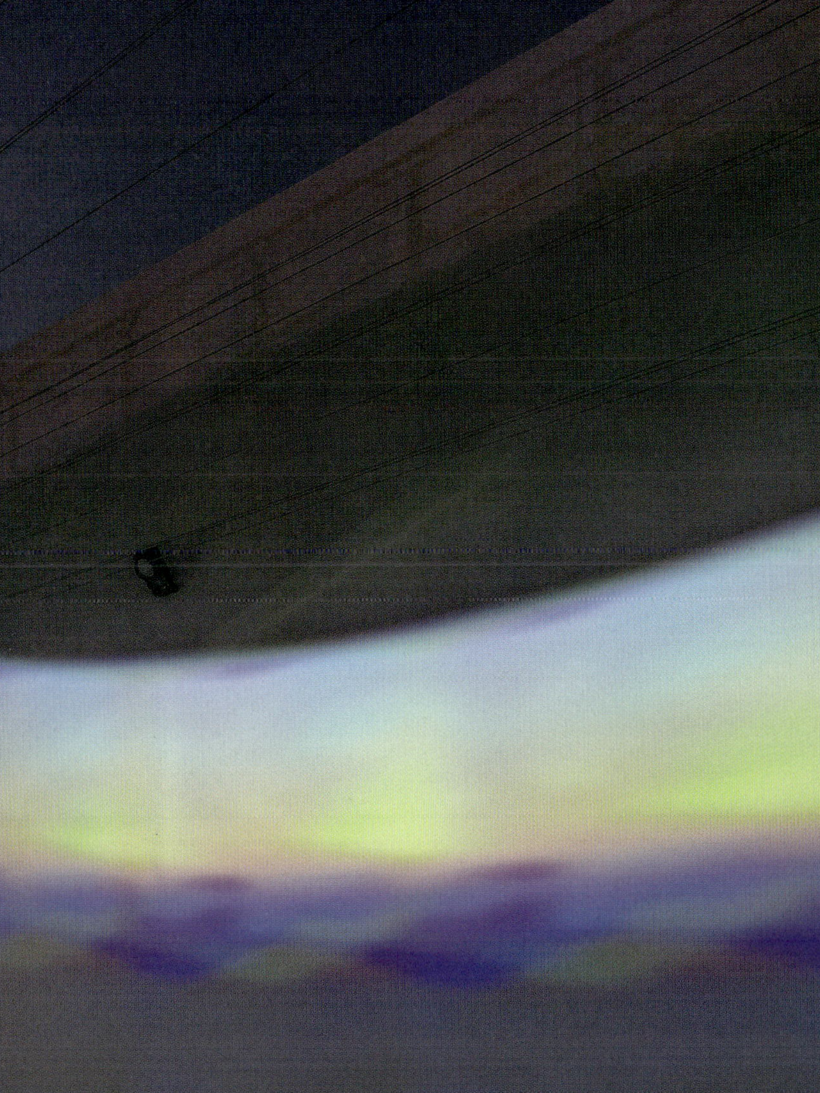

"Photography is truth, and cinema is truth 24 times a second."

Jean-Luc Godard

Time Travel features four projectors spinning at the equivalent of 24 frames per second, the timing necessary for digital moving images to appear visually fluid and continuous. The conceived projector-spinning machine also uses the internet to livestream the artist's surroundings in Beirut onto the walls of a courtyard. Throughout the duration of the 2019 Sharjah Biennial, the camera's location in Beirut changed daily, capturing the last twenty minutes of daylight. Thus, each day, the projectors would start to spin 20 minutes before sunset. Aoun playfully proposes to "Leave the Echo Chamber"—a play on the title of the Biennial—through a kind of time travel, in order to return to "material truths." In the end, the images produced are the live projection of active photons pulsing at 24 times per second: "truth 24 times per second." The whirlwind effect of the immersive images allowed viewers to reflect upon the sensation of a collapsing of space and time—of speed transmuting distance into time to enable a state of instantaneous communication—and to consider the cumulative effects of such forces on a body moving through space.

„Die Fotografie, das ist die Wahrheit, und das Kino ist 24 Mal die Wahrheit in der Sekunde."   Jean-Luc Godard

Die vier Projektoren von *Time Travel* drehen sich in einer Geschwindigkeit von 24 Bildern pro Sekunde, der Frequenz, die digitale Bewegtbilder in einem Fluss erscheinen lässt. Der Apparat, der die Drehung der Projektoren steuert, ist darüber hinaus mit dem Internet verbunden: Auf den Wänden in Sharjah ist ein Livestream aus der Umgebung der Künstlerin in Beirut zu sehen. Während der Laufzeit der Biennale wechselte der Standort der Kamera in Beirut täglich. Zu sehen waren jeweils die letzten zwanzig Minuten vor dem Sonnenuntergang und die Projektoren begannen, sich zum Zeitpunkt des Sonnenuntergangs zu drehen. Spielerisch schlug Aoun vor, auf einer Art Zeitreise „die Echokammer zu verlassen" und zu den „materiellen Wahrheiten" zurückzukehren. Letztendlich lassen sich diese Bilder als das unmittelbare Ergebnis eines Prozesses betrachten, bei dem ein Photon durch den Raum reist und dabei 24 Mal in der Sekunde Daten überträgt: „Wahrheit, 24 Mal in der Sekunde." Umgeben von diesem Bilderwirbel lässt sich reflektieren über das über das Gefühl des Zusammenbruchs von Raum und Zeit, der Umwandlung von Entfernung in Zeit durch Geschwindigkeit genauso wie über die Formen von Kommunikation heute und ihre Auswirkung auf einen Körper, der sich durch den Raum bewegt.

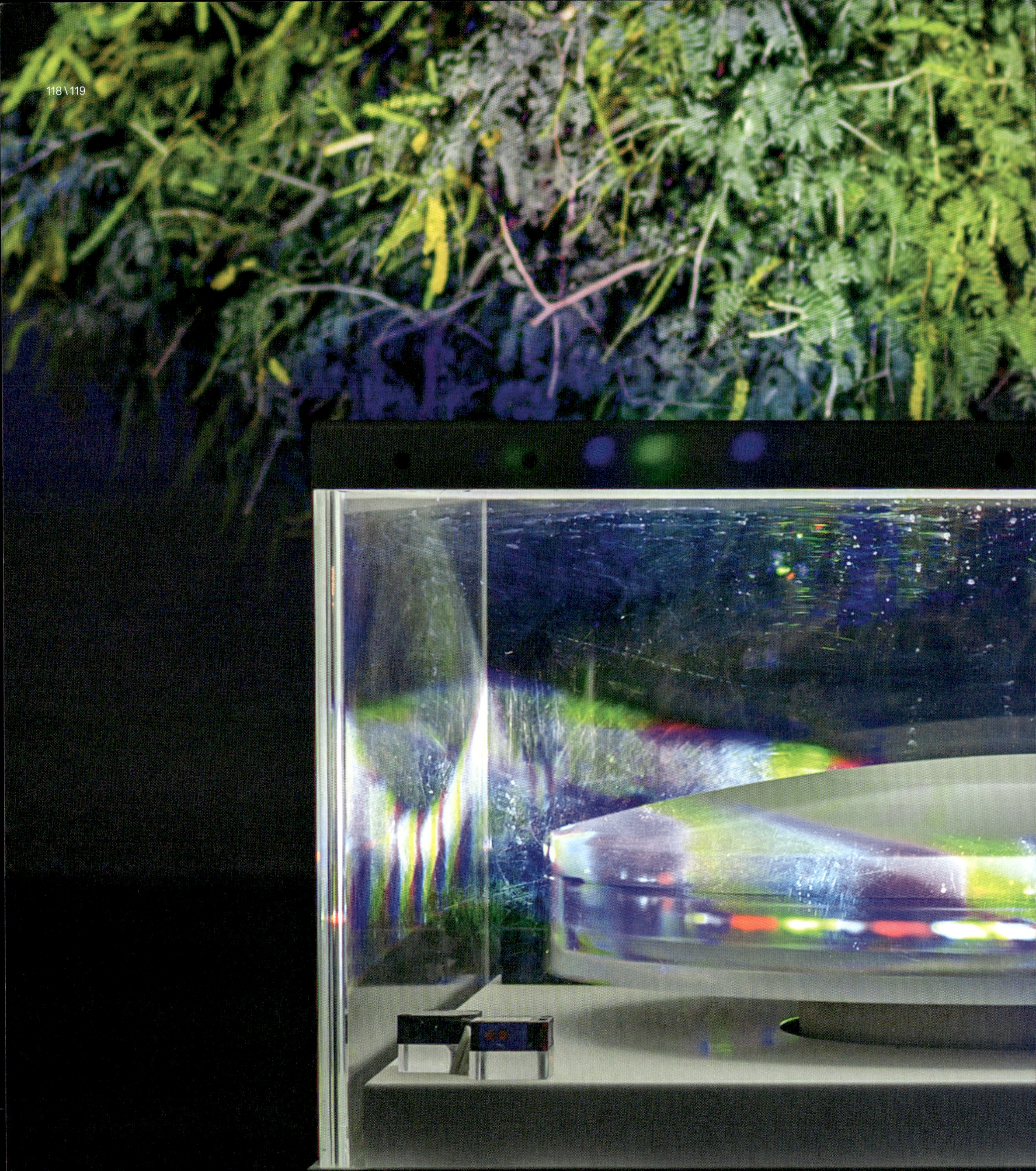

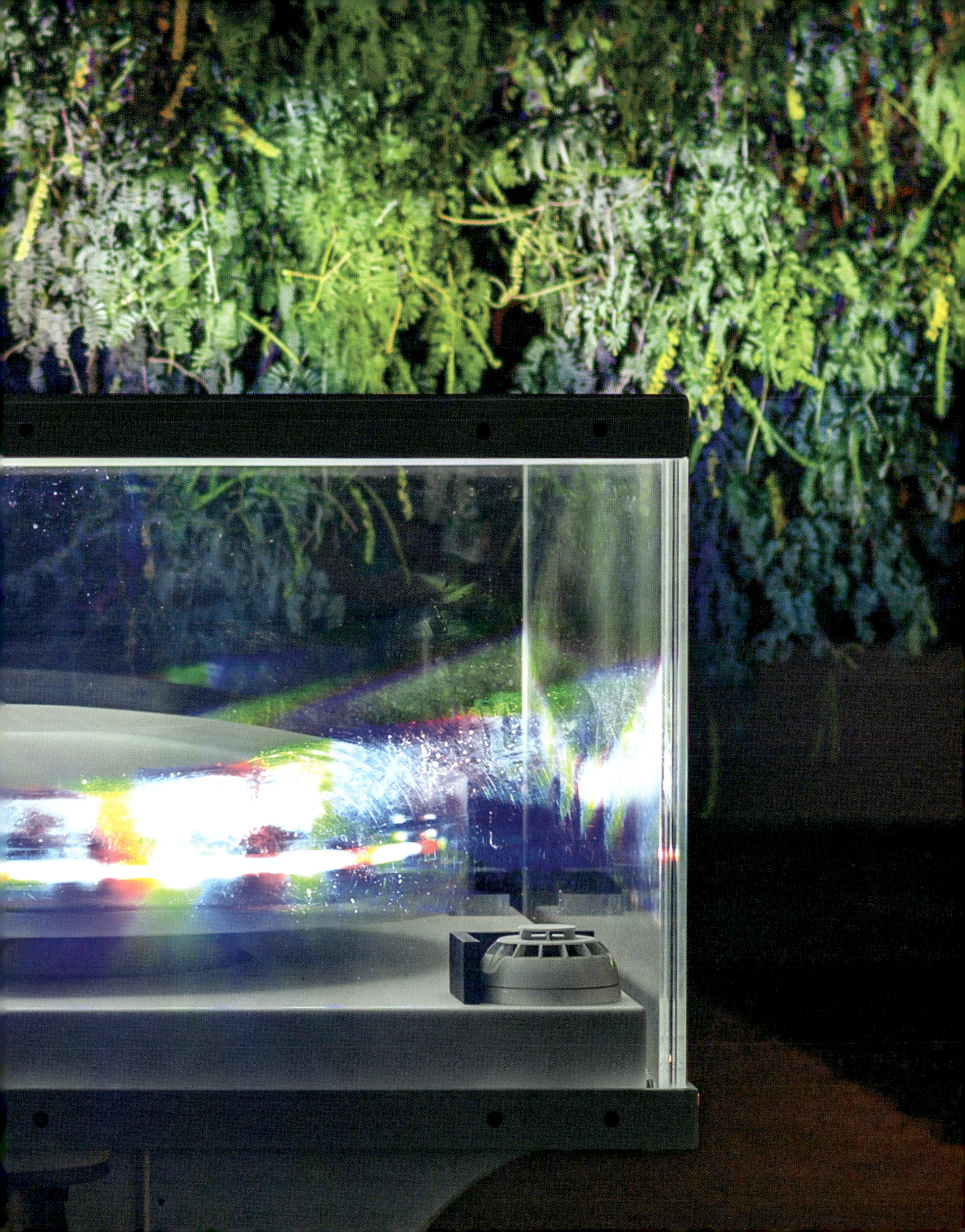

*Sunset at 24 Frames a Second
(After Time Travel)*, 2019

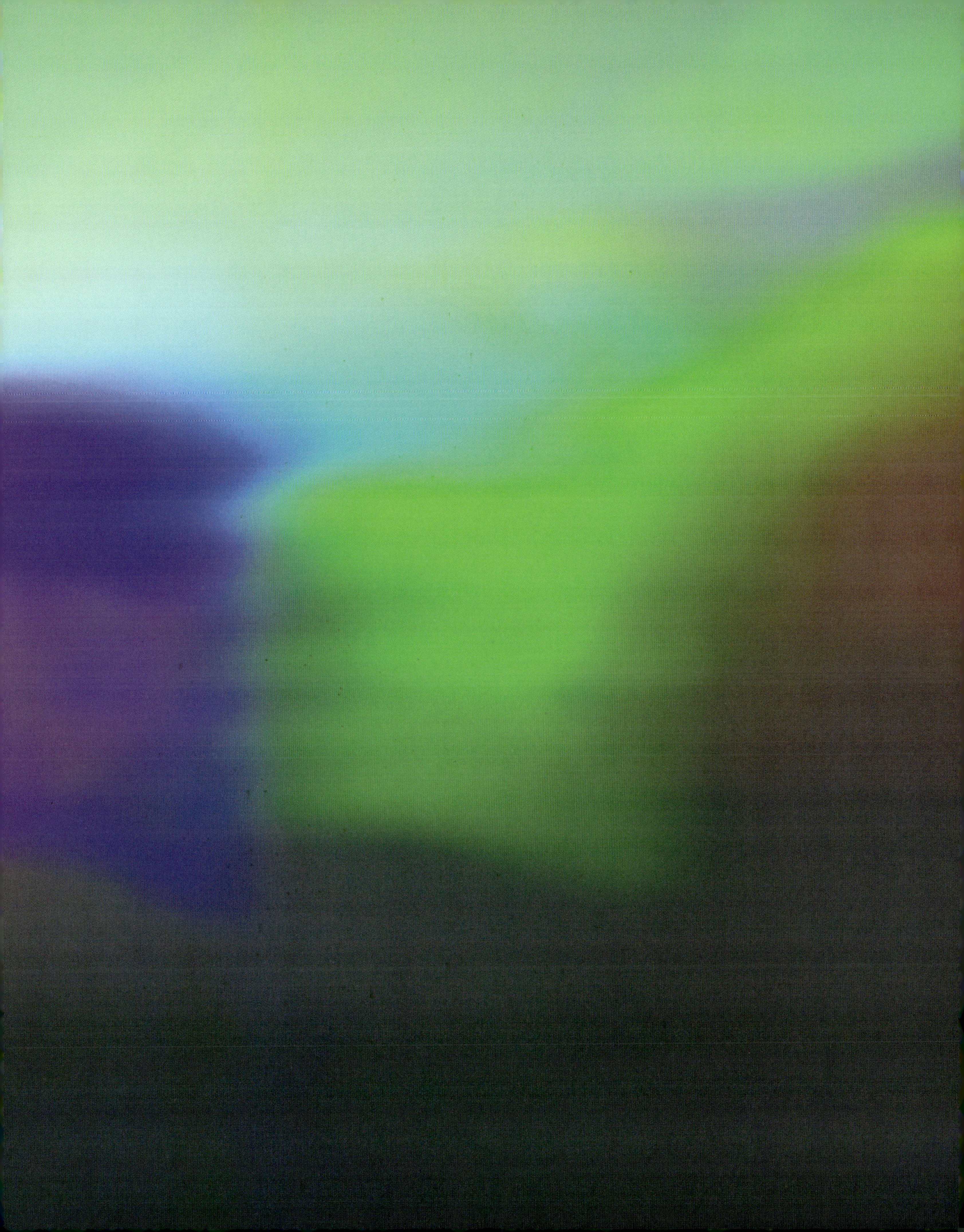

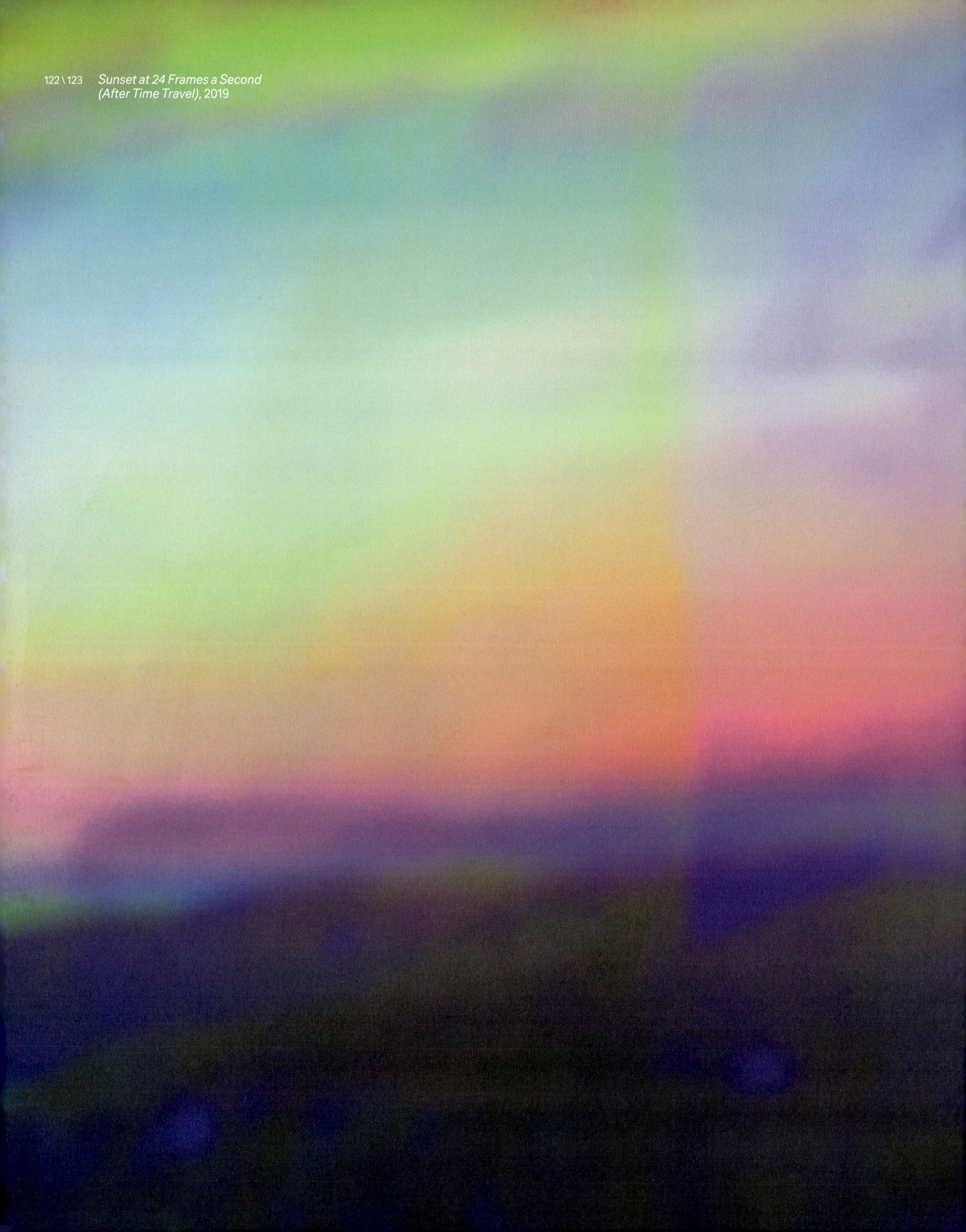

*Sunset at 24 Frames a Second
(After Time Travel)*, 2019

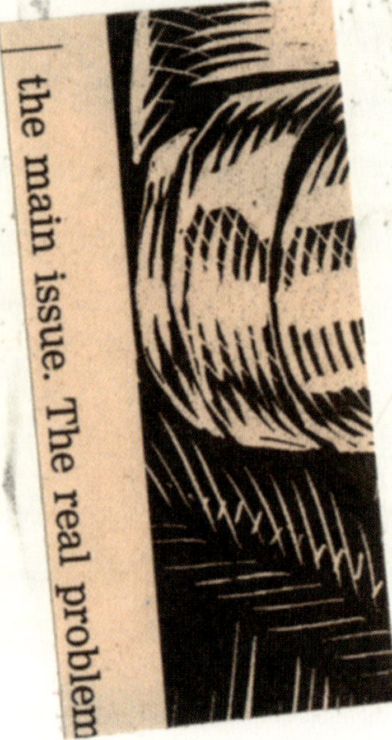
the main issue. The real problem

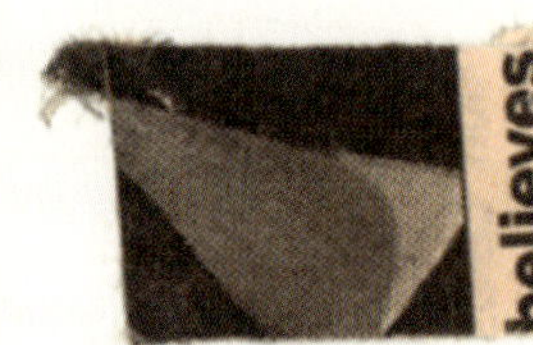
believes

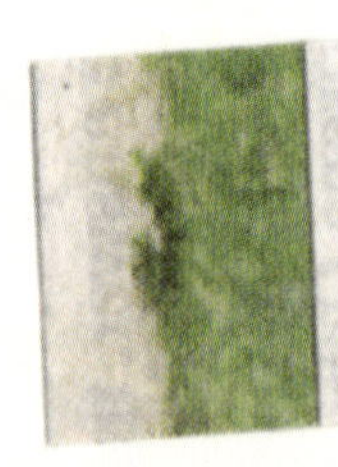
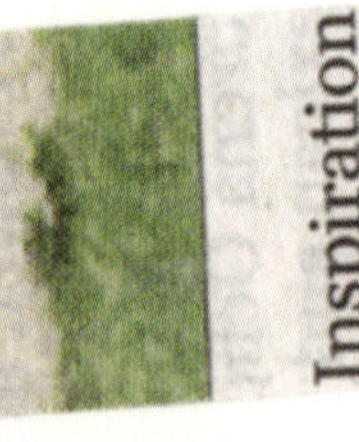
Inspiration

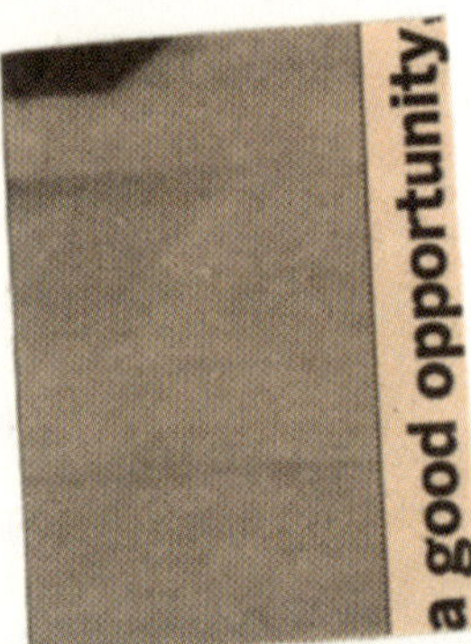
a good opportunity

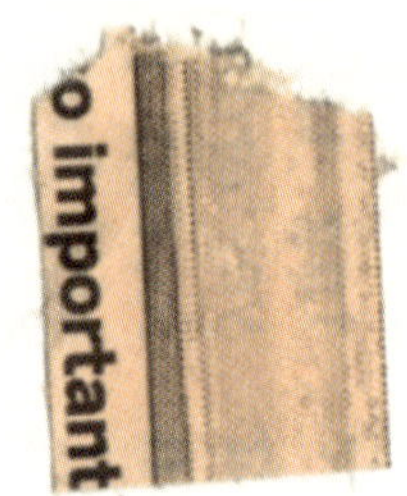
o important

criticise

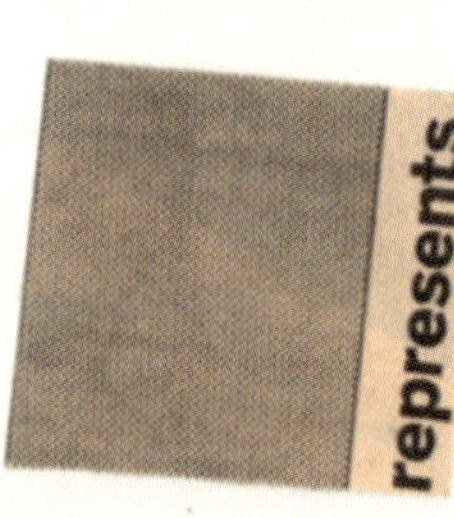
represents

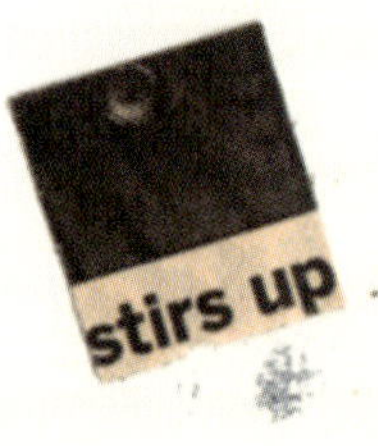
stirs up

focuses

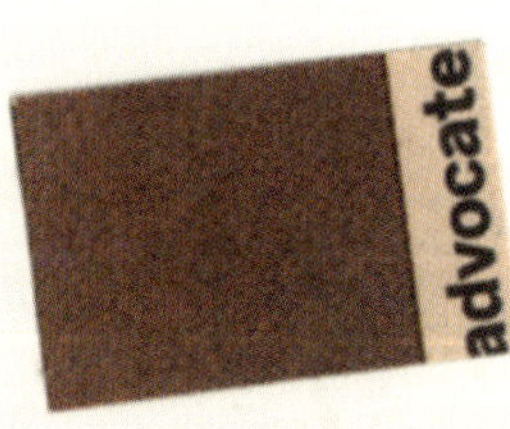
advocate

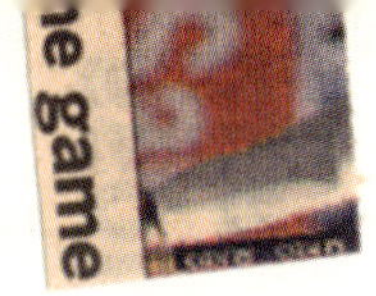

e game

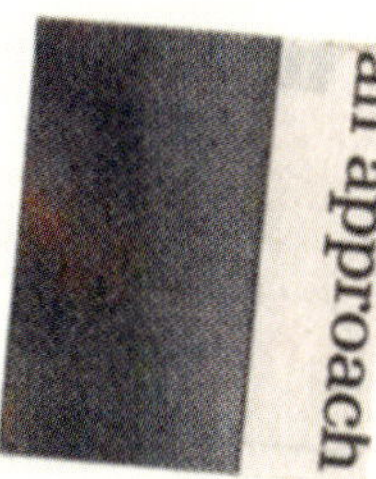

an approach

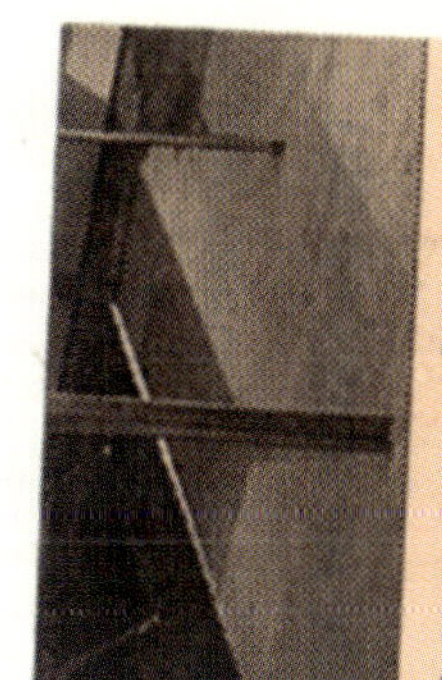

a new environment

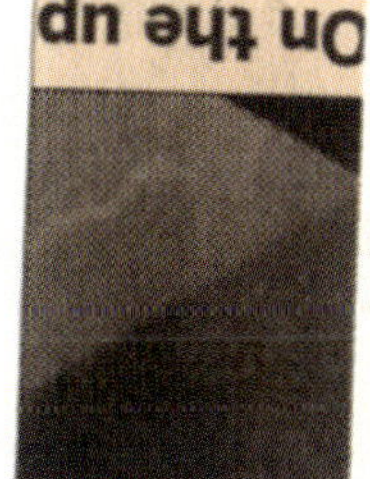

On the up

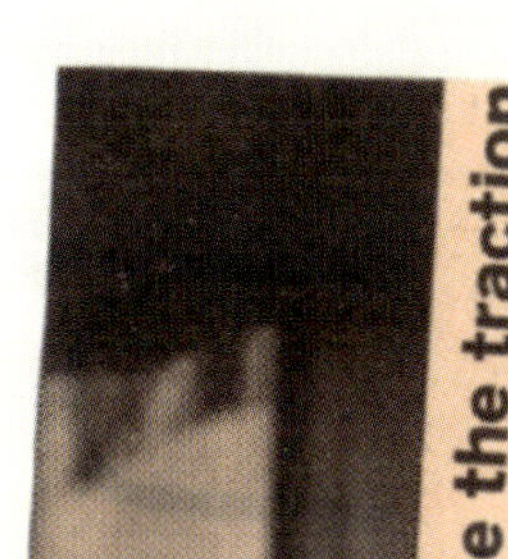

like the traction

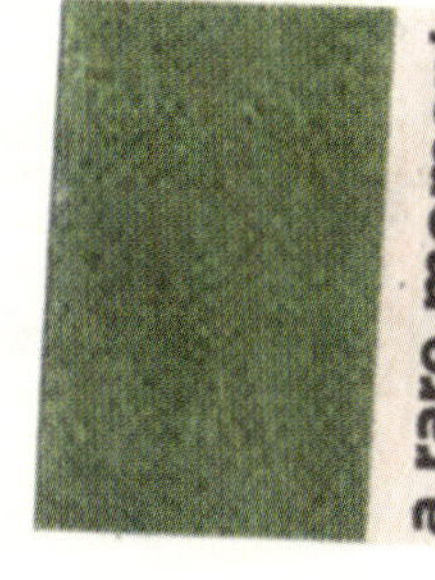

a rare moment

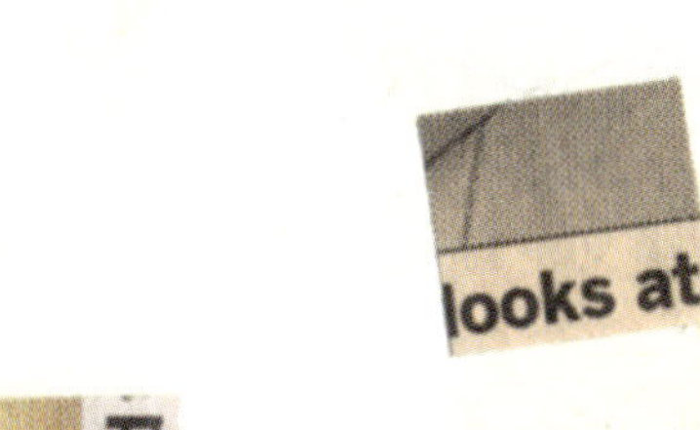

looks at

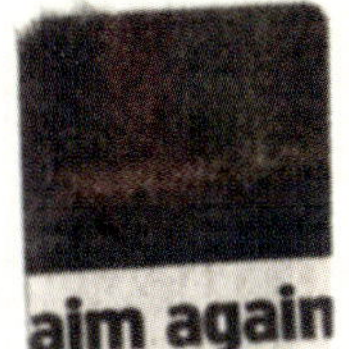
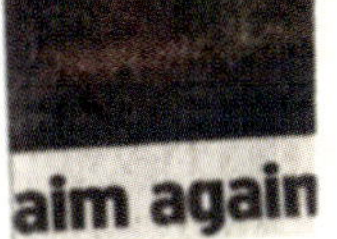

aim again

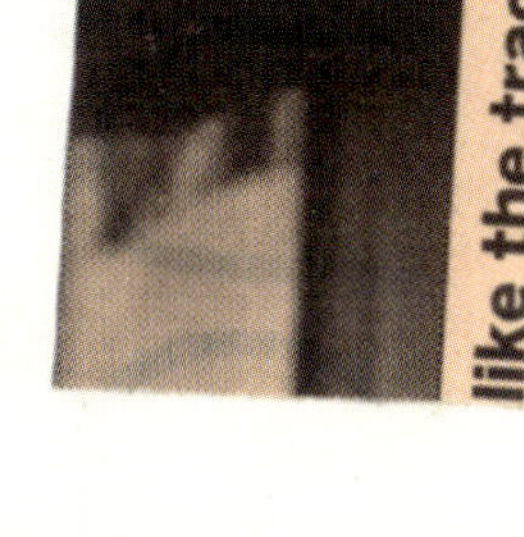

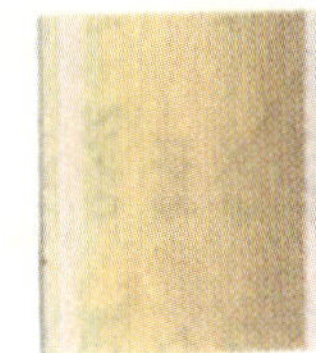

struggled

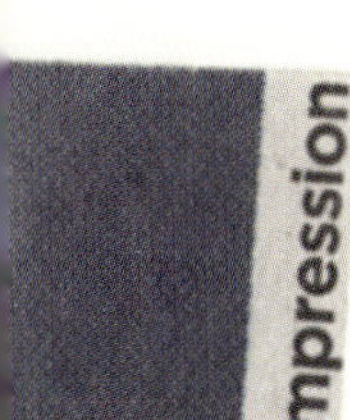

impression

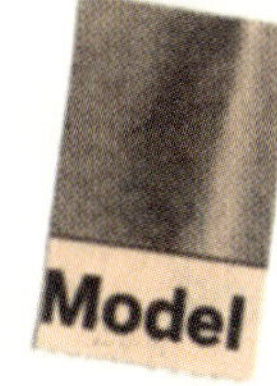

Model

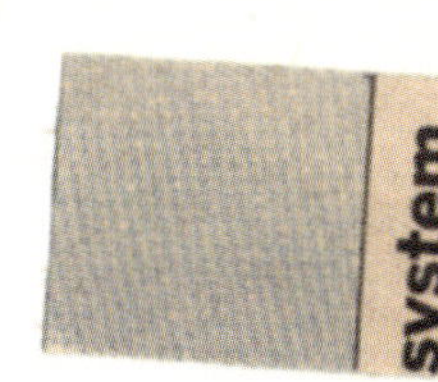

system

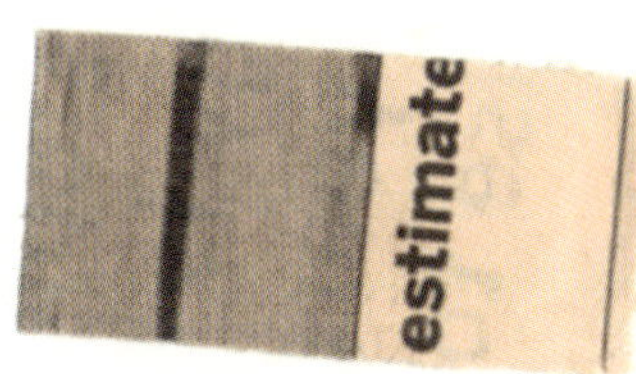

estimate

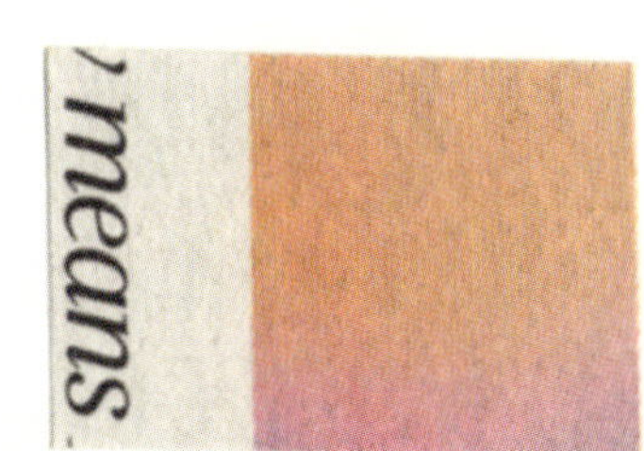

means

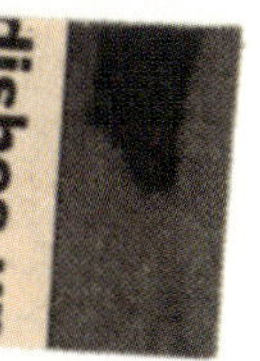

dishes up

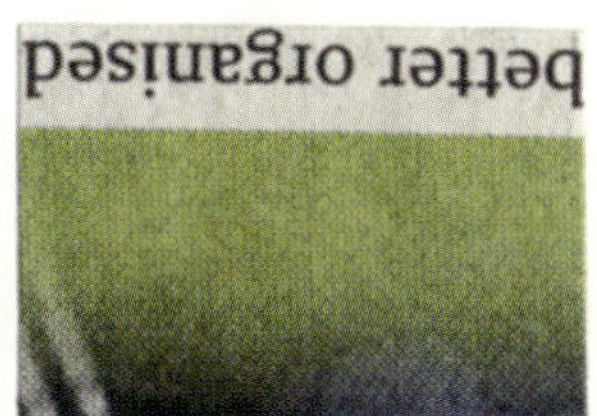

better organised

look at the moon,

Hello.

LIST OF WORKS
WERKLISTE

Cover, inside Cover innen,
1, 52 \ 53
*Contemplating Dispersions,
536 ml*, 2018
Unique inkjet print on
Hahnemühle rice paper
Inkjetdruck auf Hahnemühle-
Reispapier, Unikate
Dimensions variable
Maße variabel
Installation view Installations-
ansicht *Caline Aoun: seeing
is believing*, MAXXI, Rome
Rom 2018

44 \ 45, 46 \ 47*
*Contemplating Dispersions,
2*, 2018 / 2019
Inkjet print on Hahnemühle
rice paper 100 g/m^2,
Filmoplast p-90 plus tape
Inkjetdruck auf Hahnemühle-
Reispapier 100 g/m^2,
Filmoplast P 90 plus Tape
Installation
Dimensions variable
Maße variabel
Installation view Installations-
ansicht *Caline Aoun: seeing
is believing*, PalaisPopulaire,
Berlin 2019

8 \ 9, 24 \ 25, 36 \ 37, 126 \ 127,
132 \ 133, 136 \ 137
Silver Scratch, 2016
Silver scratch ink
Silberner Rubbellack
Dimensions variable
Maße variabel

38 \ 39*
Lands of Matter 2003–2018,
2019
Inkjet print on Somerset
Enhanced Radiant White
Velvet paper Inkjetdruck auf
Somerset Enhanced Radiant
White Velvet Papier
192 sheets, each Blätter, je
32.9 × 48.3 cm
Installation
Dimensions variable Maße
variabel
Deutsche Bank Collection
K20190053–64
Installation view Installations-
ansicht PalaisPopulaire,
Berlin 2019

39, 96 \ 97*
Seascape, 2016 / 2019
24h livestreaming video
24-Stunden-Livestream-
Video
Dimensions variable Maße
variabel
Installation view Installations-
ansicht PalaisPopulaire,
Berlin 2019

40 \ 41, 42 \ 43, 44 \ 45, 48 \ 49*
Infinite Energy, Finite Time,
2019
Plexiglas, aluminum, pump
system, water-based inkjet
ink, pipes, solenoid valves,
timer Plexiglas, Aluminium,
Pumpensystem, Drucker-
tinte auf Wasserbasis,
Schläuche, Magnetventile,
Schaltuhren
Four fountains, each
Ø 114 cm (base) Vier Brunnen,
je Ø 114 cm (Sockel)
Installation
Dimensions variable
Maße variabel
Installation view Installations-
ansicht PalaisPopulaire,
Berlin 2019

41, 42 \ 43, 48 \ 49*
Traces of Unseeable Excess,
2019
Carpet (polypropylene),
water-based inkjet ink
Teppich (Polypropylen),
Druckertinte auf Wasser-
basis
Dimensions variable
Maße variabel
Installation view Installations-
ansicht PalaisPopulaire,
Berlin 2019

42*
Becoming Otherwise,
2018 / 2019
Carbon copy paper pulp and
EVA glue Kohlepapierpulpe
und EVAC-Kleber
210 × 315, 230 × 325 cm
Installation view Installations-
ansicht PalaisPopulaire,
Berlin 2019

46 \ 47*
The Kinetics of the Invisible,
2019
Refrigeration compressor,
copper pipe, timer
Kühlaggregat, Kupferrohr,
Zeituhr
50 × 50 × 160 cm
Installation view Installations-
ansicht PalaisPopulaire,
Berlin 2019

48 \ 49*
Rock, 2019
Carbon copy paper pulp and
EVA glue Kohlepapierpulpe
und EVAC-Kleber
90 × 80 × 90 cm
Installation view Installations-
ansicht PalaisPopulaire,
Berlin 2019

50 \ 51
Paperplane (Blue Paperplane 1–5), 2018
Unique inkjet print on folded Hahnemühle paper Inkjetdruck auf gefaltetem Hahnemühle-Papier, Unikate
Each Je 158 × 109.4 cm
Installation view Installationsansicht *Caline Aoun: seeing is believing*, MAXXI, Rome Rom 2018
Blue Paperplane 1, 3, 5, 2018
Deutsche Bank Collection K20180051–53

68 \ 69
Paperplane, 2018
Unique inkjet print on folded paper Inkjetdruck auf gefaltetem Papier, Unikat
105 × 146 cm

52 \ 53, 54 \ 55
Fountain, the Ripples on the Surface of Duration, 2018
Plexiglas, steel, aluminum, pump, water-based inkjet ink Plexiglas, Aluminium, Pumpe, Druckertinte auf Wasserbasis
Dimensions variable
Installation view Rome Installationsansicht Rom 2018
On the wall An der Wand *Contemplating Dispersions, 536 ml*, 2018

55
Heavy Duration, Brief Glance, 2018
Paper, carbon paper pulp and EVA glue Papier, Kohlepapierpulpe und EVAC-Kleber
Dimensions variable Maße variabel
Installation view Rome Installationsansicht Rom 2018

56 \ 57, 102 \ 103, 106 \ 107 *
Pine Needles, 2015
Copper casts Kupferguss
Installation Dimensions variabel Maße variabel
The Museum of Fine Arts, Houston, museum purchase funded by Chris Urbanczyk, with matching funds from Chevron, and by the MuseumCollectors

58 \ 59
Lighter Later, 2009
Digital image Digitalbild

60 \ 61
At a Glance, 2009
Unique inkjet print on Financial Times newsprint Inkjetdruck auf Financial-Times-Zeitung, Unikat
250 × 500 cm

62 \ 63
Sliding Gazes, 2010
Unique inkjet print on Sommerset paper Inkjetdruck auf Somerset-Paper, Unikat
98.7 × 144.9 cm

Brighter Beams, 2010
Unique inkjet print (layers of printed yellow gradients for printing shadows) on postal cardboard tubes Inkjetdrucke, Unikate (Schichten von gedruckten Gelbabstufungen für Schattendrucke)
Height Höhe 100 cm, Ø 10 cm

64 \ 65, 66 \ 67
Excess, Repeat, 2009
Unique inkjet prints on vinyl Inkjetdruck auf Vinyl, Unikate
Dimensions variable Maße variabel

70 \ 71
Niagara Falls Realtime Webcam, February 25, 2012, 16:36
Double-spread from Doppelseite aus *Schizm Magazine*, No Nr. 4
Schizm Magazine is a London-based project conceived, produced and edited by Emma Holmes. *Schizm Magazine* ist ein Projekt in London, konzipiert, produziert und herausgegeben von Emma Holmes.

72 \ 73
Portal, 2015
Unique inkjet print on vinyl Inkjetdruck auf Vinyl, Unikat
33 × 45.5 cm
Installation view Installationsansicht *Dust*, Ujazdowski Castle Centre for Contemporary Art, Warsaw Warschau, 2015

74 \ 75, 76 \ 77
Beirut Art Center Square Meters, 2012
Paper pulp (blue envelopes, receipts, and invoice slips) Papierpulpe (blaue Umschläge, Quittungen und Rechnungsbelege)
Installation view Installationsansicht *Exposure 2012*, Beirut Art Center, Beirut 2012

78 \ 79
Beirut Art Center Square Meters, 2012
Paper pulp (yellow telephone book pages) Papierpulpe (gelbe Telefonbuchseiten)

80 \ 81
Untitled Ohne Titel, 2013
Unique inkjet print on digital transfer film Inkjetdruck auf Digitaltransferfilm, Unikate
Dimensions variable Maße variabel
Installation view Installationsansicht *We Hesitated Between Arrangements, Modulations and Manoeuvres*, curated by kuratiert von Amanda Abi Khalil, Minus 5, Beirut 2013

82 \ 83, 84 \ 85
Untitled Ohne Titel, 2013
Unique inkjet print on digital transfer film Inkjetdruck auf Digitaltransferfilm, Unikate
A3

86, 88 \ 89, 91
A Moment of Singularity in the Cyclical Rhythm of the Sun, 2013
Video projection Videoprojektion HDVD

87
Dissipation, 2, 2013
Unique inkjet prints on vinyl Inkjetdrucke auf Vinyl, Unikate
Dimensions variable Maße variabel
Installation view Installationsansicht Minus 5, Beirut 2013

90
Untitled Ohne Titel, 2013
Unique inkjet print on Permajet transfer film Inkjetdruck auf Permajettransferfilm, Unikat
61 × 108.5 cm

Untitled Ohne Titel, 2013
Unique inkjet print on Permajet transfer film Inkjetdruck auf Permajettransferfilm, Unikat
61 × 111.7 cm

Installation view Installationsansicht *The Future of Smart Technology in Your Hands*, Noshowspace, London 2013
Courtesy of Noshowspace, London

92
Untitled Ohne Titel, 2013
Unique inkjet print on Permajet transfer film Inkjetdruck auf Permajettransferfilm, Unikat
61 × 121 cm
Courtesy of Noshowspace, London

92 \ 93
Pallets, 2013
Inkjet print on vinyl Inkjetdruck auf Vinyl
Dimensions variable Maße variabel
Installation view Installationsansicht Noshowspace, London 2013
Courtesy of Noshowspace, London

94 \ 95
Pallets 2, 2016
Inkjet print on Hahnemühle Fine Art Baryta paper 325 Inkjetdruck auf Hahnemühle Fine Art Baryta Papier 325
72 × 102 cm (framed gerahmt)

98 \ 99, 100 \ 101
Shipping Container Floor, 2016
Detail
Carbon paper pulp Kohlepapierpulpe
234 × 590 cm
Courtesy of Marfa' Projects, Beirut

104 \ 105
Roads, 2015
Detail
Carbon paper pulp, tree leaves, and EVA glue Kohlepapierpulpe, Baumblätter und EVAC-Kleber
Dimensions variable Maße variabel

108 \ 109
Remote Local: Statements—Art | Basel, 2015
Installation view Installationsansicht Grey Noise, Basel 2015
Courtesy of Grey Noise, Dubai

110 \ 111, 112 \ 113
Rhythm Breakers, 2015
Concrete Beton
Dimensions variable Maße variabel
Processing Days and Nights 1, 2015
Unique inkjet prints on Permajet negative transfer film Inkjetdruck auf Permajet-Negativtransferfilm
Dimensions variable Maße variabel
Installation view Installationsansicht *Concrete Layers*, Grey Noise, Dubai 2015
Courtesy of Grey Noise, Dubai

114 \ 115
Beer Bottle, 2017
Cement, beer bottle Zement, Bierflasche
Dimensions variable Maße variabel

116–119
Time Travel, 2019
Multimedia Installation
Commissioned by Sharjah Art Foundation, 2019
Installation view Installationsansicht *Leaving the Echo Chamber—Look For Me All Around You*, Sharjah Biennial 14, Sharjah 2019

120 \ 121, 122 \ 123
Sunset at 24 Frames a Second (After Time Travel), 2019
Poster

124 \ 125
Untitled (Ongoing Project), 2009 – ongoing fortlaufend
Scan of newspaper crops Scan von Zeitungsausschnitten

* Works exhibited at Werke der Ausstellung im PalaisPopulaire, Berlin 2019 / 2020

Photo credit Fotonachweis
Page Seite
38–49: Mathias Schormann
50–57: Luis Do Rosario
60–61: Marcus J Leith, Royal Academy of Arts
64–67: John Lindquist
74–81, 86–87, 102–103, 106–107: George Eid
98–101: Nabu Productions
108–109: Dawn Blackman

If not mentioned otherwise, all works courtesy of the artist. Wenn nicht anders aufgeführt, alle Werke Courtesy der Künstlerin.

Texts Texte
58 \ 59 *Testcard*, 31 January Januar – 28 February Februar 2009
Internet project with Internetprojekt mit Francesca Anfossi, Caline Aoun, Simon and und Tom Bloor, Cut Up, Ruairiadh O'Connell, Karen Tang, Bedwyr Williams, and und Simon Woolham

62 \ 63 "La photographie, c'est la vérité et le cinéma, c'est vingt-quatre fois la vérité par seconde."
Jean-Luc Godard, *Le Petit Soldat*, 1960

74 \ 75 Text for the exhibition Text für die Ausstellung *Exposure*, Beirut Art Center, Beirut 2012

CALINE AOUN BIOGRAPHY
BIOGRAFIE

1983 Born in Beirut, Lebanon
Geboren in Beirut, Libanon

Lives and works near Beirut, Lebanon Lebt und arbeitet bei Beirut, Libanon

2009–2012

Professional Doctorate, Fine Art, University of East London, London

2006–2009

Postgraduate Fine Art, Royal Academy Schools, London

2002–2005

Central Saint Martin's School of Art and Design, London

Award Auszeichnung

Deutsche Bank "Artist of the Year" 2018/2019

2019–2020

seeing is believing, PalaisPopulaire, Berlin

2019

Marfa' Projects solo booth Einzelkoje, *Artissima*, Turin

2018

seeing is believing, MAXXI—Museo nazionale delle arti del XXI secolo, Rome Rom

2016

Fields of Space, Marfa' Projects, Beirut

2015

Concrete Layers, Grey Noise, Dubai

Remote / Local, Art | Basel—Statements, Basel

2013

The Future of Smart Technology in Your Hands, Noshowspace, London

2009

Scape, Sartorial Project Space, London

2006

New Paintings, Store Gallery, London

2019

Leaving the Echo Chamber—Look For Me All Around You, Sharjah Biennial 14, Sharjah

2017

Home Beirut—Sounding the Neighbours, MAXXI—Museo nazionale delle arti del XXI secolo, Rome Rom

Untitled, Liste—Marfa' Projects booth, Basel

Kunsthalle 3000, Public Space Intervention—Dalieh, Beirut

2016

Works on Paper, Intervention in *L'Orient Le Jour* newspaper—T.A.P., Beirut

2015

Grey Noise booth Koje, *Frieze*, London

I Spy With My Little Eye…, Casa Arabe, Madrid

Dust, Centre for Contemporary Art at Ujazdowski Castle, Warsaw Warschau

I Spy With My Little Eye…, Mosaic Rooms, London

2014

Flat Packed / Wrapped / Stacked, Punk & Sheep, London

2013

Stopped Clocks in Places of Busyness, Fold Gallery, London

Observations du Divan Oriental Occidental Multilogue en Art Video, Château Mercier, Sierre

Crisis Practice, Workshop Gallery, Beirut

We Hesitated Between Arrangements, Modulations and Manoeuvres, Minus 5, Beirut

Trajector Intermezzo, Hotel Bloom, Brussels Brüssel

2012

Exposure, Beirut Art Center, Beirut

Now (Obsolescence, Regeneration & Criticality), SCHIZM magazine issue four, London

---

2011

Matter, APT, London

Friendship of the Peoples, Simon Oldfield, London

Liquid Space, Nettie Horn, London

2010

Bloomberg New Contemporaries, ICA—Institute of Contemporary Arts, London

Bloomberg New Contemporaries, A Foundation, Liverpool

Show One, Art First Projects, London

paperplane, Occupy Space, Limerick

paperplane, The Joinery, Dublin

2009

Returning to Form, Store Gallery, London

RA Schools Show, Royal Academy Schools, London

The Little Shop on Hoxton Street, Limoncello, London

Testcard Online Project, London

DON'T Dream JUST FLY

look at the moon

Hello

Mike

KiKi
Aurora
Serina

ARTIST OF THE YEAR
GLOBAL ART ADVISORY COUNCIL

Spotlight on young art: Like its corporate collection, Deutsche Bank's "Artist of the Year" award is committed to the present. The aim is to acquaint a wide public with new and exciting artistic positions. Based on the recommendation of Deutsche Bank's Global Art Advisory Council—with the internationally renowned curators Victoria Noorthoorn, Hou Hanru, Udo Kittelmann, and formerly Okwui Enwezor, who died in 2019—the bank honors an emerging artist, who has created an artistically, as well as socially relevant, oeuvre, one integrating the media of paper and photography—the two main areas of focus of the Deutsche Bank Collection.

After Wangechi Mutu (Kenya / USA), Yto Barrada (France / Morocco), Roman Ondak (Slovakia), Imran Qureshi (Pakistan), Victor Man (Romania), Koki Tanaka (Japan), Basim Magdy (Egypt), and Kemang Wa Lehulere (South Africa), Caline Aoun (Lebanon) is the Deutsche Bank's "Artist of the Year."

Unlike many other prizes, "Artist of the Year" is not based on a financial reward, but is positioned as an integral part of the Deutsche Bank art program, which has been opening up the world of contemporary art to the public for forty years—through Deutsche Bank's own substantial collection, its exhibitions, and its joint projects with partners. Each "Artist of the Year" is presented in a solo exhibition at the Deutsche Bank KunstHalle (until 2017) and currently at the PalaisPopulaire in Berlin.

Okwui Enwezor   1963 Calabar, Nigeria – 2019 Munich, Germany. Enwezor was Artistic Director of Visual Arts of 56th Venice Biennale in 2015, and from 2011 to 2018 Director of Haus der Kunst, Munich. He was the founder and an editor of *Nka: Journal of Contemporary African Art*.

Hou Hanru   Born 1963 in Guangzhou, China. Lives and works in Paris and Rome. Hanru works as a curator and critic, and is Artistic Director of MAXXI, the National Museum of 21st Century Arts, Rome.

Udo Kittelmann   Born 1958 in Düsseldorf, Germany. Lives and works in Berlin. Udo Kittelmann has been Director of the Nationalgalerie, Staatliche Museen zu Berlin, since 2008.

Victoria Noorthoorn   Born in 1971 in Buenos Aires, Argentina. Lives and works in Buenos Aires. Noorthoorn works as a curator and art historian and is Director of the Museo de Arte Moderno de Buenos Aires.

Aktuelle Positionen im Fokus: Wie die Unternehmenssammlung ist auch „Artist of the Year", die Auszeichnung der Deutschen Bank, ganz der Gegenwart verpflichtet. Es gilt neue, spannende Positionen einem breiten Publikum bekannt zu machen. Auf Empfehlung des Deutsche Bank Global Art Advisory Council – mit den renommierten Kuratoren Victoria Noorthoorn, Hou Hanru, Udo Kittelmann und dem 2019 verstorbenen Okwui Enwezor – ehrt die Bank vielversprechende internationale Künstlerinnen und Künstler, die bereits ein künstlerisch wie auch gesellschaftlich relevantes Werk geschaffen haben. Wichtig ist, dass die beiden Schwerpunkte der Sammlung Deutsche Bank einbezogen sind: Arbeiten auf Papier oder Fotografie.

Nach Wangechi Mutu (Kenia / USA), Yto Barrada (Frankreich / Marokko), Roman Ondak (Slowakei), Imran Qureshi (Pakistan), Victor Man (Rumänien), Koki Tanaka (Japan), Basim Magdy (Ägypten) und Kemang Wa Lehulere (Südafrika) ist nun Caline Aoun (Libanon) „Artist of the Year" der Deutschen Bank.

Im Unterschied zu vielen anderen Auszeichnungen ist „Artist of the Year" nicht mit einer finanziellen Förderung verbunden, sondern steht für die Philosophie der Deutschen Bank seit 40 Jahren weltweit Zugang zu aktueller Gegenwartskunst zu ermöglichen – sei dies durch ihre Kunstsammlung, durch Ausstellungen oder Kooperationen. Höhepunkt ist die Einzelausstellung des „Artist of the Year" in der Deutsche Bank KunstHalle (bis 2017) und aktuell im PalaisPopulaire in Berlin.

Okwui Enwezor 1963 Calabar, Nigeria–2019 München, Deutschland. Enwezor war von 2011 bis 2018 Direktor am Haus der Kunst, München, und Künstlerischer Direktor der Bildenden Künste der 56. Biennale Venedig 2015. Er war Grunder und Mitherausgeber von *Nka: Journal of Contemporary African Art*.

Hou Hanru Geboren 1963 in Guangzhou, China. Lebt in Paris und Rom. Hou Hanru arbeitet als Kritiker und Kurator und ist Künstlerischer Direktor des MAXXI (Museo nazionale delle arti del XXI secolo) in Rom.

Udo Kittelmann Geboren 1958 in Düsseldorf, Deutschland. Lebt in Berlin. Udo Kittelmann ist Direktor der Nationalgalerie, Staatliche Museen zu Berlin.

Victoria Noorthoorn Geboren 1971 in Buenos Aires, Argentinien. Lebt in Buenos Aires. Victoria Noorthoorn arbeitet als Kuratorin und Kunsthistorikerin und ist Direktorin des Museo de Arte Moderno de Buenos Aires.

DON'T Dream JUST FLY

look at the moon

The bra

Hello

سكي عابد ابل

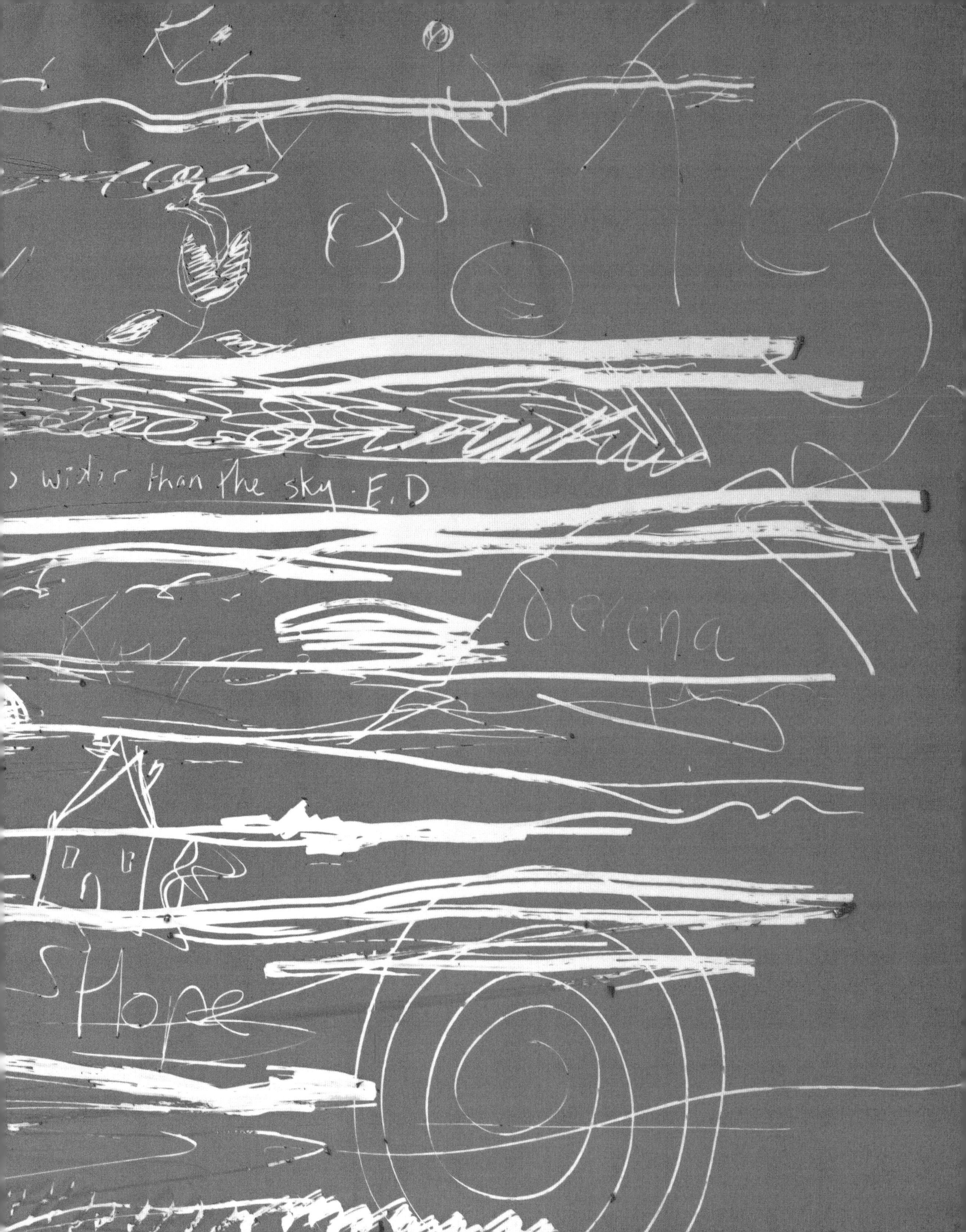
wider than the sky . E.D

THANK YOU
DANK AN

Caline Aoun
Okwui Enwezor
Hou Hanru
Udo Kittelmann
Victoria Noorthoorn

Fabienne Alexopoulos
Sabine Bachmann
Mingus Ballhaus
Burke Barrett
Nathalie Baudy
Katharina Behling
Felix v. Boehm
Andreas Berkemeier
Meryem Berker
Cornelia Bertram
Sara Bernshausen
Roland Bittner
Eva Castringius
Kathrin Conrad
Bahadar Dorani
Achim Drucks
Hayat Ebert

Michela Filippini
Sarah Fricke
Ingeborg Fries
Mirko Frohne
Lydia Fuchs
Viktória Gere
Markus Giese
Angelika Golembiewski
Team Gonder
Toni Greulich
Olaf Hartmann
Theres Heise
Jacqueline Hermann
Gero Heschl
Hildegard Homburger
Friedhelm Hütte
Annette Jentsch
Zahirat Juseinov
Bettina Kabot
Amrei Kahl
Stefan Keßel
Jörg Klambt
Elisabeth Klotz

Oliver Koerner von Gustorf
Veronika Kranzpiller
Birte Kreft
Steffen Lang
Cornelia Laufer
Julia Magnus
Nicole Nitzsche
Andreas Mantyk
Irina Marschall
Daniela Mewes
Oliver Mewes
Claude Mollinari
Annekathrin Müller
Serdar Özdemir
Doro Petersen
Marta Pihelgas
Denny Pöhle
Tahir Qasim
Anna Raum
Marc Reckling
Svenja v. Reichenbach
Rachel Riddell
Kerstin Riedel

Aurelia Rist
Peter Rode
Uwe Rommel
Serge Romzpa
Julia Rosenbaum
Mike Schärfke
Kathrin Schmidt
Norbert Schmidt
Claudia Schmidt-Matthiesen
Mathias Schormann
Jon Shelton
Lea Sievertsen
Marie Splawski
Bruno Spath
Senad Suljic
Angelika Thill
Frank Tornow
Murtaza Vali
Sadaf Vasaei
Dean Weiß
Sven Wieker
Klaus Winker
Steffen Zarutzki

CALINE AOUN WOULD LIKE TO WARMLY THANK
BEDANKT SICH HERZLICH BEI

Hou Hanru, Udo Kittelmann, Victoria Noorthoorn, and the late und dem 2019 verstorbenen Okwui Enwezor
For the incredible opportunity of being selected Artist of the Year Für die unglaubliche Chance, als Künstlerin des Jahres ausgewählt zu werden

Britta Färber
For the rich exchanges leading to the final exhibitions Für den intensiven Austausch, ohne den die finalen Ausstellungen nicht denkbar gewesen wären

Bechara Aoun
For his infinite and tremendous support, which made all this work possible Für seine unendliche und großzügige Unterstützung, die dieses Werk ermöglicht hat

Friedhelm Hütte, Svenja Gräfin v. Reichenbach, Sara Bernhausen, Annekathrin Müller, Steffen Zarutzki, and the entire team at the PalaisPopulaire und das ganze Team des PalaisPopulaire
For their trust, extensive support and collaboration behind the scenes Für ihr Vertrauen, ihre umfassende Unterstützung und die Zusammenarbeit hinter den Kulissen

Oliver Koerner von Gustorf and und Murtaza Vali
For the insightful texts accompanying the exhibition Für die aufschlussreichen Texte, die die Ausstellung begleiten

Angelika Thill from Thill Verlagsbüro
For intricately holding the whole catalog together Dass sie alle Fäden des Katalogs zusammengehalten hat

Kerstin Riedel
For her unique perceptions into the design of this catalog Für ihre außergewöhnliche visuelle Auffassungsgabe bei der Gestaltung dieses Katalogs

Frank Tornow, Peter Rode, and the entire team of und dem gesamten Team von RT Ausstellungstechnik Berlin
For concretely making the complex installation possible Für die konkrete Umsetzung der komplexen Installation

Anne Palopoli and the entire MAXXI museum exhibition team und das ganze Ausstellungsteam des MAXXI
For all the help and support for the exhibition Für alle Hilfe und Unterstützung der Ausstellung *seeing is believing*, MAXXI, 2018

Joumana Asseily (Marfa' Projects) and und Umer Butt and und Hetal Pawani (Grey Noise)
For their trust, support, and the continuous exposure of my work Für ihr Vertrauen, ihre Unterstützung und die fortdauernde Präsentation meines Werkes

Avedis Kupeyan
For production, technical expertise, making the seemingly impossible possible, and designing solutions for challenging details Für Produktion, technische Expertise, die das scheinbar Unmögliche ermöglicht, und Umsetzung sehr herausfordernder Details

Christianne Boulos
For her energetic assistance in the studio Für ihre tatkräftige Unterstützung im Studio

Lody Aoun, Carol Aoun, Stefano Rabolli Pansera, Cecilia Rabolli Pansera, Lara Aoun, Raymond Noujaim
For their limitless support Für ihre unbegrenzte Unterstützung

A special thank you to Bachar Attieh for his immeasurable love and support help making it all possible and to our beautiful boys Georges and Mikael. Ein besonderer Dank an Bachar Attieh für seine unermessliche Liebe und Unterstützung, die all das ermöglicht, und an unsere wunderbaren Söhne Georges und Mikael.

COLOPHON
IMPRESSUM

This book is published
in conjunction with the
exhibition
Diese Publikation erscheint
anlässlich der Ausstellung

*Caline Aoun
seeing is believing*
Artist of the Year
Künstlerin des Jahres

MAXXI—Museo nazionale
delle arti del XXI secolo,
Rome Rom
28.9.–18.11.2018
Curators Kuratorinnen
Britta Färber, Anne Palopoli

PalaisPopulaire, Berlin
15.11.2019–2.3.2020
Curator Kuratorin
Britta Färber

PalaisPopulaire
Unter den Linden 5
10117 Berlin
db-palaispopulaire.de
db-palaispopulaire.com

Head Leitung
Svenja Gräfin v. Reichenbach

Deputy
Stellvertretende Leitung
Sara Bernshausen

Catalog Katalog

Editor Herausgeber
Deutsche Bank AG
Art, Culture & Sports
Thorsten Strauß

Editing Redaktion
Britta Färber / Julia Magnus

Copyediting Lektorat
Thill Verlagsbüro Cologne
Köln with mit Jon Shelton

Translation from English to
German Übersetzung aus
dem Englischen ins Deutsche
Thill Verlagsburo and und
Achim Drucks

Translation from German
to English Übersetzung
aus dem Deutschen ins
Englische
Burke Barrett

Graphic design
Grafische Gestaltung
Kerstin Riedel, Berlin

Typeface Schrift
Beatrice Headline
Deutsche Bank Text

Reproductions
Reproduktionen
max-color, Berlin

Paper Papier
Profibulk 1.1, 170 g/m²

Project management
Projektmanagement
Kerber Verlag
Lydia Fuchs

Production Herstellung
Kerber Verlag
Jens Bartneck

Please find more information
on Deutsche Bank's art
program at db.com/art and
db-artmag.com

Informationen über das
Kunstprogramm der
Deutschen Bank finden
Sie unter deutsche-bank.de/
kunst und db-artmag.de

The Deutsche Nationalbiblio-
thek lists this publication in
the Deutsche Nationalbibliografie; detailed bibliographic
data is available on the
internet at http://dnb.dnb.de.
Die Deutsche National-
bibliothek verzeichnet diese
Publikation in der Deutschen
Nationalbibliografie;
detaillierte bibliografische
Daten sind im Internet über
http://dnb.dnb.de abrufbar.

Printed and published by
Gesamtherstellung
und Vertrieb
Kerber Verlag, Bielefeld
Windelsbleicher Str. 166–170
33659 Bielefeld
Germany
Tel. +49 (0) 5 21/9 50 08-10
Fax +49 (0) 5 21/9 50 08-88
info@kerberverlag.com

Kerber, US Distribution
ARTBOOK | D.A.P.
75 Broad Street, Suite 630
New York, NY 10004
Tel. +1 (212) 627-1999
Fax +1 (212) 627-9484

Kerber publications are
available in selected book-
stores and museum shops
worldwide (distributed
in Europe, Asia, South and
North America).
Kerber-Publikationen wer-
den weltweit in führenden
Buchhandlungen und
Museumsshops angeboten
(Vertrieb in Europa, Asien,
Nord- und Südamerika).

All rights reserved. No part
of this publication may be
reproduced, translated,
stored in a retrieval system
or transmitted in any form
or by any means, electronic,
mechanical, photocopying
or recording or otherwise,
without the prior permission
of the publisher.
Alle Rechte, insbesondere
das Recht auf Vervielfälti-
gung und Verbreitung sowie
Übersetzung, vorbehalten.
Kein Teil dieses Werkes darf
in irgendeiner Form ohne
schriftliche Genehmigung
des Verlages reproduziert
oder unter Verwendung
elektronischer Systeme ver-
arbeitet, vervielfältigt oder
verbreitet werden.

© 2020 Deutsche Bank AG,
Kerber Verlag, Caline Aoun
and the authors und Autoren

Edition Ausgabe
PalaisPopulaire
ISBN 978-3-942294-33-1

Trade edition
Verlagsausgabe
ISBN 978-3-7356-0642-6

www.kerberverlag.com

Printed in Germany

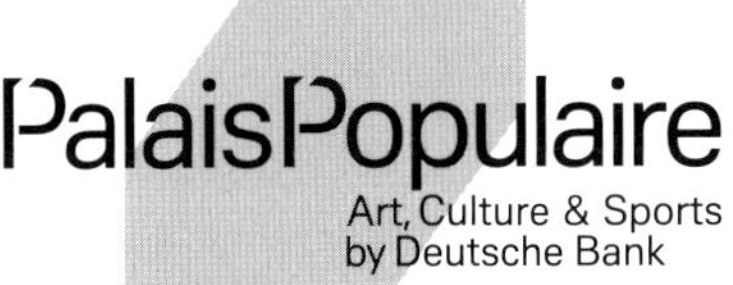